SUMMER HEAT
and the
CHALLENGER

DR. ROBERT F. BOLLENDORF, EDD, CADC

authorHOUSE®

AuthorHouse™
1663 Liberty Drive
Bloomington, IN 47403
www.authorhouse.com
Phone: 1 (800) 839-8640

Published by AuthorHouse 12/11/2017

ISBN: 978-1-5462-1679-7 (sc)
ISBN: 978-1-5462-1678-0 (e)

I had the privilege of sharing the first four books by Robert Bollendorf with my high school students with special needs. Immediately intrigued by the Brandt family, the students were able to connect with the realistic life journeys of the characters. We now all better understand that growth, change, and recovery are truly possible. Reading these books has given us an educational experience we will not forget. I can't wait to share Summer Heat *with my class.*

—Robin Reif
Special Education Teacher
Tremper High School
Kenosha, Wisconsin

To Ray, Maggie, and Rick

ACKNOWLEDGMENTS

WE HAD A HARD TIME coming up with a title for this book. For a long time we had a working title of *Summer's Journey*, but that didn't seem to fit with the experiences of our characters in the story. What is true is that with each book we go through a journey, one where we learn more about the Menominee culture, about ourselves, and in this case about gambling. We want to be clear first off that we are not opposed to gambling. Quite the contrary, we are pleased with what the casino has been able to provide for the Menominee people and other tribes throughout Wisconsin and the United States. Like alcohol, which, if used in moderation, seems not to present a problem for many people, gambling is a source of fun and entertainment, but it is a problem for others. This book attempts to tell a story about a person who becomes addicted to gambling.

Secondarily, we introduce the possibility that some people might also become addicted to exercise. Each of these is what we call process addictions, in which the body creates its own chemicals. (Someday we could do a book on sexual addiction, maybe about a famous golfer.) At any rate, the Menominee Reservation and Legend Lake again provide a wonderful backdrop for our story.

We would again like to thank the tribal police, the Menominee Tribal/ County Library, The Menominee Historic Preservation Department, Maehnowesekiyah, and the Legend Lake Property Owners Association not only for their help in research but also in promoting the books.

We would especially like to thank our friends at the College of Menominee Nation, including Debbie Downs, Maria Escalante, and Susan Waukau for promoting the books and encouraging us to write a book about gambling.

Rob would like to thank his neighbors on Legend Lake, Neil and Suki Eigenfeld, for sharing their insights into the history of the area and Neil for his knowledge of vegetation and wildlife. Rob would also like to thank his brothers and sisters for their support and encouragement. They are always the first to read his books and ask for more. It would be worth it to write books just for the joy it gives him to hear kind words from them.

Rob would also like to thank his friends and family: Tom Lindblade, for information on canoeing and kayaking; Alan Bergeson, for help with editing; his son Bryan, for help with information about mountain biking; and, of course, his wife Linda, for support and encouragement, but also for her help with words he botched so badly that even spell-check couldn't help. Rob would also like to thank Kathy Quinn for her research help, as well as John Teller, Celeste Hockings, Alan Caldwell, and Andy Gokee for their gracious help on the Ojibwe language.

Donna would like to express deep gratitude to all who inspired, supported, educated, and encouraged her. She would also like to thank Jon, who has given unconditional hugs, smiles, and the gentle shove that was needed to move forward.

Finally we would like to thank April, Joe, and our students, who are a constant source of feedback, encouragement, and support.

Thank you for all the times we heard or read, "I picked this book up with little enthusiasm, thinking it would be like another textbook, but once I started, I didn't put it down till I was finished."

IT WAS EARLY MORNING, AND Legend Lake was dead calm. In spots, the placid water accurately reflected the cool green trees that surrounded it and the horsetail clouds that floated overhead, foretelling an upcoming change in the string of calm, dry, hot summer days. Legend Lake even reflected the eagle that was soaring lazily above the smooth waters. If the eagle had not been so concerned with finding his morning meal, he might have noticed disturbances in the water. Four different wakes could be discerned—all racing toward a collision that would bring dramatic change to the lives of many innocent and unsuspecting people.

Police Officer Lucy Teller and her children, Jerrod and Tara, were the causes of two of the wakes. Lucy was in the water, swimming, while her children drove the tribal police WaveRunner beside her. It was an important safety precaution, but Lucy was beginning to regret it.

From the sound of the children's screams, Lucy might well have thought her children were being murdered. She figured they were back to the bickering they typically used to get her attention.

The interruption was irritating, to say the least. Lucy had been training for months to participate in the first Experience the Reservation competition. Developing and organizing the competition was one of the most ambitious projects the Menominee had taken on since regaining their reservation status back in the sixties. The race would involve swimming, road biking, mountain biking, kayaking, whitewater canoeing, in-line skating, and running—over seventy-five miles in all. The competition would be grueling. Lucy loved a challenge, and pushing her body hard helped prepare her for each of the challenges in her life.

There were certainly many challenges in her life. Not only did she have to work to maintain her sobriety, which was a challenge she faced one day at a time, she also faced the demands of being a Menominee Tribal Police officer, and, finally, the struggle of being a single parent, which at the moment was the biggest test.

Having the children drive alongside her as she swam a mile was a wise measure, in theory; there was a "no wake" rule on Legend Lake until ten a.m. to give the fishermen a crack at the lake before being swamped by skiers and wake boarders. Unfortunately, not everyone followed the rules. A swimmer was difficult to see on the lake, especially if a boat was cruising slowly and had not planed out—which meant its bow was riding out of the water and obstructing vision close to the boat. Jerrod and Tara were her eyes and ears, but at the moment they were a huge distraction. Now that they were getting older, their fighting and bickering had decreased considerably and had become almost tolerable; still, at times, as now, their bickering pushed Lucy to the edge. She really needed this workout. Couldn't the children even stop fighting to help her? Back in her drinking and using days she too often would say to them, "Do that again and I'll kill you." That voice still inside beckoned to be heard but she choked it. As she turned her head to the side to take a breath, Lucy tried to let them know of her displeasure.

"Jerrod!" she yelled. Then she put her head back under water and stroked once or twice before raising her head again to breathe and shout.

"Tara!" she called out, following her cry with a couple more strokes. "Stop it!"

Then she, and, it seemed, the world, fell silent for the next two strokes. The silence was broken, on the next stroke, when her hand hit the WaveRunner that they had abruptly turned in front of her. She lifted her head from the water, breathing fire.

Maybe, she fumed to herself in a moment of angry fantasy, I'll just have to kill them in order to get in a good workout.

But her fury melted when she saw the look of fear and panic in Jerrod's eyes. He was fourteen years old, and hovered over his little sister like a hawk on its nest. It was appropriate; at his naming ceremony he had been given a tribal name that meant Hawk Soaring Seeing Much. He was clearly seeing something now. Her eyes followed his finger where it was pointing.

"Mom," he shouted, "the weed cutter is heading right toward that swimmer!"

Lucy's anger turned quickly to fear.

The long-time residents of Legend Lake say there was a time when you could practically walk across the lake on top of the thick and matted weeds.

But the property owners had found a way to make lemonade from their lemons, purchasing weed cutters and selling the weeds to a fertilizer plant.

The weed cutter was a combination of a potato harvester and old-time riverboat. The front of the boats displayed long blades that could be raised and lowered to cut the vegetation, working in a manner similar to the blades of a hedge trimmer. These blades would cut the aquatic plants, and then they would be picked up by a conveyer made of long bars that allowed the water to flow through but trapped the weeds and sent them to the back of the weed cutter where they were collected on a flatbed. After a large pile was collected, a second boat would come and pick up the soggy mess and transfer it to a truck on shore to be hauled away. On the side of the weed cutter was a large paddle wheel that propelled it forward or backward.

It was a machine that could easily kill an unsuspecting swimmer.

Struggling to swim in place, Lucy's attention focused on the driver, who sat high above the conveyer, a good ten feet above the water. He had an excellent view of everything around him. How could he not see the swimmer?

The swimmer, on the other hand, was not aware of the situation. The weed cutter was approaching him quickly from behind. He was swimming freestyle, with his face in the water, only turning his head from side to side and occasionally looking forward. Even if he heard the sound of the machine or felt the vibration, he would probably assume it was a fisherman looking for a new fishing spot. The swimmer had no idea of the imminent danger he was in, and the weed cutter was catching up to him quickly—much too quickly, Lucy thought in horror.

Lucy pulled herself from the water in one fluid motion, her newly acquired muscles rippling in her back and shoulders. She had made fitness part of her recovery program since leaving treatment for drug and alcohol addiction; with additional training in swimming, biking, and weights, her muscles were rock hard and toned.

Jerrod, terrified, moved back as his mother roughly took control of the WaveRunner. She quickly accelerated the machine toward the swimmer. The weed cutter was now only twenty yards behind the swimmer, who continued to stroke efficiently through the water but soon would be no match for the speed of the slashing machine.

It was gaining on him steadily, and Lucy was still several hundred yards away. She blew the horn of the WaveRunner, and her children, holding on tightly to the edges of the WaveRunner, screamed loudly along with the horn. As the weed cutter narrowed the gap to ten feet, the driver turned to look at her. She could not quite make out his features, but from what she saw all he did was give her a blank, emotionless stare.

She blew the horn again. This time the swimmer heard it. He rolled over on his back just in time to see the huge weed cutter nearly on top of him. Lucy could only imagine his terror. Then the swimmer rolled and dived just as the weed cutter crossed over him. There was no way of knowing if he had moved in time to avoid the sharp blades—blades that would cut sharply and very deeply, Lucy reckoned.

The weed cutter passed over the spot where the swimmer had disappeared. Lucy scanned the water frantically, holding her breath, waiting to see if the swimmer's head emerged behind in the weed cutter's wake.

There was no sign of life. No sign of the swimmer. Seconds later, she arrived at the point of impact. Blood was already spreading across the surface of the water. The children, who had continued to hang on and scream as their mother raced toward the swimmer, now sat in silence with their eyes and mouths wide open. Tara was crying silently.

Lucy slowed the WaveRunner and without another thought dived into the middle of the blood-stained water.

The lake was about twelve feet deep where she entered. She soon reached the bottom and began to feel for the swimmer's body. Her own body felt tangled in the thick weeds and mud. In her head she screamed, "God, save us! Move, Lucy, move!"

The deadly weeds seemed to multiply, wrapping around her feet and legs like a hungry octopus. Just as she was running out of oxygen, she felt a pair of hands clinging to the weeds on the bottom of the lake. With all her strength she grabbed the hands and attempted to push off with her feet from the bottom. She felt as if her energy were being absorbed by the muck, and she had to kick hard to free herself from the decaying weeds that had built up over so many years. Her lungs ached. All she could think about was reaching the surface for fresh, life-giving air.

After what seemed like an eternity, Lucy struggled up to the surface, pulling the body of the limp swimmer with her. As they broke through the surface plane of the water, Lucy and the swimmer both took a deep and desperate breath. Even as she gasped for air, Lucy was relieved to hear the swimmer's cough and gasp beside her. But when she saw his stunned face, relief melted away and she felt chill instead.

It was Dr. Meany. The man who had once saved her life. If it were possible, Lucy now felt an even greater sense of urgency to save his.

Jerrod pulled the WaveRunner next to his mother, and within moments they had the wounded swimmer on board. They laid Dr. Meany on his stomach perpendicular to the WaveRunner, exposing the cuts on his back. With a mixture of blood, water, and weeds covering them, it was difficult to tell how serious they were. His legs and head dangled from the WaveRunner. Lucy had to remain in the water because there was no room left on the seat. Jerrod drove carefully back to the lodge while Tara used the radio to call an ambulance. Her young voice was trembling, but she was very thorough in her description. Even in the midst of her worry about Dr. Meany, Lucy thought of Tara—she seemed to be going through a hard time. She seemed lost somehow, on the brink of maturing a step out of childhood. Perhaps soon she would be ready for her own naming ceremony. Experiences like this would certainly mature her, Lucy thought grimly, and not in a healthy way, perhaps.

She looked up to watch the weed cutter as it moved toward the bay where it was usually parked. As the driver disembarked, she was unable to get a good look at him but figured he wouldn't be hard to track down. She would never forget his cold and vacant eyes.

To Lucy, it seemed to take forever for the WaveRunner to reach shore, but Jerrod did his best to combine speed with safety.

By the time the WaveRunner reached shore, the ambulance and the tribal police were arriving at the lake parking lot, and the swimmer was gently loaded on board the ambulance. Ray Waupuse was the first to respond to the call from the police dispatcher. He was not in the least surprised to see Lucy at the scene. He was getting used to her being in the middle of most of the commotion on the reservation. She seemed to be a magnet for trouble. He was relieved to see her all in one piece and wondered—not for the first time—how the hell she had gotten herself involved in this one.

As he stood close to Lucy, wanting to touch her and comfort her, she was deep in her own thoughts and Ray knew better.

Doc was barely conscious as the ambulance was pulling away—but conscious enough to smile weakly at Lucy before the doors closed.

"You're going to be fine, Dr. Meany," she said in what she hoped was a cheerful voice. "I'll see you at the hospital." As she watched the ambulance leave the parking lot, she kept on repeating it to herself: "You're going to be fine. You're going to be fine. You are going to be fine."

Dr. Meany wasn't his real name. He was Dr. Wolf, the addictionologist at the Maehnowesekiyah Treatment Center just outside Keshena.

Lucy knew Maehnowesekiyah well. She had been taken there after she agreed to go to treatment—though "agreed" might not have been the best word for it. At the time, she had very little choice in the matter. She was told bluntly by the Department of Children and Family Services worker that Tara and Jerrod would be taken away from her until she got help for her addiction to heroin and alcohol.

At the center, Dr. Meany had taken charge of dispensing medication to her. Like all addicts in withdrawal, she frequently felt he was far too stingy with the drugs used to manage her symptoms. Hence the nickname Lucy had herself made up.

Each time he visited her, she would describe a list of aches and pains, which to her were excruciating, and attempt to convince him to give her more drugs.

Each time he calmly told her she was already at the maximum that he felt comfortable prescribing.

"Well, the goal here, Dr. Meany," Lucy would spit back at him, "isn't for you to be comfortable. It's for me to be comfortable."

Lucy smiled as she remembered it now—smiled at her obvious sense of entitlement and blatant immaturity. She recognized now she had needed to re-build a tolerance for pain. Lucy took heroin—the most powerful painkiller—all the time, so even everyday aches and pains were foreign to her. Whatever a drug does going in, she had learned, it does the opposite going out. A depressant effectively becomes a stimulant as the body rebounds. So on top of the pain, Lucy attempted desperately to score more drugs and still felt she couldn't sleep.

Although years passed before Lucy began to sleep well, she learned new ways to cope with her pain and began to embrace recovery. In time, she began to volunteer at Maehnowesekiyah, and eventually she and "Dr. Meany" became close friends.

After the ambulance left, Lucy asked Jerrod and Tara to walk home. A friend of the children, Jeffery, happened to be playing alone nearby. She called the trusted older boy over and asked him to make sure her children arrived home safely. Lucy's mother would be waiting, and they were close to their home, which was only a couple of blocks from the lodge.

Then she turned to Ray. "Would you meet me on Highway VV? I want to check out where the weed cutter would probably be parked." She grinned. "I'm not armed," she added, "and don't know what I'll find at the site. I could use some back up."

"You've got it," said Ray simply.

Lucy jumped on the WaveRunner and sped off toward where she thought she would find the weed cutter.

Most of Legend Lake was lined with cabins, but where the weed cutter was tied to shore the lake was only a few feet from the road. Lucy circled the bay until she saw Ray pull off the road nearby. He drew his gun and searched the weeds near the machine and then waved for her to come ashore. As she expected, the driver was nowhere in sight.

Alone and away from the lodge where there were nosy onlookers, Lucy ran to Ray and kissed him warmly, her wet suit leaving an outline on his uniform. She smiled as he pulled away. "Better keep your window down so that dries before you see the captain."

Even though they unearthed no clues at the weed cutter, she thought to herself, it was always worthwhile to steal a few moments with Ray.

After a parting kiss, Lucy raced back to the lodge. Dave, the manager of the homeowners association, was just opening up the office. She explained to him what had happened and asked for the name and address of the driver.

Then Dave told her his regular driver had called in sick the night before.

"He was going to his mother's funeral at the reservation at Lac du Flambeau," Dave explained. Lac du Flambeau, they both knew, was about two-and-a-half hours northwest of the Menominee Reservation. "The guy told me that the engine was running rough, the hydraulics were sticking, and he was going to have a mechanic work on it today."

"Who was the mechanic?" Lucy asked loudly.

"I don't know," Dave answered. "He said he had a friend in from out of town who had actually worked at the factory where the weed cutters were made, and he was down on his luck lately and needed an opportunity to make some money. He said the guy would stop by the lodge to fill out the necessary paperwork."

Lucy looked sharply at him, but before she could tell him that he should have known better, he shook his head apologetically.

"Yeah, I know it wasn't exactly according to proper procedure and I'm sorry I can't help you more. But I didn't know I should expect this sort of thing. Sometimes I just hope people are going to do what they are supposed to do. Or at least what I think they should do—like their job! Looks like this guy found better pay than what mechanics make, if that's possible."

Lucy frowned. "On a clear day," she said meditatively to herself, "sitting ten feet off the water, how do you not see a swimmer right in front of you?"

Dave watched her. He had known Lucy since she and her friends would go swimming off the dock owned by the lodge. That was back in the day when boys were just swimming companions and drugs were something you took when you were sick.

"Unless..." she said slowly, "unless you don't want to see him."

Dave shrugged. "These are folks I hire to add to people's enjoyment of the lake, not to muck it up with blood and attempted murder."

Lucy awoke from her thoughtfulness. "I've got to go," she said. "Thanks, Dave."

Leaving the lodge, she quickly drove to Shawano Hospital. Dr. Wolf was just being released from the emergency room. Thankfully, his cuts were minor, and only one required stitches. When she found him, he was sitting on a table in the emergency room still in his swimming suit. He was alone and looked deeply troubled. As she stood in the doorway, she realized that this was the first time she had ever seen him without a shirt. Lucy was taken aback at how good he looked.

John Wolf had a full head of gray hair and just a little bit of loose skin under his chin, which was the only indication that he was approaching fifty. He had the body of a prizefighter. Even as he sat, there were no rolls of fat on his stomach, and small movements caused muscles to ripple, showing which muscles were involved in each movement. Doc looked better than most of the men his age—or even Lucy's age—on the rez. Many of his and her peers had the bodies of old men due to the ravages of excessive smoking and drinking.

"Hi, Dr. Meany," Lucy said from the doorway.

He looked up smiling and jumped off the examining table to give her a hug.

"My heroine," he said with a sincere smile.

Lucy could still smell the bottom of Legend Lake as he hugged her. She vividly recalled her frantic feelings in searching for a man in the weeds—a stranger, she thought.

"I'm so glad you're okay," she said. "Have you called Gayle to bring you some dry clothes, or are you going to sit around here and turn on the nurses with your bare chest?" She thought she felt his body stiffen ever so slightly as she mentioned his wife's name—but perhaps that was her imagination.

"Actually," he said, "I was hoping you could give me a ride to where I left my sweats back at the lake. I haven't called Gayle—I don't want to bother her. Anyway, she already complains enough about my exercise routine without adding a run-in with a weed cutter."

Lucy wondered how he was going to explain the stitches on his back to her, but decided not to ask. It was an awkward thought, but maybe his wife would not even know the stitches were there. Maybe she wasn't in the habit of seeing much of his bare back and chest.

The brief checkout procedure was made even briefer because the Doc was well-known at Shawano Hospital. Within a few minutes, they were in Lucy's truck heading for the lake.

They drove in silence.

When they arrived where John Wolf had started his swim that morning, fully expecting to be back to his clothes twenty minutes later, Lucy was wondering how to ask him the question that was in her mind. She finally decided there was no gentle way. "Do you think it's possible that the guy driving the weed cutter didn't see you this morning?"

"I was wondering that myself," John Wolf answered casually, almost as if someone else's life was in the balance. "I guess it fits with a number of unusual experiences I've been having lately. I just have not been able to sort it all out."

"What do you mean?" Lucy asked.

"Well, it all seemed to begin this winter. I don't know if you remember, but for the first time since I started working at the treatment center, I took two weeks off. Gayle and I were going to celebrate being empty nesters for the first time in twenty-five years with both kids in college. At the last minute, a big event came up at her job at the casino, and she couldn't get away for two whole weeks. So the plan was that I'd fly down to Sanibel

Island in Florida and stay there for a week by myself, then meet her at the airport, and we'd spend the second week together."

"I remember that time," Lucy said, "because I began to think you lived at the treatment center. No matter when I went there, you were there. Then all of a sudden you weren't there at all. I asked one of the nurses where you were, and when she said vacation, my first thought was that they shouldn't have hallucinatory people working at a treatment center. Then other staff confirmed her story. Was it lonely the first week without Gayle?"

"I was excited about staying there because I could work on most of the events that I can't do up here in the winter. That first week I didn't have to worry about leaving Gayle alone, so I worked out hard so I could ease off after she got there. There's a nice bay for kayaking and canoeing, bike trails, and lots of beaches for running. After I arrived the first night, I sat outside by the pool and listened to a one-man band play a lot of Jimmy Buffet music, which I enjoy. After dark, and when the music ended, I went to my room and called Gayle. She wasn't home, but that's not unusual because lately she's had late meetings and often stays and plays the slots. Anyway, I went to bed and the next morning I got up early, wanting to run along the beach at sunrise. I ran a mile or two and was lost in thought. I was feeling in rhythm with the whole world. The tide was out, I had an expressway of smooth sand to run on, and it was like my breathing was in time with the waves."

"Sounds like a good combination of exercise and quiet time," Lucy noted.

"It was at first," he agreed. "There were a few people out shelling, and some fishing boats out a quarter mile from shore. Everyone was focusing on his own obsession. I began running by some of the hotels, but most of the guests were still fast asleep. Anyway, a young woman came running from one of the larger places on the beach. She was only wearing a bikini and running shoes without socks. A blonde with a dark tan. I could tell she worked out regularly because she had that line running from the top of her bikini to the bottoms, right in the middle of her stomach. I see a number of young women at the treatment center, but for most of them the drugs have already taken a toll on their appearance. This young woman was the picture of youth, beauty, and health. I tell you all this because of what happened next."

"Well, it's nice to know you are human and notice these things," said

Lucy with light sarcasm. "I only get to see you in your clinical role, where your most obvious feeling is empathy and compassion."

Dr. Wolf ignored the comment and continued on. "She began running alongside me and commented about the pace at which I was running. She asked if she could run with me for a while and asked how far I was going. I told her I wasn't sure, because I hadn't been to Sanibel before, but I planned to run till I ran out of beach. She suggested I run to the lighthouse at the east end of the island and back, which would be about ten miles.

"I figured that would be the end of it. I thought she'd speed up or slow down or go a different direction, but she stayed with me and we ran ten miles together. She told me all about Sanibel and asked a lot about my life. I was confused why she stayed near me. At one point she even told me a bug flew in her eye, and I stopped to look. She didn't seem to have any difficulty leaving her eyes open, and she looked deep into mine. I bent her head back to see better. It was almost surreal, but that's when I noticed that submissive movement we see so often in women who've been sexually abused. She kind of shrunk right into herself. It is hard to explain, but I have seen it many times. I got quieter after that for a while, trying to figure out what was going on with her, trying to figure out what to say to her. Toward the end of the run, she asked me why I had gotten quieter, and I told her I was wondering why a young lady her age was wasting her time with a man old enough to be her father. She told me she found me quite attractive and had been fantasizing about the two of us going to her room and showering together after our run. Usually I have no difficulty ignoring the seductive behavior of young women at the treatment center because I know they have no interest in me. And they only see me as a vehicle to get the drugs they want. But I was confused by this woman's behavior.

"I told her I felt very flattered by her attention, but I didn't want to be another man who exploited her sexually. She looked both surprised and afraid. I found it an interesting combination. She said she wasn't used to being turned down and told me I was passing up a chance to indulge in any fantasy that I wanted. I told her I thought she was too attractive and personable to be offering herself like that to any man she found attractive. I told her I wasn't sure what her motive was but that I didn't believe it was sex with me."

Lucy, having just seen him without his shirt, thought Doc might be selling himself short but decided not to comment on that and let Doc continue.

"She got very agitated at that point and seemed quite anxious all of a sudden to leave. Without another word, she was gone. I saw that same young woman at the airport when I went to pick up Gayle although she didn't see me or at least pretended not to see me. She had a black eye with what looked like minor abrasions on her face."

"That's an interesting combination of feelings," noted Lucy, "—agitated, surprised, and afraid. Do you think she ended up with the wrong guy or that her beating was somehow connected with you?"

"It was weird because she was also wearing long sleeves and pants, not typical clothes for hot Florida weather. Lucy, I wasn't really sure what to think of it. I wondered what else she was hiding. Gayle even asked me what I was thinking about. She said I seemed preoccupied or worried about something. She recognized that look from the times at work when I've had a tough patient or two at the clinic—probably a look she saw in me after having you as a patient. Remember what a difficult time you gave me? Do you remember the stuff you said to the staff and me? Okay, I can tell by the look on your face you want me to get back to my story."

"No, keep talking about me and what a bitch I was," Lucy said sarcastically. "Yes, Doc, of course I want you to get back to the story."

"Well," he said, "then I will need a cup of coffee. Because the story just gets weirder."

THEY STOPPED AT A CAFÉ. Equipped with tall steaming cups, they settled at a table near the window. Doc took a couple of deep breaths and then began again, from where he had left off.

"A few days after the encounter with the blonde, I was out running again and two guys who were standing on the beach drinking water began to run behind me about a hundred yards back. They might have been in their early thirties and in excellent shape, but they weren't runners. They had the big, bulky muscles of bodybuilders. I didn't think too much of it until I made the mistake of turning away from the beach to run in the nature preserve off Tarpon Bay Road, and they followed me. All of a sudden, we were alone in a swampy area, and they had picked up the pace and were only about fifty yards behind me now. One of them had the large thighs and small calves of a sprinter, and I could tell he was having difficulty with the pace. He probably could have caught me if we had run one hundred yards, but we had already run a mile and he'd already used up the oxygen in those red fast-twitch muscles. I decided to pick up the pace and see what happened, and sure enough, they picked up theirs also. I picked it up again, and this time they couldn't keep up with me. And soon I saw them stop.

"After that, I ran in the early evening and stayed on the beach. I saw them one other time when I was biking through Ding Darling Nature Preserve, but I made sure I stayed with a tour group from Germany that was also biking through. It was all very confusing to me so I wrote it off. I really don't like it if I can't figure something out."

As Doc finished up, Lucy thought to herself that this was the most she had ever heard him say about himself and his own experiences, with the exception of the time she heard him tell his personal story at an open AA meeting. She remembered the details now. He had grown up on the Menominee Reservation with emotionally absent alcoholic parents—like many others in his generation and those that followed. Luckily, he was gifted with intelligence and, unlike so many other young Indians, he avoided the traps of alcohol. He got a scholarship to the University of Wisconsin and took a pre-med path. He maintained an A average and was accepted to medical school at the University of Chicago. This was a huge compliment, as many of his peers never left the rez, let alone attended a university.

After medical school, he decided to specialize in neurosurgery, and while doing his residency, he met a young nurse named Gayle. She was impressed with his promising talents and apparent ambition and believed that he had every intention, like her, to be rich someday and belong to an exclusive country club. Soon they married. They were filled with big dreams and high hopes. But the pressure of long hours and little cash began to weigh heavily on them. Success seemed to be taking longer than his new wife wanted to wait.

Then one day he discovered that just a little valium made the pressures of his residency go so much smoother. After all, it wasn't like alcohol.

He had taken enough classes in chemistry to know that the only difference in the formula for alcohol and valium was water, but the denial was already beginning. The road to addiction was a short one, and a couple of DUIs landed him in treatment. Not only was the treatment successful the first time, but he became fascinated with the process, and his whole life changed. Surprising even himself, he changed his specialty to addictionology and decided to go where he was needed most—the rez.

He and Gayle had two children. Gayle begrudgingly worked at the tribal clinic as a nurse. She became bored and recently had decided a career change was in order. She began working at the Menominee Casino, first as a cashier, and then as a manager.

"Lucy?" Suddenly she was aware of Dr. Wolf watching her. When she had refocused on him, letting go of her wandering remembrances, she smiled apologetically.

"Sorry, Doc. Your story has given me a lot of food for thought. I was just processing the Sanibel business a bit more. So, did you ever bother to tell anyone about this?" Then she added with a hint of sarcasm: "—like the Sanibel police, maybe?"

"What was I supposed to tell them? That a young lady tried to seduce me, and two men with lots of muscles were running behind me on the beach?"

"Well, did anything else happen in Sanibel, or since you've been back? That is, before today's incident? Now would be a good time to tell me everything, John."

"Nothing else happened in Sanibel, but the other day when I was out riding my bike along Highway 55, I think a truck tried purposely to hit me."

"What happened?" Lucy pretended not to show the growing surprise and alarm that she felt creeping into her mind and body.

"Well, I was riding out near Wayca Creek, not too far from where that young man hit a tree a few years ago. What was his name? He was a white kid. Scott?" He continued without waiting for an answer. "I know a lot of people, including my wife, who think I'm crazy for doing some things like biking on highways and swimming alone, but I do take precautions. When I bike, I always wear a helmet, and I have a rearview mirror on it so I can see cars coming on the road behind me." "I see it all the time from my squad car," Lucy said. "More and more people are giving bikes the room they deserve as they pass. Some people still pass way too close and occasionally bikers get the people who are drunk or psychopaths who try to run them off the road, or pull up close and then swing open their passenger side doors. Some idiots find that sort of dangerous behavior amusing."

"Well," Doc continued, "I could see this red truck coming up behind me and he wasn't moving over, so at the last minute, I veered off and he missed me. I fell when I left the road, so by the time I looked up, the truck was well down the road. I don't think the truck had a license plate. There were no injuries sustained, so no problem, right? You can't think there is a connection."

Lucy asked if he had reported this incident either and he just shook his head.

"Listen, Lucy, nothing happened, and I'm sure the police would say if someone truly wanted to hurt you, they could have shot you out there by Wayca Creek, and there would have been no witnesses. Even if you put all four of these incidents together, it makes no sense. First of all, they seem to be different people, and secondly they chose odd methods. And why would they even want to hurt me? It makes no sense at all, Lucy."

"Okay, I've got to ask, is there anyone you know who'd like to hurt you?"

Lucy realized the question was a difficult one because of what Dr. Wolf did for a living. So many people including Lucy owed Dr. Wolf their lives, yet the drug dealers (and maybe even husbands, wives, boyfriends, or girlfriends still using) resented the changes that come with sobriety. Many people, for other reasons, could be angry with him. There wasn't a lot of motivation for a drug dealer to kill Dr. Wolf. He wasn't single-handedly winning the war on drugs; as a matter of fact, the dealers were probably winning in spite of his best efforts. They were more likely to spend their energy just finding new users or getting the old ones to relapse, which was a common occurrence as well.

Doc shook his head again. "You know the answer to that, Lucy. For every person that is helped in treatment, there is likely one or two that are angry about it. Many of those people are abusers or dope dealers that are not above violence. But there are a hundred people who work there, not just me."

Lucy smiled. She knew the quickest way to kill any living thing was to cut off its head, and Dr. Wolf was definitely the head of Maehnowesekiyah Treatment Center, but she knew that he didn't place his role above anyone else's. His humility was one of the things that made him so well-loved and respected. "Is there anyone else outside of work that might want to harm you?" she asked.

John Wolf smiled. "Only if people like you are taking this race coming up a lot more seriously than I think you are."

Lucy chuckled. "You forget I'm participating in the team portion. I'm not competing with one of you whackos that do the whole thing yourself. And speaking of doing things your self, you are done working out alone until we get to the bottom of this."

"Now wait just a minute here!" said Doc, setting his cup back down rather emphatically. "I'm not dropping out of the race and I won't quit training. I'm also not going to slow down and work out with people who can't keep up with me."

She shook her head at that. It would certainly be hard to find someone who would be able to keep up with Doc. "Well," she said. "Enough talking. Let's go find your sweats."

Back at Legend Lake, Lucy parked on Tall Moon Road. They walked together in silence through the gate at the beach club that prohibited the snowmobiles and four-wheelers from using it.

To the developers' credit, some of the nicest land on Legend Lake was reserved for the beach clubs, which were used by property owners who lived on lots off the lake. The beach club sat high above the water on a point, which created bays on either side. From there, Lucy looked down at two loons fishing in the middle of the lake. She was reminded of the story she was told as a little girl.

The Great Spirit had created the eagle, and the eagle was alive and loved to soar above and below the clouds. He celebrated his freedom, enjoying the land as well as the skies. The eagle was happy except for a loneliness that could only be filled by a mate. So the Great Spirit created a female mate for him. These two danced in the sky. He provided food and protection for his cherished partner. She gave him love and companionship. They played, danced, and mated with great passion. Flying high in the sky, the eagle would roll onto his back, and they would touch chest to chest. As the couple clutched talon to talon, they would freefall moving quickly toward the ground. At the last minute they would let go of each other and take off toward the heavens.

A trickster who lived alone on Mother Earth was jealous and hated the love he saw in the eagles, knowing he could never have a partner. He changed the female eagle into a loon. She was in great pain; she could not fly with her mate. She would cry out to her love. The fact that she would never be able to fly with him and that he could not live on the water caused them both to suffer. She would mourn in a song. He was heartbroken and made the choice to give up his great freedom of the sky to be with her. The Great Spirit transformed him into a loon. Every time Lucy heard the cry of the loon, she remembered this love story.

Smiling to herself, she wondered if she was really a loon— or had she had found her Eagle in Ray. The smile brought her back to the lake and to Doc. The loons were hooting at one another to stay in contact while they took turns diving for food. The lake was calm and reflected a few fair-weather clouds that floated above. From Lucy's perspective, it appeared the loons were diving into the clouds.

That's when another warm memory hit her. It was hard to believe that it was two years ago this fall since she had met the Brandts at the funeral for their son, Scott. She was the first to arrive at the scene after he had smashed into a tree. At first glance, it looked like an accident, but from the start Lucy was convinced otherwise. She went to the funeral to learn that Scott had been on his way home and on the path toward recovery from drug addiction. She helped prove that Scott had been murdered and that the cocaine in his system was not self- administered.

Since that time she and her children stayed in close touch with the Brandts. Hank and Bobbie had helped her locate a kidnapped child the winter after Scott's death, and she thought they might provide the answer for her current dilemma.

"Are you done working out for the day?" she asked Doc.

"Well, I might have time to ride the stationary bike in my office, but I should be pretty safe there, don't you think?"

"I'll send one of our interns to stand guard," Lucy said with a smile. "What were you planning to do tomorrow?"

"Well, I like to start off each day with a swim, but the emergency room doctor told me not to get my stitches wet for a couple of days, so I thought I'd do some canoeing or kayaking instead and then do some speed work at the high school track."

"I'll have people there to work out with you," Lucy said,
hoping desperately she could keep her promise.

CHAPTER 4

SHORTLY AFTER LEAVING DR. WOLF, Lucy went to the station to speak to her supervisor. The lieutenant was sitting at his desk with the same expression he always seemed to have when Lucy entered the room. It appeared to her that his entire body stiffened, as if he were preparing himself for some sort of onslaught.

He spoke in a pleasant tone, but Lucy could hear just the slightest bit of sarcasm in his tone. She could never be sure if he didn't like her and pretended he did, or did like her and pretended he didn't.

"Officer Teller, I hear your day has had its share of excitement already." His open palm pointed to a chair. "Please have a seat and fill me in on the details. Please, sit."

Lucy started out by telling what happened at the lake, trying hard not to make herself sound like a hero. She did not want or need any more attention. Then she filled him in on the events Dr. Wolf had shared with her in the ride back from the hospital. Each time she departed from the facts and added her own opinion, the lieutenant would look over his glasses at her, a gesture she always read as disapproval.

"This sounds like a lot of speculation on your part, Officer Teller," he remarked as she finished. "May I once again remind you that you are a patrol officer and not a detective."

"I just wanted to inform you of what has been happening. I'm not interested in investigating, and I know there's not enough evidence to provide any protection for Dr. Wolf. That's why I thought I'd go ask the Brandts if they'd be willing to work out with Dr. Wolf while he's training for the Experience the Rez race."

Then he not only looked over his glasses but also shook his head at the same time. "Officer Teller," he said in a forced, patient voice, "Is one person in harm's way not enough for you? Do you want to get more people hurt or killed? What are you thinking—this time?"

"But you said yourself that the evidence was flimsy and I'm just speculating. Besides, it appears if anyone is trying to do harm to the doctor, they want it to look like an accident. I don't think they can do that if there is a group of people. I will also make it very clear to the Brandts that there are risks involved. I will tell them that I'm acting as a friend of Dr. Wolf's and not as a police officer. I just want to make sure that I'm keeping you in the loop." When she finished, she sat with her fingers crossed.

"Well," said the lieutenant finally, "there is nothing we can do as a department to protect him, and he is so important to this community. If they are willing to take the risk, I for one would feel safer. Go talk with them. But remember you are doing this as a private citizen."

Lucy thought she could see a few more hairs turning gray on the lieutenant's head as she left.

When she called Hank Brandt, he suggested they meet at Pine Hills for ice cream after dinner. She told him she would bring her children since they never would pass up any kind of ice cream. Luckily, all the Brandts would be available that evening.

Pine Hills was a golf club owned by the Mohican nation. The Mohicans had purchased Pine Hills several years ago from a private owner and built a brand new clubhouse and restaurant. It was built with huge pine logs and large windows on a rise that gave a beautiful view of the lush surrounding forest. Lucy liked to go there with her family, especially on Friday evenings for the fish fry.

The club was only a mile or two away from the Maehnowesekiyah Treatment Center, where Lucy had been in drug treatment. Going out for a treat with her children so close to where she had been in such bad shape was a bittersweet experience. She was grateful for having her life saved yet sad at all the special times lost with her children. There had been full days and nights when all her energy and focus was on getting high. So many precious moments with her kids were lost forever. But tonight Pine Hills, with ice cream and good friends, was the final destination.

Thank you, Great Spirit, she prayed silently, for giving me another day here on earth.

The restaurant wasn't crowded, and since it was a pleasant evening, they moved toward a table on the balcony. While Tara instructed people where to sit and what ice cream she thought everyone should order, they all watched the golfers finishing up their last holes in the dusk.

It was a large group around the table, including Lucy's mother, with whom Lucy had lived ever since finishing treatment. Hank and Molly Brandt were the head of a large family of four living children. Bobbie was finishing up her last year of college. She had taken some time off after her brother, Scott, was killed. Ryan, now the oldest son, was a junior in college. He had brought his friend, Zack, with him. The two swam on the same college swim team and had been best friends since grade school. The next child, Paul, was just finishing his freshman year in college, majoring in environmental studies at a school in Colorado. The youngest was Sally, who had just finished her senior year of high school and was still on a high after winning state in both cross-country and the sixteen hundred meters in track. Lucy had also invited Kathy and Brad. Kathy was Scott's former girlfriend, and Brad, who had been Scott's best friend for many years, was now dating Kathy.

Lucy enjoyed getting together with all of them. Their lively conversations on every subject were filled with teasing and laughter and always involved several of them talking at the same time. But it was growing dark quickly, and after about twenty minutes of pleasantries Lucy thought it was time to address the reason why she had brought them together.

So sticking her fingers in her teeth, she let out with a loud whistle and then raised her hand. After a few conversations finished up, she finally had their attention. She told them first about Dr. Wolf and his significance to her and to her community. She told them about the events of that morning and some of the incidents that Dr. Wolf had described to her. Finally she described Experience the Rez and his commitment to it.

"I need people who would be willing to train with him and participate in the race, staying by him at all times. I thought of you guys since you are about the only ones I know who can keep up with him, and some of you have helped me out at other times. I won't lie to you. I don't know what sort of danger I might be placing you in."

Lucy couldn't help but notice Molly's body stiffen. She seemed to be shaking her head side to side at Hank, who sat across the table from her. He, for his part, tried to ignore her by looking at Lucy.

"I talked with my lieutenant this morning," Lucy continued, "and he can't commit any officers to this because we don't even know if a crime has been committed or if Dr. Wolf's in any real danger. I believe he is though, so if you help you might also be in danger. On the other hand, these people seem to go to great lengths to make things look like an accident, so I believe that if there are witnesses, they won't try anything. I'd be glad to answer any questions you have, but I don't want you to give me an answer now. I'd like you to talk about this among yourselves and give me your answer by showing up tomorrow at Legend Lake Lodge. Then if you want to participate, we will figure out who will be with him in which event."

Molly was the first to ask a question. "Isn't it possible that these people could stage an 'accident'" (Molly used her fingers for quotes as she said) "for more than one person?"

"Since I have no idea who we are dealing with here, I'd have to say yes it is. But they haven't even been successful with one person. So I'd like to think that more than one would be a strong deterrent, but I can't be sure. That's why I want you to think about this and not take it lightly. This is also not sanctioned by the Menominee Tribal Police. We'd be acting on our own." There was a moment of silence then, and as Lucy looked at all the faces, she could tell they were taking this seriously. And she was very glad. They did not need anyone half-heartedly involved. But, as she thought about it, she could not think of anything the Brandts did half-heartedly.

Hank was the next one to ask a question. "Is this the same director of the treatment center when Scott was an outpatient there, the one who helped him get sober?"

"He was there then," Lucy answered. "I don't know how much contact he had with Scott, but he would have done his examination and oversaw any meds he may have needed."

Hank started to speak, but after looking at Molly, he decided that he'd better wait.

"So you aren't sure whether we are putting our lives in danger," Molly began, "...or are just wasting our time driving an hour a day to work out with a guy who's in no danger at all?"

"That's it in a nutshell," Lucy answered. After a short pause, she asked, "Any other questions?"

They were silent, so she went on: "Then I think we will leave you now and let you talk among yourselves. You may want to talk more on your way home and after you arrive, for that matter. You can call me if you decide not to participate. Otherwise, show up at Legend Lake Lodge at seven tomorrow morning. It was good to see you all again. We will remain friends whatever you decide."

They all started to get up from the table.

"Oh," said Lucy, "one more thing. Though I can't offer you police protection, I have friends in the department. I will make sure they make a point of driving by in the patrol car wherever you are. And Ray will be watching from a distance whenever he can. You won't see him, but he'll be there, and he'll be armed. I'm also going to see our old friend Ezra." With a huge smile and wink she continued, "I think you all remember Ezra. As you know, he knows this area better than anyone, and I think he will be willing to help as well."

The evening ended with hugs all around, and Lucy and her family left for home.

When the Brandt family arrived home, everyone was lost in his or her own thoughts. After a long silence that seemed to go on forever, Molly spoke. "I might as well speak first because I know I'm going to be in the minority, but before you get caught up in the intrigue of all of this, would you think about my feelings? I've buried a son whose life was lost way too early because of evil people with bad intentions."

At that point everyone looked down toward the floor, thinking about Scott. Brad peeked at Kathy, who had tears in her eyes, but she caught Brad's look and gave him a reassuring rub on his shoulder.

"Having to bury your child changes the way you see the world for the rest of your life," Molly continued. "I'm telling you this for a number of reasons. First, before you go risking your lives for someone you don't even know, how about considering saving your lives for me. I love each and every one of you. Secondly, you are all young and maybe too quick to forget that there is real evil in the world, and though part of this involves participating in a game, death is very real and not a game."

Molly looked around the room. What she noticed was what she didn't see. No one rolled eyes at what she had said. No one looked as though the lights were on but no one was home, the way it often happens when a parent makes a point to a child. Molly was pleased. She doubted that she was changing any minds, but at least she was convincing them of the serious decision they were about to make.

"If any one of you dies," she continued, "it will affect the rest of us forever. Every one of us loved Scott, and we all will feel pain from his death forever. I just don't think I could go through that again. I'm not sure if I could make it through. Now I'm open to discussion here because I can see the other side too, but don't insult me or any of the rest of us by bringing up some crap like: 'Oh, Mom, nothing will happen.' That is probably what Scott thought when he was driving down that road in the falling snow. But we will never know what Scott thought because he's dead, and that's forever." Molly's voice cracked, and she hesitated a moment before continuing.

"One other thing. We've had this discussion once before, and I lost. I will probably lose this one too, but in that case it was an innocent baby who had no choice in the matter. This time we are dealing with a grown man who is a doctor, and not only a doctor but also an addiction specialist. He continues to participate in an activity in spite of the fact he may be risking his life. Maybe instead of exercising with this guy, we should be doing one of those interventions we're all becoming so familiar with because that sounds like an addiction to me. I say this because I see our whole family getting the same way. I remember back when you were drinking, Hank, and always at the bar on Sunday afternoons in the summer. I'd think to myself how nice it would be to take a bike ride around the neighborhood. Now you're not happy unless we do thirty miles on the tandem before breakfast on Sunday. You have to go to church on Saturday night so it doesn't get in the way of our ride. Even then you're not happy unless we bike to church, and I have to carry my music in our panniers."

Hank tried to interrupt, but Molly held up her hand.

"I'm almost finished. I can see all of you thinking, well, of course he exercises. Know why you think that? Because you are as crazy as he is."

"I can add my own experience to what Mom is saying," Bobbie added after waiting for Molly to take a breath. "I volunteered the last time Lucy asked for help. Though I admit I was excited at first and almost changed my major to law enforcement, there were times when I was scared to death, not to mention almost dying. That whole thing was seriously dangerous!"

Hank spoke next. "You're right, Molly, about everything. First, we must take this seriously. When I heard he helped Scott, I was ready to say I would help. He provided treatment for Scott, however briefly, and I feel I owe him for that. I don't mind risking my life, but when I think of those I love risking theirs, I don't like the way it feels. It actually makes me sick to my stomach when the thought enters my mind. This may sound contradictory, but I hope whatever we decide, we're all in or all out. I think the worst scenario of all would be wondering for the rest of our lives if we could have made a difference, even if something happens to one of us. I still live with guilt about Scott, and I don't know if I could take much more of the responsibility I feel for his death."

Scott had been dead for three years. The family had talked frequently about their feelings for the first year and less frequently the second. In the last year their feelings had become more private. This was the first time in many months that they had exposed their own pain to one another. Each began to believe that perhaps he or she was the only one still haunted by these feelings. In a way, it was reassuring to all of them that Scott still lived in all of their hearts.

"Well," said Sally, "I'd like to speak to the addiction piece because out of everybody in this family, I'm probably the worst. I've had two. I had an eating disorder, which some consider an addiction, and now I'm addicted to running. And yes, Mother, I'd rather die than quit. But that's where their similarities end. The eating disorder made me crabby and irritable. Running makes me feel good. I isolated myself and lied so no one would know about my crazy eating rituals. I still like to run with Paul," Sally added, smiling, "even though he's getting slower and slower."

Paul smiled back.

"I feel closer to him when we run," Sally continued, "and I love the talks we have when we're running. I might have to live someday with quitting because of an injury. But I will be damned if I'd let some creep keep me from it. And one other thing, you say there is evil in the world, and we might minimize that, Mom. Perhaps sometimes I do, but I don't think after Scott's death I could ever forget or forgive wicked behavior. But I will be damned if I will let it win. If this guy quits, evil wins. And, Dad, you shouldn't feel guilty."

"Yeah," Paul commented, joining in to put a political spin on it as he often did, "just like if we stopped riding airplanes because of terrorism, they'd win." He was secretly hoping to start an argument. He loved to debate any time, any place.

Getting back to the subject at hand, Brad chimed in. "I'd like to do this because he helped Scott. Because of Doc and his treatment center, I had my friend back for a while before he died. It would give me a chance to thank Scott again for his friendship and to relieve some of the guilt I feel for loving his girlfriend and having her love me back." He looked deeply into Kathy's eyes, and they smiled at one another.

"Oh, that's nonsense, Brad," said Molly, rubbing his short-cropped hair. "No angel smiles brighter seeing you two together than Scott does up in heaven."

"Thanks, Mrs. Brandt," said Kathy. "That means a lot coming from you. I'd like to do it for Scott, but also for Lucy. She and I have been through a lot together, and her friendship means so much to me. I know how indebted she feels to Dr. Wolf and how much he means to the community. I really like her and want to be there for her."

After a short silence, Ryan spoke—or, rather, shouted. "Okay," he said, pumping the air with his fist, "I say we do this thing! You ready, Zack?"

"I better pass this by my parents first, but I think if you guys decide to do it, they would be okay with it."

"Just a minute now," said Molly, "We haven't decided anything yet."

"Well, does anyone have anything else to add?" Hank asked. "If not, how about going around and simply saying in or out? How about you, Molly?"

"I want to go last," she answered softly, looking down solemnly.

One by one they all said they were in. Last of all, Molly also agreed.

"We can decide how to divide up who will do what when we get together tomorrow," Hank said, "but you may be thinking about it tonight. I have a pretty good idea how it will shake out now, I think," he added, with a mixture of excitement and fear in his voice.

THE NEXT MORNING THEY ALL met at Legend Lake Lodge at seven a.m. Lucy introduced Dr. Wolf to each of the people present, and he responded cordially. As it turned out, he did remember Scott and had several nice things to say about him while he was in treatment. "The thing that stands out the most was that he never asked for more drugs than what I prescribed. I can count on one hand the people who have done that, and trust me Lucy wasn't one of them, but Scott was. Once he got it in his head he was going to recover, he never wavered. He was a very strong young man–very determined to do the right thing and set things straight."

Scott's family and friends just shook their heads.

"Yes, that was Scott," Hank said, sticking his chest out just a little with pride.

When Doc had a chance, however, he whispered firmly to Lucy. "Remember what I said, these people need to go at my pace."

Lucy just smiled, holding back a laugh. "I already told them they might have to slow down for you."

Her friend just stared at her with a hint of disbelief.

Next they developed a training schedule for the month that remained before the race. Dr. Wolf planned to practice three events a day in addition to using the stationary bike in his office. They coordinated it so that the Brandts would make just one trip a day from their town an hour north. It was agreed that Sally would run with him, and on some days the youngest son, Paul, would join them. Ryan and his friend Zack would swim with Doc.

Hank and Molly would bike the roads with him on their tandem along with Paul, who had taken up mountain biking while at college in Colorado. Kathy and Brad would join him for in-line skating. Like so many kids in Wisconsin, Brad had played hockey in elementary school and would switch to in-line skates in the summertime to reduce expensive rink time. Since he could skate uphill with the in-line skates, it improved his conditioning.

Kathy had taken up the sport to spend time with Brad, and it was easier on her knees than running. So much for the easy events.

The most difficult events for the group to cover would be kayaking and canoeing. Bobbie had taken a kayaking class in college, but most of the training had been in a pool, and she had little experience with whitewater. Since she was such a good swimmer, the group decided she'd be the best kayaker. Hank and Molly mostly paddled their canoe on flat water and had little whitewater experience. All in all, none of the three had enough experience to be of much help, so Lucy would have to look elsewhere. She asked her mother, her sponsor Sophie, and friends Dawn and Bill to help her find someone with skills in this area. Lucy would keep looking for more help in these events especially since they were potentially the most dangerous.

This had become a full time job for her. Organizing and making schedules was not the easiest thing for Lucy. She had a hard enough time keeping track of her two busy children and her own schedule. Thank goodness for Mom, Lucy often thought. Even though she and her mother faced some old unhealed wounds between them, her mother made it possible for Lucy to focus on getting and staying clean and sober.

After they had sorted all of this out, John Wolf decided to begin his training with running, in-line skating, and swimming. The day was already beginning to heat up when Doc started out on his run, and Sally and Paul happily joined him. The sun had been up since five, and the long shadows had disappeared as they turned east down South Branch Road. The bright sun split the trees on either side of them. Even though it was only seven thirty, they could already feel the heat of the sun on their bodies, and Doc was looking forward to the swim. Doc started out at the speed that had left the two weightlifters in Sanibel gasping for breath as they followed him ominously down the beach. He looked up hopefully to the heavens for a friendly cloud but saw nothing but blue sky.

Paul had grown since the year he first protected the endangered loons that landed in the lake just outside of town. That battle over the loons really inspired him to fight for a good cause. Though he was late with puberty, he finally started to mature in high school and grew to five feet ten inches. He now weighed a lean one hundred and forty pounds. He didn't have the rippled body of his older brother Scott, who at six feet and two hundred pounds, revealed the bulging muscles of a college football running back when he died. Ryan was also six feet tall and carried one hundred and eighty pounds of long, hard swimmer's muscles on his supple frame. Different from both his elder brothers, Paul displayed the thin and gaunt look of a runner. In addition to his fascination with loons, he had broadened his interest to other endangered species and ultimately to the entire environment. He loved the outdoors and was very concerned with the direction of the world and the crisis of global warming. All of this helped him in the decision to major in environmental studies. He hoped someday to work for the EPA or a lobbying group that focused on environmental issues like the Sierra Club.

Sally, who had earned a running scholarship to the University of Wisconsin scholarship, ran both cross-country and track. Not sure of a major, she was leaning toward teaching and coaching. She had overcome her eating disorder and now focused on a healthy lifestyle that incorporated both nutrition and running.

At five feet four and just over one hundred pounds, she clearly carried the look of a distance runner. She had tiny breasts and very little body fat, but she ate whatever she wanted, which usually involved healthy choices—but with no fear foods. She loved to eat pizza and ice cream and occasionally indulged with her girlfriends. Like Paul, she was later than some in developing a romantic interest, but she had plenty of male friends and seemed to be in no hurry to fall in love.

Paul and Sally started out running on either side of John Wolf, who seemed to look a little confined with two people running next to him. He quickened the pace still again when Sally asked him if he was a pronator or a supinator.

"I don't know, I just run," he responded with mild irritation. He smiled when Sally said she was going to fall back. He picked up the pace again, but Paul stayed right with him. In a moment he was surprised to see Sally next to him again.

"You have shoes for pronating, but actually you supinate.

I bet you have knee pain," she said.

"You're right, I do," Dr. Wolf said, looking surprised.

Sally recommended a running shoe that she thought would take care of the problem. "I also think you are overstriding. Look at that speed limit sign up the road. Does it bounce up and down?"

"Yes, it does!" Doc answered, sounding surprised.

"You may want to shorten your stride a little," Sally diagnosed matter-of-factly. "If the bouncing stops, I think you will be more comfortable and reduce your chance of injury."

"If you are done warming up," Paul broke in, "we're ready when you are, Dr. Wolf."

"Actually, I'm thinking I will take it easy today," he answered with a smile. "You guys are good. I think I'm going to enjoy this more than I thought."

They ran about three miles down Old South Branch Road, to the spot where Lucy often turned off for her morning smudging ceremony, and then turned around and ran back.

The sight of that spot made Sally thoughtful. She respected Lucy for her discipline when it came to spiritual practices. Lucy offered up her prayers for the day by burning sage. The cleansing effect and ritual of smudging helped her stay connected to the Creator and to stay focused on the important stuff. The smoke from her smudging was carried to the eagle, and the eagle carried her request to live another day to the Creator.

High above them, the eagle once again had the perfect vantage point. He could observe Ray Waupuse searching through the scope of a rifle as he hid camouflaged in the woods. Ray was also a member of the Menominee Tribal Police and one of the important persons in Lucy's life. He had served in Special Forces during Desert Storm as a sharpshooter. He once had Saddam Hussein in his cross hairs, but it was against international law to assassinate another country's leader, so he was not given the order to engage his target. He still had nightmares about the people dying in roadside and car bombs and wondered for hours at night what might have happened if he had ignored his orders. He secretly wished he had pulled the trigger.

That day, Ray stayed well hidden and none of the three runners knew he was there. He didn't know that someone else was also watching him— and the eagle watched them all.

When the three reached the lodge, Doc had to bend down and keep his hands on his knees to catch his breath. Paul was breathing hard too, but Sally looked as if she had just stepped off a bus. She suggested next time they meet at the high school track in town so they could do some speed work.

Doc couldn't believe he was now going to lace up his skates and pursue the same route again with Kathy and Brad. The day was getting hotter, but he could already notice a drop in humidity as the storms from the night before had ushered in a high-pressure system. He found the skating more relaxing as Kathy and Brad didn't push the envelope and the conversation was pleasant. Kathy was a gymnast in college, and though she never looked anorexic like many gymnasts, she appeared athletic.

With each stride, her leg and arm muscles rippled, and she moved with grace and beauty. Brad, on the other hand, looked like a house being moved on skates. Brad was a heavy- weight wrestler in college and played offensive and defensive line in high school. In spite of his size, he moved well.

"So you are here not only to protect me from bad guys, but to protect me from the sun as well," Doc remarked as he skated in Brad's shadow.

"Not only that," said Brad with a smile, "but we can talk science. I teach science in Shawano, and I'm taking some grad level biology classes to see if I might like med school."

Doc didn't have to bend over to catch his breath after the skate. Still, the cool waters of Legend Lake felt soothing as he eagerly ran into the shallow water next to Ryan and Zack. The sand quickly changed to weeds and muck, and each of the three swimmers planed out in the water.

During the swim, Doc did freestyle, while Zack did the breaststroke so he could look forward, and Ryan did the backstroke so he could look backward. Both had just finished their junior year of college. Zack was the more serious of the two, but both enjoyed college. Since Zack was in recovery, he didn't drink alcohol or do drugs, and as his close friend, Ryan consequently didn't drink much either. Considering his family history of addictions, that was probably a good thing for Ryan. But that didn't let that stop them from enjoying college life. They would work out with the girls swim team, which gave them an opportunity to meet girls who had other interests besides drinking. They both studied hard enough to stay eligible for sports and keep their parents happy, but fun was part of their college experience, and they resolved to cash in on their share.

As they swam, Hank and Molly canoed nearby, watching them closely. "What are we looking for?" Molly asked her husband. "I'm not sure," Hank answered honestly. "I would guess we want to keep an eye out for boats going faster than they should heading for the swimmers. I don't think we have to worry too much without many people around."

They passed the time by practicing some maneuvers that Doc showed them. First, they practiced gaining speed and then making tight turns, which allows whitewater paddlers to move more slowly down a rapid and engage in eddy turns. Such turns are utilized so the paddler can rest in the calm water behind some of the larger rocks. Then they practiced moving the canoe sideways as they were moving forward, which is called "side slipping". This maneuver allows paddlers to avoid big rocks by moving to one side or the other. They looked forward to practicing these moves in flowing water, which of course would be much more difficult than on the lake.

From the shore, Lucy watched Doc participate with mixed feelings. She was enjoying the interaction of those participating but was worried because the next day would include the rapids events, and there they still needed help. Her own team could not help. They were all police officers and they would have different schedules than Doc. Besides, they were doing the race for fun and didn't have Doc's expertise. Little did she know that the answer would come to her and provide more danger than a solution. And little did she know that the very real danger in which Doc found himself would strike painfully close to home—his home.

While the Brandts were working out with Doc, Lucy spread the word that she needed someone who could paddle canoes and kayaks in whitewater. Later that evening, she was attending a meeting with her sponsor, Sophie, when a man who was in town for the powwows approached her. He was tall, thin, and wiry, with dark skin and eyes that were almost black. She recognized him immediately; he was a storyteller who visited each of the powwows, both telling stories and learning new ones from the elders. "I hear you're looking for someone who can teach whitewater canoeing and kayaking. I'm certified in both, and I'm available."

He reached out a big hand with long fingers to Lucy. "My name is Dean Swank, but most people call me 'Fiddler'."

"I can't pay you, Dean," Lucy answered.

"I'm not looking for money. I heard some of the story and want to help."

"I appreciate that, but I would need to check you out,"

Lucy answered.

Fiddler provided his American Canoe Association number and even his social security number so she could run a background check on him. When she entered the name and numbers into the computers, she found out that he was indeed certified in both whitewater canoeing and kayaking. She also found that besides a few minor brushes with the law, he had a clean record. He had been a Navy Seal and had served with some distinction, receiving a number of medals and citations. He seemed a perfect fit, but there was so much the computer couldn't tell her, and a great deal that Fiddler did not mention.

His mother was a full-blooded Cheyenne, but he didn't grow up on the reservation—she liked to drink and found it was easier to get white men to buy her drinks than the men from her reservation.

She met his father in a bar and married him a month later. She was pregnant before she realized she was married to an abuser. When Fiddler grew old enough to understand, he would often try to protect his mother only to have his father turn his anger and violence on him. He soon learned that he could draw his father's rage and hide out in the hills and woods of Montana while his drunk and angry father would tramp through the woods trying to find him. Finally, exhausted and needing a drink, his father would give up, return home, and pass out in a drunken stupor. Fiddler's mother would turn off the light as a signal that it was safe for him to return. He would hide in the woods until the lights went out, and then he would sneak inside.

The first night he stayed in the woods overnight he was petrified. His mother had also passed out on the couch and didn't turn off the lights. The harmless sounds that he heard through his bedroom window were now so much closer and ominous. Each time a large branch broke near him, he was sure it was a grizzly. He knew bears could see and smell much better than he could. Still, the threat of wild animals was nothing compared to the dread of returning home. As he got older, he stashed a sleeping bag in the woods and began staying out all night frequently. His mother died when he was twelve, and the abuse grew more intense. He spent more time in the woods and came home only for food and clothing when his father was working.

At fourteen, he was kicked out of school for fighting, and by sixteen he devised a plan to kill his father. He stole a rifle from his father's gun collection and killed a bear. After eating the meat, Fiddler cut off one of its paws and tied it to a sturdy stick. He waited until he knew his father had been drinking and went home. The usual argument started; it never took much. His father would just look at him and punch him. Dark thoughts always ran through his mind at times like these. Did his father feel powerful and free when he hit and kicked his son in the face? Did he feel a sense of justification or domination?

That night the boy ran out as he often did, and his father chased after him with a loaded gun in his unsteady hand. Fiddler stayed visible but never gave his father a good shot. Even after all the years of abuse, he was still shocked that his drunken father actually shot at him. As Fiddler approached a steep cliff, he suddenly turned and caught his father off guard. With all his strength, he hit his father hard in the face and neck with the bear paw. His father shrieked as he fell to the ground, the sound of the blows combining with the sound of tearing flesh. He heard his father groan as he rolled off the cliff and landed on the canyon floor below with a sickening thud. Then he began to call to his son, at first loudly and then angrily. Soon his pleas were frightened and pitiful.

"I can't move and I'm bleeding bad! Help me, son!"

Fiddler wondered if this cruel man was that stupid. Did he really think he would help him?

He stood his ground and watched and listened to his father die. In a couple of days the animals began to eat him. It was then that Fiddler called the police and reported his father missing. They soon found the body and came to the conclusion consistent with his elaborate plan. It was a tragic and fatal accident, the result of an unusual and unfortunate attack by a marauding black bear. By then, Fiddler had dismantled the bear claw and burned it in the woods. The remains would look like what hunters might leave. He hoped he covered all his tracks.

He then became curious about his Cheyenne roots. He visited the Flathead Reservation and began to listen to stories of the elders. He developed from them an identity that he had been seeking all his life. He took his mother's last name of Swank and developed a new sense of morality, though it was much different from White Man's laws. Since he didn't have a home, he would move from reservation to reservation, following the seasons. He visited the Navaho and Zuni reservations in the Southwest and the Seminoles in Florida in the winters, and the Sioux and other Northern Indians in the summers. He worked jobs that interested him, especially those that would teach him skills for surviving in nature. He spent several summers guiding and teaching whitewater canoeing and kayaking in the West. He studied for his GED and passed. And at nineteen he met a recruiter who convinced him to join the military.

The Navy recognized his potential and trained him to be a Seal. After his tour ended, he was recruited for covert intelligence. His superiors began using him to carry out undercover operations that would involve the disappearance of people some called enemies. He had a knack for making the deaths look accidental, and his reputation soon spread. He learned he could make much more money from private concerns, and he became a favorite of organized crime. Though he had little interest in getting rich, he liked using his money to help kids improve their lives. He had a particular interest in spousal and child abuse. He would donate money to family shelters on the reservations he would visit. He learned to drink in the service and soon had a problem stopping. One night while out with some of his fellow Seals, he saw a man get abusive with a woman in a bar. He intervened and would have killed the man had his friends not stopped him. The charges were dropped, but the Navy ordered him into treatment, and he found he actually enjoyed AA. It gave him fellowship wherever he visited, plus he learned new boundaries to his behavior and added another dimension to his unique code of ethics.

THAT NIGHT, JOHN AND GAYLE Wolf sat uncomfortably across from one another at the dinner table. It was a scene both took every opportunity to avoid. There was so much to think about and yet so little to talk about. Both thought about how different it was when the children were still home. Then the table was filled with excitement and conversation and laughter. Now the ticking grandfather clock was so much louder than it ever seemed before. The pauses in conversation far exceeded the conversation; all of a sudden, John noticed how much noise his knife made on the plate as he cut his steak.

He thought about his day. He wanted to tell Gayle about the Brandt family and how much he enjoyed the children and what he had learned from them about running and swimming, but the filter of his brain thought ahead. She might ask why he was suddenly working out with other people, and he knew he couldn't lie. Oh, it's just that I think some people are trying to kill me. What he most feared was not her worries, but how it might fuel her desire for him to stop obsessing so much about exercise and this silly race. At least Gayle thought it was silly. He didn't want to sit there while he talked about running and swimming only to see that same bored look on her face whenever he discussed just about anything he found interesting.

Little did he realize his story was insignificant compared to the secret Gayle was keeping from him; but unlike John, Gayle had become a quite proficient liar. It all went back to the surprises she'd had starting a few years back. Prior to that, she had no understanding or compassion for addiction. It wasn't that she wasn't exposed to it—her father was an alcoholic. But he was different from some others. He wasn't abusive, and he didn't lose his job or his family. He was a loving man who was successful with everything but battling alcohol. She had tried alcohol as a kid, but she didn't like the taste, and it almost made her sick. She also thought drugs were stupid and certainly didn't understand how her husband got so hooked on them. All of that changed innocently enough when she and some of her nursing friends spent an evening at the casino.

Back in 1976, only thirteen states had lotteries, two had off-track betting, and there were no casinos outside Las Vegas. Today a person can make a legal wager in every state but three. Thirty-seven states have lotteries, twenty-eight have casinos, and twenty-two have off-track betting. Perhaps no group has benefited from this as much as Native Americans, but it is a mixed blessing that comes at a price for everyone. It is estimated that problem gambling costs each taxpayer over a thousand dollars a year in lost jobs, court expenditures, jail time, and prison costs. This financial and social burden does not include the cost for divorce and counseling, nor the personal pain of families in these situations.

That night she took a dollar coin, placed it in the slot machine, and pulled the lever. It was a combination of cherries lined up one after another. The thrill of watching the coins falling in the tray below and the sound of coins bouncing off of one another hypnotized her. Soon she would have dreams of scooping up coins she found lying on the floor after overflowing the basket beneath the slot machine. There was attention too as people gathered around and watched as the rotating light and the siren signaled a big winner. That night, before all was said and done, she had won five thousand dollars, and her life would never be the same. Suddenly, a life that seemed so dull found excitement and passion. Her life had a purpose— to win more money. Gayle loved money. She always wanted more. She didn't need drugs or any artificial stimulation. When she gambled, her body produced its own.

She decided not to tell her family about her winnings. She would use it as a base to make even more money.

Power, wealth, and acquisition were Gayle's driving goals for her entire life. To some extent, she developed this neediness when she was young. Her parents didn't get along well, and each tried to bribe their only child in return for her attention. Her mother didn't care for men much and needed Gayle to be her girlfriend instead of being her daughter. They'd go shopping together, and her mother thought everything looked stunning on her little girl. When she turned sixteen, her father took her shopping for a car, and he beamed at how great she looked in the red convertible she chose. He had started to tell her it was too expensive, but when he saw a tear roll down her cheek, he took out his checkbook. But her parents had limited resources and her desires went much further. When she met John

Wolf in college and realized he wanted to be a neurosurgeon, she was sure she hit the mother lode.

By the time he was addicted to drugs and then recovering with a dream of saving the First People one drug addict at a time, John and Gayle had two children. Her modeling career, which helped her through college and helped pay for her husband's drug abuse, was ruined by the obscurity of the reservation. Gayle didn't like the idea of being poor, and raising two children on a nurse's salary was not very appealing to her.

That was why her win at the casino was so thrilling. The next day, Gayle went back to the casino to add to her earnings. Each time she put a coin in the slot machine, her heart would pound waiting for the next big payoff. She won sometimes, but she lost more frequently and in one day her five thousand was down to four thousand. But now she was hooked by the thrill of it all.

Like so many addictions, it wasn't just the time at the casino that excited her. She began to think about gambling all the time and to explore other options. She learned she could play poker and bet on games from her home computer. She found that buying stocks and watching them rise from day to day in the newspaper was just as exciting. Since she was in charge of the family finances anyway and John paid no attention to them, she soon just comingled *her* money with *their* money. She began to read books about gambling, and when a job opened up at the casino she took it. She was careful to never gamble while she worked, but that didn't keep her from studying the scene and talking to people who worked and played there.

Gayle was an attractive woman with natural red hair and the fair complexion that went with it. Even though she had two children, she took good care of herself. At five feet two inches and one hundred and ten pounds, she was a forty-something who looked like a thirty-something. She was vivacious with a laugh for every occasion, and she was smart. It didn't take her long to move into management. She soon learned there was no way to win in the long run if you played games against the house. The house had the odds and was always going to win. The only game she could win at was poker, since there the house just took a cut, and the competition was against the other players. She began to focus her reading on books about poker tips and strategies. She learned the odds of each hand and even read a book on tells, or the psychology of judging how other players tipped off their hands. Her background as a nurse who paid attention to blood pressure, pulse, and skin conditions made her a natural at reading tells.

She noticed one man would purse his lips when he held winning cards. She would usually fold if she had a poor hand. But when he would raise the pot and he didn't purse his lips, she knew he was bluffing. Gayle would win big. Another man, she noticed, spent less time looking at his cards and more time looking at her cleavage. He didn't seem to mind losing as long as she bent forward to scoop up the pot. She made sure she faced him and smiled and took considerable time to gather up her winnings.

Learning to control tells was more difficult, particularly controlling her excitement when she had a good hand. If she gave it away, other players with good hands would fold.

Gayle started playing on her days off at the low-stakes tables with amateurs and found she could usually win. But as the stakes got higher with the better players, she'd often lose and lose big. There were always two or three at the table with lots of money who liked to show how much they could afford to lose. And then there were the professional gamblers, who were only too happy to take that money. But Gayle didn't have it to lose, and each table usually had just one or two winners. Gayle began to travel to the Oneida Casino in Green Bay and the North Star Casino owned by the Mohicans on the other side of the Menominee Reservation. That way she could avoid suspicion from her neighbors and coworkers and also play for bigger pots. Her husband could have explained this to her: whether drugs or alcohol, the addict develops a tolerance and needs more and more to get high; with gamblers, it takes a larger and larger pot.

-One day Gayle was playing at the high-stakes table when she noticed a new player. He was near her age and impeccably dressed. She could tell right away he was a professional because she could not spot any tells, and he won several hands that he should have lost. She had gone through all of the family savings by this point and was playing with next year's college tuition for the children. When Gayle lost the last of her money to the stranger, she left the table for the washroom and, once inside, began to sob. Minutes later, she composed herself and reapplied her makeup. The face she saw in the mirror looked strange to her—a mask that she put on and took off. If the mask came off, what would exist underneath? She didn't know. Perhaps she never knew, and that was part of the problem. But then her addictive behaviors took over. Your luck is bound to change, she thought to herself. And when she walked from the restroom, it did change. It got worse.

The professional gambler was waiting for her. "I know what you are doing wrong," he announced. "Do you?" she said coldly.

"Let's go to my room," he said, leading her by the arm. "I know how to improve your game."

She pulled back, but in a hesitating sort of way.

"I don't do sex for money," she said sharply.

"Who said anything about sex? I'm suggesting a card game."

"I don't have any money left," she responded immediately.

"You let me worry about that," he said with a confidence she found irresistible.

Gayle flushed. "I don't go with strangers to their rooms," she said, "not for card games or for anything else." "Don't you." It was a statement, not a question.

They stood there for a long time, his hand on her arm. Gayle's mind whirled. She thought of many things that were seemingly unconnected— her wedding dress, the boys she had known in high school, the first boy she had slept with, the sound coins made when they fell into the slot. When she tried to think of Doc or the children, she felt nothing.

"You want to come with me," said the gambler in her ear. "You want to take the risk and come with me. That's because you are a gambler too. You wouldn't be able to bear knowing that you could have come with me—and didn't. You want the adventure and the thrill as much as I do. And more. That's why you'll come with me."

Once again they stood in silence.

"What's your name," Gayle asked finally. "Slade. Jack Slade."

She laughed. "It sounds like a private eye in an old movie."

He smiled, but did not respond. For some reason she felt certain that it was his not his real name.

Gambling. Adventure. Thrills. A man whose real name she would not know. Perhaps a man who was worth surrendering to.

What's one more lie, Gayle thought to herself, one of many more to come.

Once they got to his room, Slade pulled out a deck of cards. "We'll play for your clothes. If you win, I pay you back some of what you lost. If I win, you're naked." Then he added, as if it had already been decided, "Along the way I will tell you what you are doing wrong."

Gayle was at a low point and getting desperate. She had lost her family's savings and now the money for her kids' tuition. Not only that, but the game sounded appealing. "Aren't we talking apples and oranges here? What are my clothes worth?"

"For each of your bids, say, a button, a zipper, a snap, or a take-off, I'll bid a thousand dollars."

"Plus you give me tips for free?"

"This is as close to a sure win as you are ever going to get in poker."

"You could lose more to me than I lost to you. I have more than five buttons on my blouse alone," she cautioned hopefully.

"Yes, but I don't plan on losing. That's your first lesson. It's not about the cards."

They sat at a small table in his room. He shuffled the deck one-handed and then handed her the cards. "You can deal first. What's your game?"

Gayle took the cards and named five-card draw. "Aren't you going to ante?"

"One button?"

"Already I know I have you. You're playing not to lose instead of playing to win."

She dealt the first five cards and dealt herself three eights.

"Your bet," she said. "I fold," he said.

Gayle's disappointment was obvious and clearly written on her face.

"See how important that ante was," he said. "If you had anted more, you could have won all you had lost tonight or maybe kept me in the game. You could have made better use of that hand."

"How do you know what kind of hand I have? I never even had a chance to bid?"

"I'm sure that red hair and complexion of yours has served you well your whole life. You are a beautiful woman, who needs little makeup, but when you have a good hand, your fair complexion gives it away. Right next to your temple there is a slight color change." "You mean like a blush?" "Yes," he answered.

"How can I control that?"

"You can't make it stop, but you can make it lie for you. You have to make yourself look like a good hand when you don't have one. You have to practice in the mirror."

"How do I control it?"

"Think exciting thoughts that have nothing to do with the cards, or imagine you have all aces when you've got two deuces. People have different ways. You will have to learn your own methods."

"I thought you said the cards don't matter. You could win any hand. Why did you quit so early?"

"I can win any game, and maybe I could have won that hand. But you would have had to give up too many clothes, and I want this to go slow."

Gayle shivered. Did she feel fear or excitement? Slade dealt the next hand. "Ante three," he said. Gayle was dealt a hand with few possibilities. "Your bet."

"I fold," she said.

"You owe me three buttons," He responded with some huskiness in his voice.

Gayle undid the three buttons on one cuff. Then she looked at him and smiled in defiance. He showed no expression.

In the next hand, Gayle had good cards and bid high but lost. She removed her shoes but still owed more. So she began removing her blouse as she might in her own bedroom. She was looking down and moving fast to remove her top.

"Ah, ah! Slow down!" he demanded.

Gayle looked him in the eye and slowly undid the rest of her buttons. Then she ever so slowly took her blouse off of each shoulder using only two fingers to expose a sexy black bra. She then slowly removed each sleeve and let the blouse fall to the floor. She felt his gaze burning into her skin. This time she was sure where the shivers came from. She was becoming very interested in this game.

Slade lost five thousand in the next hand.

Gayle was now up a thousand dollars and could have left up a grand, but if the thought entered her mind, it didn't show. Her pulse and sexual arousal were both rising and intense, and she did not want to leave. A tiny, almost imperceptible grin crossed Slade's face ever so briefly. He won the next hand, and Gayle was down to her bra and panties. It was her deal.

"I can only ante two," she said.

"We can start with you removing my clothes now," Slade said.

"I get to choose," Gayle smiled.

They continued to play well into the night. Gayle won several more hands and was up several thousand dollars. When she lost all she gave up a little more respect and dignity but was too excited to notice. Even that first night in the casino could not top this. Gambling gave her a high, but add to that an attractive man with the power and wealth she always dreamed of, who was able to touch her emotionally and physically again and again, Gayle was now hooked twice.

THE NEXT MORNING, WHEN HANK, Molly, and Bobbie met Doc at the Wolf River, Lucy was there to introduce them to Fiddler. She watched for an hour to verify whether he had the skill on the river that he promised. He was good. He was even better than Lucy had hoped. He taught Molly and Bobbie to get more strength in their strokes by keeping their paddles vertical. He also taught them to twist with their torso and use their oblique muscle for extra power.

He taught Hank and Bobbie skills in reading the river. They learned they could tell when a rapid was approaching not only from the sound it made but also by watching for a horizon line as they looked downstream. The smooth water made a downstream "V" at the head of a rapid, and it was the place to enter. Now that they were in moving water, they could practice turning into the calm eddies behind rocks where they could rest and watch the current go by. Most of all, they acquired new river skills by simply watching Fiddler play easily with the river. And play he did.

It was clear, calm day with just a few puffy clouds overhead. The sun sparkled on the water. The strong thundershowers that were moving through regularly in the late afternoon kept the river high and the power of the current strong, especially in the rapids. High water made the river change. In some ways it made certain rapids easier because there were fewer rocks to navigate around, but it also made the river more powerful and mistakes potentially deadly.

After they finished their workout, they stopped at the Wild Wolf Inn for breakfast. Bobbie found she had a strange reaction to Fiddler. Her first impression was fear, and she was reminded of Ezra, whom she met the last time she helped Lucy. She had fallen off her snowmobile and was trapped underneath it when Ezra came along and pulled her out. At that time, she understood and knew real fear. Was he going to save her or kill her?

Fiddler had fierceness in his eyes, and yet there was sadness there as well. He had somehow heard about Scott and began asking questions about their family. Molly was impressed with his intensity as he listened and paid attention to each word. Like a man in the hot desert who comes upon the cool water of an oasis, he seemed to drink in every syllable and yet focus most on the meaning. His face would change to match each different emotion in the story. If he asked a question, it was only to clarify or deepen his understanding. There was never a hint of judgment. Molly also noticed, however, that it was difficult to learn much about Fiddler. Though she was convinced he had lived an interesting life from what he did share, he was an expert at refocusing the conversation back onto them. Most people would enjoy the attention. In the end he asked if he could use their life in his stories and songs.

"If you want to," was the usual response, "but I'm not a Native American."

Then Fiddler would smile and say, "I know that. I like the lives of all people. Every person's life is a story. I think God created people because of His love of stories."

After she was convinced that the Brandts and Doc were safe with Fiddler, Lucy went to the storage area where the weed cutters were kept in Legend Lake. There was a small parking lot off of Highway VV where the drivers could park their cars and board their machines. She got there just as the two men and one woman were getting ready to start work. The woman and one of the men had been in another lake the day of Doc's injuries, and so Lucy focused on the man who had just returned to work after burying his mother. He had only just arrived home after spending some time alone in the woods of Lac du Flambeau after her burial. His friends had built a sweat lodge and arranged a feast in honor of his mother's spirit. He was tired and perhaps a little irritable from grief and the stress of travel.

"I'm sorry about your mom," Lucy began.

The man simply shrugged his shoulders. "Look," he said, "I'm sorry about what happened to Doc. My friend told me he had been working on the cutter but had stopped to go pick up some parts for the engine in Shawano. He didn't bother taking the keys because the engine had parts missing. Besides, how would anyone be able to steal this big thing anyway? When he got back he was surprised to see it was working, and then Dave told him about Doc. As I guess you heard, this is a guy who's had some bad luck already, so he left town. I told him you'd probably want to speak to him, but he didn't care. He didn't even wait to get paid for his work. He said he'd call me later to see if he was in any trouble. If not, then he'd tell me where to mail his check."

It was another dead end. Lucy swallowed her frustration and left.

In her car, she sat for a while wondering where she could go next to solve this mystery. She didn't have a clue. She wanted to go to the casino and talk with Gayle, but Doc had been so determined to keep the whole thing from his wife. Since Lucy wasn't sure a crime had been committed, she had to respect Doc's wishes.

Damn it, she thought. Why do I have to listen and follow the rules? I just want to get everything out into the open and help a friend. A host of questions plagued her mind, all centering around Gayle: why didn't Doc want his wife to know? Why did he obviously expect her not to see the scars on his body from the attack at the lake?

Then she thought of a way to find out more about Gayle without talking directly to her. She had a great source in her sponsor Sophie, who knew everything happening on the reservation. Lucy stopped by the little store on Highway 47 and picked up some tobacco and a couple of sweet rolls.

Then she continued just a few blocks further down to Sophie's. As usual on a nice day, Sophie was out on the porch drinking her morning coffee and enjoying a cigarette.

"Hi, Auntie," Lucy said as she handed her the tobacco and a sweet roll.

"*Boozhoo! Miigwech*, Lucy," Sophie responded, thanking her for the gifts. "Cigarettes are tobacco too, you know."

Lucy just rolled her eyes. They had been over this a number of times. Lucy disapproved of her smoking and would only bring her tobacco for her offering to the Great Spirit in the morning. Each day she would start a tiny fire and would sprinkle tobacco, sweet grass, and sage onto it while she asked the Spirit for the opportunity to live another day. The Eagle would then take the smoke up to the heavens, and the Spirit would be pleased with the offering and grant the request of another day. This was the only tobacco that Lucy would bring. It came loose in a pouch and was not rolled in cigarette paper.

"You bring me sweet rolls. They can kill me too," Sophie said with a smile. She swirled her arm for emphasis, dropping a long stream of ash on the porch floor.

"You're right, but I just bring you one of those, not a pack of twenty. Besides," she said, smiling, "if I eat sweet rolls, they have to be good for you, right?"

"Why am I blessed with this wonderful visit criticizing my lifestyle? You must be in some sort of trouble."

"Are you saying I never stop by just to chat, Auntie?"

Lucy asked, rubbing Sophie's arm.

"Yes, that's pretty much what I'm saying."

"Well, I'm not in trouble, but as you know, Doc is, and I've hit a dead end in trying to figure out who might be behind it. I'd like to talk with his wife about this and the people at the clinic, but he won't let me. So I came to you as a source of information, because no one has a hand on the pulse of this community like you do."

"If Doc asked you not to investigate this, shouldn't you respect his wishes?"

"He didn't ask me that," Lucy replied promptly. "He just asked me not to bother his wife or the treatment staff."

"What do you hope to find out from talking to them? Do you think that one of them is trying to kill him?"

"No, but I think they might have some ideas about who might be trying. This is weird. Doc is the person who saved my life, and now I'm trying to do the same for him, but I feel like I'm meeting resistance."

"And do you think it was probably what he felt when he was working with you?" Sophie countered.

Lucy just stuck her tongue out. "How about the treatment center? Who there might have reason to harm him?"

"Too many people to count. Think about it, how many times has Doc recommended that a woman not return to her husband because he also uses or because he is abusive? How often does the court refer people, and then Doc reports that they are not complying with the court order?"

"You're right, there," Lucy said with a shiver. "I hate to think what I would have done to him if he had testified that I shouldn't have my children back."

"What about his wife at the casino? Does she ever throw people out of there or fire someone that might get back at her by hurting Doc?"

There was a long pause before Sophie spoke. "I think you need to know that what I'm about to tell you is only what I've heard from some pretty unreliable sources. Gayle has been spending a lot of time at the casino."

"Of course she has. She works there now," Lucy said. "Even I know that."

"Yes, but she is there before and after her shift."

"Well, she's in management now. I'm sure she's just conscientious."

"Is she conscientious to the point that she's using her own money to see if the slot machines work, and that no one is cheating at the poker tables?"

"Oh!" Lucy exclaimed.

After another long pause, "There's more. There is a gambler in town who has been here before, but he usually stays a week or two and moves on. This time he has stayed for six months. Gayle has been seen going to his room on more than one occasion." Sophie added sarcastically, "I know she's in management now, but I don't think she works for housekeeping. Even if she did, would she just keep inspecting the same room? For a cop, you are awfully naive."

"I guess Doc has been a hero of mine for so long now I don't want to admit that anything could be wrong in his life. So you think she may have a gambling problem and is having an affair? Do you think Doc knows?"

"I don't think he does. Sometimes even the best of us can be in denial, and remember, there are always people who want to hurt him. Of course," she added, crushing her cigarette into a rusty ashtray, "Maybe this is just a vicious rumor made up by people who don't like him."

Lucy's head was spinning! How could she find out the truth, and even if she did, could she talk to Doc about it? Could she continue to investigate this without jeopardizing her own recovery? The casino was a place she liked to avoid. It attracted too many elements that were bad for her. Was that a lesson Gayle was learning? Would she learn the truth before it was too late?

DOC WAS NOT THINKING ABOUT his wife at all, and certainly not about any secrets she might be keeping from him, when he met Paul at the trailhead of the mountain bike trail at seven a.m. They waited about fifteen minutes for Fiddler to show up, but they finally decided he must have overslept or was tied up with some other business. "He probably met an interesting person on the way here," said Doc. "He's too busy listening to his story to come with us."

They decided not to wait any longer and took off down the trail.

Mountain biking is dangerous even if no one is trying to kill you. As the term indicates, it is usually done in mountainous or at least hilly terrain. The trails are usually little more than hiking trails. Often rocks and logs are embedded on the narrow pathways that traverse steep up-and-down terrain. The trail up requires strong legs, great aerobic capacity, and the skill to keep your weight balanced enough to create traction on both tires—particularly on the front tire, which has a tendency to rise on the way up a hill. If it spikes too high, the biker will sail over backward. It is difficult to maintain speed, and if the biker stops, he probably will be forced to walk the remainder of the way up the hill because it is too difficult to start in the middle of a steep incline. Downhill the challenges are the opposite. It is tough to keep from going too fast. You may find yourself flying over the handlebars if you shift your weight too far forward or hit a rock or log. Racers and even casual riders who participate in this sport are usually well acquainted with slings, casts, and stitches. This was the one event that Doc was willing to concede time just to survive. He was practicing to improve his time as much as his skill.

"I'm not very good at this event," he told Paul as they were starting out. "Any tips you can give me would be greatly appreciated."

"I've only been doing it for a year myself, but doing it in Colorado demands that you learn in a hurry. I also spent my spring break in Moab, Utah. Those Utah riders were really skilled, so I learned a lot."

For the first few miles, the trail passed through gentle rolling hills, and the path was clear and wide. They biked side by side and talked about their appreciation of nature and their concern for what was happening to the environment. Both were well versed in both the biological and political forces that were impacting it.

At the third mile marker, however, their concern shifted to the immediate moment. First the trail became narrower, and off in the distance they could hear a four-wheeler. Wisconsin is not unique in the conflict between those who engage in what is often referred to as silent sports and those who preferred their recreation to be loud and motorized. Their arguments would often end up in one of the branches of government. Trails such as the Mountain Bay, between Wausau and Green Bay, and the Gandy Dancer, between St. Croix and Superior, were a combination of crushed limestone and blacktop. The trails were originally designed for bikers, walkers, joggers, and equestrians in the spring, summer, and fall, and for snowmobiles in the winter. Some areas, however, were also approved for four-wheelers in the warmer months. This naturally created some conflict. Not only did the bikers and walkers like the quiet of the trail the four-wheelers interrupted, but their difference in speed created safety concerns as well.

The trail that Doc and Paul rode, however, was not a limestone trail, and the four-wheelers had as much right to it as the mountain bikers. But the narrow trail and poor visibility made riding even more hazardous, and the natural dislike between bikers and four-wheelers added to the tension. And ominously, a four-wheeler in the woods and away from traffic made a perfect murder weapon.

Paul led the way down the path that had grown increasingly steeper and filled with more rocks and fallen branches. They were now on nature's roller coaster. They no sooner made it down one hill than they found themselves heading back up a steep grade often fifteen percent or steeper. Both of them could still hear a four-wheeler getting closer, but they could not see it. It was also difficult to tell in which direction it was headed. As Paul reached the top of a hill, he looked down a steep grade to the bottom where it intersected a fire lane. The loud whine of the four-wheeler came to a halt, and they could hear it faintly idling nearby. Paul stopped at the top of the hill. The color had left his face. "For the first time, this murder stuff seems more real," he said softly in Doc's ear.

"I know what you mean," Doc said. "I have the distinct feeling that a four-wheeler is waiting at that fire lane, and as we cross we will be like ducks in a shooting gallery."

"I'm going to head down the hill like I have no concern,

but when I get to the fire lane I'll slide to a stop. So give me plenty of room," Paul said with a tremor in his voice.

Just as he was about to start down, Doc grabbed his arm.

"Why not let me go first?"

"I think I can be more convincing."

"What do you mean?" Doc asked, but Paul had already taken off down the hill.

It didn't take long for Doc to get his answer, and at the same time he realized how much Paul had been holding back on the downhill runs. He was flying downhill at about twice the speed as before and just before he reached the intersection, he slammed on his brakes and turned his bike sideways into a skidding stop. Without the extra room between them, Doc would have hit Paul for sure because there was no way he could have stopped that fast without flying over his handlebars. Sure enough, just as Paul came to a stop, the four-wheeler barreled through the intersection. They both breathed a sigh of relief until they heard the four-wheeler turn around.

Doc took off across the fire lane and yelled for Paul to follow. Just past the fire lane, Doc scrambled up a short hill and then roared down a steep hill. Paul was impressed at how quickly fear had improved his riding, but the roar of the four-wheeler was closer behind them, and moving ever closer.

Doc quickly cut off the trail onto a narrow path where the four-wheeler couldn't follow, but the four-wheeler was riding parallel to them in the woods. They caught a glimpse of him sporadically, but he was wearing a helmet with mirror- reflecting glass in front of his face. He matched their speed as if he were just looking for a place he could turn toward them and run them down. Paul looked ahead of Doc and saw the place toward which the four-wheel driver was aiming—just as he heard a gunshot ring out from a hill above them. It seemed like time stopped and then moved in slow motion. Paul and Doc held their breath. The bullet landed just in front of the four-wheeler. A second shot hit a tree inches from the helmet the rider was wearing, splattering bark against the reflecting glass. With a quick U-turn, the rider was gone.

Soon they heard another four-wheeler start up near the same place from which the shots had come. The vehicle raced toward them and

Doc smiled with relief as the rider came into view. It took Paul longer to recognize Ezra, since he met him only once. But both riders sighed and hung their heads for a moment, trying to slow their racing hearts.

Ezra lived by himself in the woods of the reservation since his wife died. He owed Lucy a favor since she helped keep him out of jail after he kidnapped a baby and gave it to his daughter. The judge took into consideration that the child was probably going to be removed by child protective services anyway because the mother was addicted to heroin. Still, Ezra was probably looking at jail time if Lucy, the mother, and even the Brandts hadn't come to his defense. A bad situation actually turned out for the better. The baby's mother entered the treatment center. When she finally got clean and came to her senses, she actually let her son stay with Ezra's daughter. She was yet another person Doc had helped.

Ezra climbed off the four-wheeler. "Felt trouble," he said simply.

"Thanks," Doc answered, equally brief.

"You two okay?" Ezra inquired after a long pause.

Paul and Doc, still breathing hard, looked at one another.

"How are you?" Doc asked Paul with concern.

Paul took a long time to answer. He had demonstrated real courage and not of a false bravado type. The amount of courage one has is in direct proportion to the amount of fear to be overcome in order to act, and Paul had plenty of fear. But he was also honest enough with himself and others not to pretend it wasn't there. "I'm okay for the moment, but I don't think there is any doubt now that someone is trying to kill you, and I don't like the fact that the guy on that four-wheeler is out there somewhere, and we don't know where."

"We'll take a different way back," Ezra said. "And I'll stay right with you."

"I'd appreciate that," Doc answered. "I guess I can't kid myself any longer. I'll talk with Lucy when we get back. I don't want to give up, but maybe we'll have to be more careful in our training. I can't jeopardize your lives like this. I will not risk your life."

Deep in thought, the three silently made their way back to Keshena.

Doc's thoughts were filled with anxiety and guilt. It was obvious now that he was not only risking his own life but that of this wonderful family of whom he'd become very fond. Paul was just a freshman in college whose intelligence and compassion gave every indication that he would one day make a strong contribution to the world. How could he allow his own ambitions to jeopardize that?

CHAPTER 9

THAT NIGHT THE STURGEON FESTIVAL began. For much of their history, the Menominee people had counted on sturgeon for a large part of their diet. Their ancestral homeland ranged from Lake Michigan to Lake Winnebago and along the Wolf River. Through treaties, the White Man slowly took more and more of the Menominee's land until they were left with a small sliver along the Wolf—from its source to about the middle part of this wild and scenic river. Still, they would fish each spring during the spawning season until the White Man eventually damned the river and cut the Menominee off from their precious sturgeon.

The sturgeon is a huge fish with a long history among the Indians. An ugly fish that can top two hundred pounds. Bottom feeders. While they have no teeth, they can, nonetheless, be intimidating based on their size alone. Legend has it that long ago the elders would cut off the head of the fish and boil it. They prized the head as a delicacy. The rest of the fish was simply thrown away. There is much speculation as to why they would not eat the whole fish, as many members of the tribe could be fed with just one catch. In recent decades, they stopped this wasteful practice. Indians used the whole sturgeon and eventually cut off and threw away the head while enjoying the flesh of this very large fish. They honored any animal that produces so much food. Many Indians offered *sama*, or tobacco, to the Great Spirit and to the animal for giving up its life to provide food. So even though the source of sturgeon was cut off, they still continued to celebrate their relationship to it during the Sturgeon Festival at the end of each June.

Doc made it a yearly tradition to attend the festival. He loved the spirituality and stories of his people. It was early evening and dark clouds and lightning dominated the horizon when Lucy ran into Doc. He shared with her the day's events. Lucy noticed that Doc did not mention Fiddler.

"Where was Fiddler?" she asked, somewhat angry and disappointed.

"I don't know," Doc said. "He planned to be there but never showed up."

"I know he's here somewhere. I'll go ask him what happened." Even then Lucy did not share with Doc the growing misgivings she had about Fiddler.

The Sturgeon Festival was held at the same location as the powwow and could rival any man-made arena. It was a natural bowl surrounded by large pine trees, the tops of which provided a natural canopy for the edges of the bowl. The center was open and used for dancing at the powwow. In between the large pines, tall grass swayed in the breeze and appeared to be dancing right along to the beat of the drums. That space was saved for the drummers and the big drums used for the festival. All participants were surrounded by mouth-watering smells originating from booths that sold traditional food.

Handmade art was displayed for sale, and the booths were strung around the rim of the bowl. Everyone from very young children to elders spent the year making the wares they would display proudly at the festival. The many bright colors and beautiful patterns danced in the sunlight. The ladies were known especially for their beadwork.

The previous year Lucy and her daughter Tara had begun to sew a traditional dress. The outfit was long and fell to the bottom of Tara's calves when they started making it; but now it was only to the top of her calves as Tara's legs grew long like her mother's. The dress was covered from top to bottom with silver tubes each about an inch long. Sewing provided an opportunity for mother and daughter to bond, and they often shared stories of their day. Tara would confide her concerns about her girlfriends. Some were becoming interested in boys, and Tara often disapproved of their choices. Lucy would occasionally ask her of her memories of her father and of her drug use when Tara was young. Tara's answers were brief and matter-of-fact, but Lucy was convinced her drug abuse had more of an effect on Tara than she would admit. Lucy suspected that was one reason Tara approached new experiences in her life cautiously, for which Lucy was thankful.

Fiddler was there and in fine form. He did some dancing in the bowl, then went to work his booth on the bowl rim where he displayed and sold CDs of his music and stories.

Lucy was downright afraid as she approached him, but he looked up and preempted her questions.

"Sorry I missed the workout," he said. "I overslept."

She didn't believe him, but she didn't let on. Little did she know that Fiddler could read her every movement like a book. He knew that she didn't trust him.

Later Lucy talked the whole business over with Ray. "I hate going behind Doc's back like this," she concluded, "but I got permission from the lieutenant to check into the bank account Doc and Gayle have at the bank in Shawano. If the rumors are true about Gayle being caught up in gambling, there might be some activity there."

"I know you and Doc are friends," said Ray stroking Lucy's hair, "but after what happened today, there is no doubt we have an attempted murder going on here. I don't think you have much choice but to try to get to the bottom of this."

"So," she said, "you think I should get a subpoena and look into Doc's bank records?"

"I think that's a start," said Ray.

"What if I find out that the rumors are true? That Gayle is gambling? Who would I tell? Would I have to tell Doc? What if he already knows and is trying to protect Gayle from an investigation? What if he doesn't know?"

"We'll cross that bridge when we come to it," said Ray. "You still have to do what you feel you must do. Doc may know—maybe he's in denial. You won't help him by supporting his denial."

Saddened and yet comforted by his strength, Lucy closed her eyes, resting against Ray. She had begun to depend on him for so many things. She had never had a relationship with a man without alcohol and drugs playing a major part in it. Ray had never been a drinker and he liked the fact that Lucy didn't drink. She had never thought she would have a man whom she would trust enough to lean on. She had always respected his advice as a cop, but now it was so much more. Her kids and even her mother had grown to love him. He was kind and gentle and never seemed to push her into more of a relationship with him than she could handle. He was patient; they never made love at her house, and they rarely spent a night together unless they had an opportunity to be away alone. It wasn't that she didn't trust him. Lucy would leave her children with him when her mother was busy, which was good for all of them. Her mother had a chance to have more free time, and the kids got a chance to know Ray away from their mother and grandmother.

She wouldn't have been attracted to him when she was younger—not that he wasn't good looking, because he was very attractive. And not that he was a sissy, because he wasn't. He was kind and patient and loving. He treated her with respect, and though he loved to laugh and have fun, he wasn't wild. He didn't live on the edge. She often wondered why so many young girls were most attracted to the men who treated them badly. It wasn't until they were older that they longed for the things that Ray could offer. Often it was too late because they were trapped in bad relationships. The times alone, making love, filled Lucy beyond her imagination. She had longed for a good man who was safe, and she found that safe, warm, accepting and exciting place lying next to Ray.

That same night across town, Doc lay in bed next to Gayle. They both were awake but pretended otherwise. After twenty-five years each knew the other was awake, but they allowed the shameful silence to continue.

Doc was busy thinking about the distance between them. He even allowed it to cross his mind that there might be someone else. Over the years there had always been logical reasons for the growing distance between them. In the beginning, they were both finishing school, and there were papers and tests. Then he suffered through his chemical dependency and a lengthy and complicated recovery. Once sober, there were kids to raise. They both had jobs, and he became increasingly absorbed in his practice. Then he started exercising to reduce the stress and fight a sedentary lifestyle and creeping middle age. His addictive personality kicked in and before he knew it he was biking, swimming, and running a combined 100 miles a week.

When the kids were younger, he'd take them along in strollers, or they would bike next to him while he ran. He even developed a raft he would pull them on as he swam. As they moved to adolescence, they would sometimes ride, run, or swim with him, but more and more they got their exercise with their sports teams or activities with their friends. He sometimes worked out with Gayle, but she rarely was interested in going the distances he did or at the intensity he desired.

In spite of all of those things, they were friends even when the passions of love came and went. They were still playful with one another despite the direction in which their relationship began to deteriorate. But for some time now, both of their minds seemed elsewhere. He knew for himself that his mind was either on work or some new residents that had just entered treatment and what he could do to reach them or on physical training and some new way he could tweak his body to get more from it. He knew Gayle was also somewhere else mentally, and maybe even physically, but he just didn't know where. He was not sure if he wanted to know. She seemed very involved with her job at the casino. What he originally thought would be less demanding on her than nursing now seemed to be more demanding. So the distance between them had reached new dimensions, both high and low.

As Gayle lay there, she was torn right down the middle. One part of her wanted to confess and ask for his forgiveness. She wanted to unload the tortured burden of having this secret life. If it were just him, she might have gone in a heartbeat, but there were children, family, and even friends to consider. She knew if she left with Slade, it would be just the two of them moving from place to place, and she would never feel a sense of belonging or community again. Though she resented her husband for moving to the rez, she had to admit she had made friends and a meaningful life here. While the rich and glamorous lifestyle was appealing, and Slade seemed to be all she needed, Gayle wondered if the passion and excitement would last. She knew so little about him, and he was always evasive about his past. Why was a man who was so good with women never married before? Maybe he was married and just hadn't told her. He would just say that he had never met the right one, that he was concentrating on his craft, or that most women just wanted to settle down and have babies. Gayle seemed to be his match; she was done with that baby stuff and now sought adventure and excitement and the thrill of that next big win.

She was restless and turned over.

Doc, who was remembering in-line skating with Brad and Kathy— remembering the playfulness and tenderness of their relationship, and realizing there was a part of him deep inside that ached for something he had lost but rarely acknowledged, the connection and intimacy he had been missing for too many years—sat up slightly in bed.

He knew his only chance for redemption involved Gayle. He felt keenly the debt he owed to her. She had stuck with him during those years of residency and drug addiction. He wasn't naive enough to believe she was motivated to stay with him by undying love. And although she had the opportunity to use guilt as a way to keep him from following his dreams of working at a treatment center, she didn't. She was his wife. She was his only hope for love. He had to find a way to regain what they had lost.

"Gayle?" he asked. "Are you awake?"

Gayle did not move or respond.

After a moment, Doc lay back down.

Soon he and Gayle drifted into fitful sleep and another opportunity had passed.

LUCY STOPPED BY THE POWWOW one afternoon to watch the preparations unfold. Tara came with her, eager to see all that was going on.

"Do you suppose I could have my naming ceremony this year?" Tara asked for the twentieth time.

"We'll see, honey." Lucy was as anxious as Tara was to have the ceremony—almost as anxious. But she was still uncertain about Tara. Sometimes she seemed to be so mature, while at others she seemed far too young. And anyway, Lucy's mind was preoccupied with thoughts of defense for Dr. Meany—but not too preoccupied for her to miss noticing Lily Pearson standing by one of the booths with her children.

She and Lily had met a few years earlier at a powwow. They were both widowed women, each with two children, a son and a daughter. Lily had begun to explore her Native roots, encouraging her kids to dance and learn from their ancestors so they might have the values they could never get from their father. Lucy's children were older, but they enjoyed taking care of Lily's children, especially Tara, who had a special love for children. Tara was into dance anyway, and the idea of teaching a young child added to her excitement. And so they all became friends. They knew they had a bond that ran deep, and they became closer than many biological siblings. It seemed so natural that no one felt a need to explain it.

Lily and Lucy had been planning to meet at the powwow for months. They had missed each other and needed to connect in a way that is difficult with so many miles between them. It was only the threat around Dr. Meany that had distracted Lucy from receiving Lily the way she should have. But she set aside feelings of guilt and hurried over to speak to Lily.

She called Lily's name three times before her friend heard her.

"Lucy! I'm so glad to see you!"

They hugged, and Lucy leaned down to speak with the children and give them a proper welcome and a hug. They were full of the sights and sounds and smells of the powwow and tripped over each other to tell her of it all.

When Lucy stood back up to face Lily again, she was startled to see the look on her friend's face. In an instant she knew that something very serious was wrong. But she didn't say anything; instead she called over to Tara.

"Tara," she said, "why don't you take the kids around and get them something to eat? Lily and I will be back in a few hours."

Tara was more than happy to oblige, and the children were soon clinging to her hands, begging to go in every direction at once.

"Now," said Lucy. "Let's go to Pine Hills and get a cup of coffee."

She waited until they were settled at a table before she asked Lily directly.

"What's wrong?" she asked gently. "You looked as if you had seen a ghost!"

"I had seen a ghost," said Lily with a sad shake of the head. "I saw a man I haven't seen for over a year, and…I don't know how I feel about seeing him again." Her eyes filled with tears.

Lucy waited patiently. She knew that Lily would tell her everything she needed to tell her, if she was just given the time to be ready.

Her friend took a few deep breaths, then spoke again. "I met him after James' death. He came to see me. He was an odd sort of friend for James, I suppose, but they were close. Maybe even closer than blood brothers. And from such different backgrounds too."

Lucy tried to remember all that Lily had told her of her dead husband. James was born into a wealthy Ivy League family from the East Coast, a handsome, light-skinned charmer. He was quick to smile and would often give a wink. He and Lily had met at Harvard. She was there on academic scholarships from Harvard and the American Indian Education Foundation, and he was there, incidentally, to play football, but also because his father and grandfather were alumnae. She was a Navaho Indian from a reservation in Arizona. He needed tutoring in English, and she was assigned to him. Soon he asked her to join him for a drink, and they became inseparable. He was always embarrassed by his money and wanted to prove he was a regular guy. He married Lily right after graduation and then enlisted in the Navy. He was gifted athletically and was assigned to training in the Seals. It was during a secret operation in South America that James had been killed.

"Well, after James was…after he died, Fiddler came to see me."

ter, since Lily was too intent on remembering to notice her friend's reaction.

"He was as different from James as anyone could possibly be. Not the sort of fellow to make friends easily. An introvert. Some would call him a 'half-breed'—his mother was a full-blooded Cheyenne, and his father was a white man she met in a bar. She was pregnant before she realized she was married to an abuser."

"I've heard that story a number of times," said Lucy with a sad shake of the head.

"That's just it—it was a compelling story. And he was a compelling man. An extraordinary sort of man. That was why—well, Lucy, it wasn't what I expected at all. If I had he never would have crossed through my door. I… I missed James so much. Terribly. And he was so gentle, and so kind. The children were in bed. I just started crying in his arms. I remember it was a cold night. I cried a lot. Then we talked— talked for hours. We didn't talk about how James had died. Instead we talked about how he had lived. First he would relate a story, and we would laugh; then I would tell a story, and we would laugh even more. Then suddenly we were kissing. Then…then we made love."

Lily fell silent. Lucy could only imagine the rush of emotions that strange couple had shared—both felt cheated of a love taken way too quickly from them, and making love together, in grief, was as close as they would come to getting it back. And it was a reassurance that they were both still alive. "The children woke up late and then we all ate breakfast together. It was so strange. But it felt right. And what had to have happened. I didn't even know his real name—just the name he has earned through his stories and his music. Then… we talked. And I sent him away. I needed time to sort it out."

A few moments passed in silence.

Lily shrugged helplessly, and her eyes were once again full of tears. "And now I have seen him again. It's like it's all coming back to me. I'm not ready to face it, Lucy. I don't know what I should do or how I should behave. My son saw Fiddler first, and wanted to run over to him—he knows him as his daddy's friend. I think he even thinks of him as a stand-in for his father. How can a toddler understand where his daddy has gone?"

"Give it time," said Lucy soothingly. "Give it time. Everything will work out in time."

"I know," said Lily, "but…" she paused, then blurted out: "…but what if, because I'm not ready to face a new relationship, I miss a chance at being really happy? The only chance I can have now James is gone? Or, worse, what if I take the chance and it turns out that the mystery that seems to surround Fiddler is something horrendous? Something I can't handle?" Lucy could not comfort Lily or guide her—these sorts of worries were too close to home for her to feel an adequate judge. And, moreover, there was her own vague, unshakable mistrust of Fiddler. He was indeed a man of mystery, and that mystery might well involve something truly dangerous.

CHAPTER 11

FIDDLER HAD NOT OVERSLEPT AS he had assured everyone the morning of Doc and Paul's adventure with mountain biking. He had slipped into Slade's room and shut off the lights, rigging them so that when Slade entered and flipped the switch, the lights would not turn on. As Fiddler waited and dawn approached, he closed the heavy curtains to keep the sunlight out. His mind flashed back to his childhood and all those nights he waited for the lights to go off in his parents' house. The light was a beacon that he was safe for another day. He had learned to be so patient, but he realized now that waiting would make him late to meet Doc and Paul. He didn't want to take the chance of being seen entering Slade's room again, so he decided to stay and make up an excuse for not meeting Doc.

At the same time, Jack Slade was thinking about his situation as he walked back to his hotel room. He had been in entangled with women before many times—*many* times. His friends said it was his weakness, but he always said he could love them and leave them as easily as he could leave the card table when departure became the most advantageous.

Gayle was different. He didn't know why. After that first night, he used all the standard techniques: flowers and jewelry which Gayle hid in a safe in her office, and promises, lots of promises. He described a lifestyle of playing cards all over the world, staying in the best hotels and resorts in the Caribbean and the south of France, and, of course, always gambling at the most exotic casinos.

Needless to say, he had made these promises dozens of times before and had always meant them, but the romance soon faded and the relationship ended. But, though Gayle came often to his room, and took part in his sexual fantasies with an almost desperate abandon, she would not agree to go away with him. If he could just get Gayle to commit to him as more than just a lover and a business partner. But as much as he knew that she was attracted to him and to the lifestyle he described, she wasn't ready to drop everything and escape. She was loyal in her own way to her family. She was concerned about how it might appear to others, particularly to her children.

"I can't stay in this place forever," he would tell her. "Some may think it is beautiful here, but I prefer tall buildings to tall trees, and ocean fronts to lakefronts, and I hate snow and cold."

"But it's plenty hot here now, isn't it?" she would say, sensuously rubbing her body against his.

It was that night that he concocted the plan to show Gayle that her husband wasn't the saint everyone believed him to be. The young woman in Sanibel was a sure bet; she would easily lure the Doc up to her room. There was a hidden video recorder there just waiting to record damning evidence.

When that failed, Slade decided to seek a more permanent solution. When the two jogging goons failed, he had to go to his cousin in Vegas. It was a dangerous chance to take. His cousin always wanted something in return. If a hit looked professional, the police would start pointing fingers at his organization. If suspicions were raised, Slade knew his life wouldn't be worth a one-dollar poker chip. So much for family loyalty.

At first he tried to convince his cousin that John Wolf was a spouse abuser who deserved to die.

"Do I look like some sort of social worker who's trying to protect the victims of this world?" was the disgusted response. "She probably deserves it. What woman is worth it?"

Eventually Slade got what he wanted, though his cousin swore this was the last time he was willing to use the organization's resources to help him with his love life.

"Look," he said, "either keep it in your pants or learn to have sex without falling in love. I don't run a dating service here. An escort service maybe, but that's different."

Then Slade was left to wait. The hit man he sent worked painfully slowly. Slade was ready to leave the rez forever. He could tolerate the spring and the summer, and even, if absolutely necessary, the fall. But the winter, all of that snow and cold—that was too much. He had been there in late January, and it had been excruciating to wait until spring, which did not come until late April. There was no way he could stand another winter.

Finally he was tired of waiting. That was when he began looking for other options to deal with his "problem".

With a collection of specialists to deal with Doc, Slade could focus on his work—work which did not bring him as much pleasure or entertainment as it once had.

Slade was feeling irritable and exhausted. Perhaps his cousin was right. No woman was worth it. Not even Gayle.

Finally Slade opened his hotel room door and walked in. As he passed through the doorway, he fumbled with the switch, then turned back in confusion when the lights didn't go on. A moment later, confusion turned to fear. The door closed behind him, plunging the room into darkness. A hand slipped over his mouth, and the cold, harsh edge of a knife was at his throat.

"You've made two big mistakes that make me question your integrity," a chilling voice whispered in his ear. "You lied about the man you asked me to kill, and I've gotten word that you've become impatient and hired amateurs to do my job. That does not make me very happy."

If there had been time to spare, Slade would have regretted his own impatience. His head swirled in the darkness. After what seemed like an eternity, the neurons in his brain began to make connections. This had to be the man his cousin had hired and for whom he had grown tired of waiting.

"I'm waiting," the voice, still icier, demanded.

The knife cut even more deeply into Slade's throat—at least that was what it felt like.

"I didn't hear from you or see any results," he said, "so I thought maybe my cousin forgot about me."

"Won't fly," the voice said, throwing Slade's mind back into the dark water.

Finally out of desperation, Slade decided on the truth. "Look, I can't stand this place anymore. I want to move on, but I don't want to leave without my woman."

"You mean the one that doesn't belong to you. The one that has a family." The menacing voice turned even colder as the knife changed position from his neck to a point directly below his chin.

Even with his life on the line, Slade was too exhausted to lie. "Yes, that one, and he doesn't abuse her, but he does ignore her and isn't that just as bad? She wants to be with me. I know she does. Help us."

A tear fell from Slade's eye and landed on the assassin's hand. His hand tightened, and his voice registered disgust.

"Call off the others."

"I can't. I don't even know who they are. I just offered a reward."

"If this gets screwed up, I will find you. Even if I have to search for you in the darkest circles of hell. Now…don't turn around."

Slade did as he was told. He would have been a fool to have done otherwise.

And anyway, there was a mirror nearby him, and Slade could see the intruder clearly as he passed out the door into the lighted corridor. He was a tall man and thin, with taut, wiry muscles, and dark skin. A Native American. And one Slade would remember.

After the door closed, Slade hurried into the bathroom and lost the expensive breakfast he had purchased with a tiny portion of his winnings from the long night of card playing. Then he lay, fully clothed, on the bed in his room. Though he was now even more exhausted, he knew he couldn't sleep. He tried in vain to collect his thoughts.

His assassin had turned rogue. Just from that glimpse, he knew the man was only too capable of carrying out any threat. If Doc were killed, Slade was as good as dead. But there was no way he could call off the others—nor did he really want to. In some perverse sort of way, the threat had made him all the more determined. He wouldn't leave without Gayle. He needed a plan.

It may have been exhaustion that made him imagine such a dramatic solution. What could he do to deal with a killer? Why not kill the killer?

Slade had a number of friends in Washington—his connections were one of the reasons his cousin put up with him. They also gave him an "in" with rising new casinos throughout the country. He was a sort of gambling kingmaker, able to get new Indian tribes declared eligible, with the casinos to follow. For a man who could mold the future of a tribe, it should have been easy to get rid of one man—or two, for that matter. It didn't have to look like an accident. Once the man was dead, Slade could smear his past and his reputation so successfully that any investigation would peter off into nothing. No one would ever suspect Slade. No one.

That was what he told himself as he picked up the phone to call in a few old debts. In such a small community, it didn't take long to find out the identity of his rogue assassin. Then he put in another call and put out a second hit—this time on Fiddler.

For his part, Fiddler also felt uneasy. He had been here longer than he liked to stay in one place. He was nervous with Lucy Teller. He figured she knew nothing, but he had lived in danger all his life. He didn't stay alive just with his physical skills but also with his canny perception and intuition. He knew Lucy had a gift not unlike his own. Some call it psychic, while he thought of it more as spiritual. Whatever it was, she saw parts of him that he hid well from others. That inevitably would lead her to dig into his past, and though she wouldn't find much to start, she would soon start to piece together what she found. Maybe he should just move on.

He could tell the people who hired him that he found out the truth of the situation, and he just didn't kill good people. That was the truth. He just never had to say it before because the people they wanted dead were always bad themselves. Besides, he didn't need the money. He would just leave.

But then he saw Lily, and of all things, she was a friend of Lucy Teller's.

HE HAD MET JAMES IN seal training, and they became friends. It took a while. Fiddler wasn't one to make friends easily, if at all. He was an introvert and usually took life very seriously. They were from very different backgrounds. James was born into a wealthy Ivy League family and Fiddler was a so-called half-breed. What brought them together indirectly was Lily.

James had met Lily at Harvard. She was there on academic scholarships, and he was there to play football. He married Lily after graduation, then enlisted in the Navy, and became a Seal. Fiddler was in James's group. At that time, both men liked to drink, and they would often engage in loud and obnoxious drinking bouts. Both of these normally respectful men acted in embarrassing ways when under the influence. Because they were so well trained physically, their conditioned and rippled bodies were lethal weapons. Alcohol removed common sense and inhibitions, and they often became ugly when drunk. They realized that alcohol didn't mix well with either of them, and started attending AA meetings together and their friendship grew. On assignment, they watched each other's back and kept each other alive; they had the best damn team in the whole military.

Unfortunately, too many opportunities arose to prove their brotherhood. But even in the worst of situations, James would joke and get Fiddler to smile. The smile, faint at first, soon became a broad grin. Fiddler even became comfortable hearing his own laugh. Of course, there was a great deal of swearing and sarcasm, but that was all done in fun. Fiddler felt for the first time that he could trust another human being. He was able to open up and let his newfound brother into his heart and life. He actually felt love for this man who appeared to be so very different from him.

They were in Columbia rooting out drug traffickers. They had been on a number of dangerous assignments like this. It was perhaps the faith they had developed in each other that made them too secure and too confident and allowed them to let their guard down just for a moment. When a drug lord and his men ambushed them, James saw a man step from behind a bush and aim at Fiddler. Almost instinctually, protecting one of his own, he stepped in front of the bullet and took it in the chest. While the other Seals and their Columbian allies gave chase, Fiddler pulled James to safety. Fiddler held his friend, tears streaming down his face. He prayed hard as he felt the warm blood of his brother on his hands. He prayed and begged with all of his being that James would live. His prayers did not work. He asked to die to save his brother, but his friend, his partner, died. James died in his arms with a wink and a smile.

When Fiddler felt the life leave his friend's body, he screamed aloud, "Why? You have everything to live for, and I have nothing!"

Then he sat for what seemed an eternity, rocking and holding his dead brother. He could feel a physical emptiness.

His heart grew cold and hard, and he was not aware of his surroundings. He should offer sama to the Great Spirit in thanks for the life that was given to save him. But he could not move his brother out of his arms. For a very long time he sat there, confused and heartbroken.

A few days later Fiddler sneaked back into the drug cartel and hunted for James's killer. He found him and for the second time in his life watched with satisfaction as a man died by his hand. He felt a debt had been paid as he watched this man take his last breath. He was not sure how, but he still felt the need to repay his brother for giving his life to save his. That was why he went to find Lily.

Though his heart was heavy when he knocked on her door, he could tell as soon as she opened it that none of the pictures his friend had showed him over and over again did her justice. Her dark eyes filled with tears because Lily immediately recognized Fiddler from pictures her husband had showed her so many times. She had cried so often since hearing that her husband had been killed in a secret operation in South America.

They hugged before they ever spoke and held each other for a long time. Fiddler smelled a fragrance from Lily he had found in no other woman, even though he would walk down crowded streets and stand in elevators and concentrate on nothing but the smell of women who were close to him. He also felt her tears and the shudder of her sobs against his chest.

It was a cold winter evening when he arrived, and Lily had already put the children to bed. They talked for hours. Fiddler dreaded telling her how James had died, so they ended up talking about how he had lived. First he would relate a story, and they would laugh; then she would tell a story, and they would laugh even more. But their hearts were heavy even as they laughed. As the stories continued, they would exchange glances, then long looks, then hugs. Both Lily and Fiddler felt incredible energy when skin would brush up against skin. Both were aware of the growing attraction toward the other. Allowing it to draw each to the other, they finally kissed, softly at first, playfully exploring each other's lips. Then, quickly, the kisses became hard and full of hungry passion. He knew it wasn't him she was kissing but his friend and brother. And though he instantly loved her, he knew, too, that it was his way of being close to his friend again. He and James would spend hours together through the night on assignments just waiting for a light to go on in a window. They got to know each other's thoughts without needing to speak them.

James touched a part of him that had been hidden and protected. They could tell by each other's breathing how they felt, and the tiniest of looks or gestures would convey their next move. Fiddler longed for the incredible connection that was becoming apparent with this woman. He wanted to feel with another person the kind of intimacy that he had never known before or since. He wanted to be vulnerable with someone again and have the trust he rarely allowed himself feel in his lifetime.

Both felt cheated of a love taken way too quickly from them, and this was as close as they would come to getting it back. Soon they were exploring each other's body and making love on the couch. Fiddler had any number of one-night stands with women all over the world, but never before had he made love like this. It was so much more than physical gratification. Touching, arousing, and causing her body to quiver under his touch, they would lock eyes. It became a spiritual experience for them. She did not make a sound louder than a whisper, and yet he knew he had touched her deeply. They would sleep for short intervals after each achieved orgasms but somehow they would wake at the same moment and start again, touching, kissing, and taking in each other's body with their eyes, mouth, and touch.

At dawn, which came late in the winter months, one of the children cried, and Lily immediately rose and dressed. Fiddler followed her and sat down to breakfast with Lily and her two children. The daughter was four and looked like a younger version of her mother with dark eyes and hair. As soon as she learned that Fiddler was a friend of her father, she became a chatterbox. Fiddler would look at Lily as her daughter talked, and Lily would roll her eyes. The second child, a two-year- old boy, never left his mother's lap while Fiddler was present. Most of the time he wouldn't even look directly at Fiddler, but every now and then he would catch the boy staring at him from the corner of his eye.

Fiddler would make a funny face, and the boy would smile and hide his face in his mother's chest. Fiddler was envious on so many levels. He wished he had had a mother like that and that he had come from a father like James. The little boy inside him that he rarely recognized still wanted a lap he could crawl upon, a place of safety and comfort where he could hide. But it also reminded him of making love the night before, and how he nuzzled his face in her breasts. He had overwhelming urges just to touch her, to kiss her, to taste her.

After breakfast the kids went to the living room to watch TV. Fiddler never stayed this long after having sex or making love to a woman. He couldn't count the times he would dress in the darkness and leave, dreading the thought of facing the woman in the morning. His body had learned the response of intimacy, but his heart and his mouth didn't know how to respond once sex was over. Today his heart nearly beat from his chest and a tiny voice inside of him kept saying, "She could teach you. Let her teach you." Still, his mind and heart couldn't find words.

Luckily she spoke first, but it wasn't the words he wanted to hear. She placed her hand on his hand and looked deep inside him. He didn't try to hide from her view. He allowed her to see the real man, the one that had fallen in love with her.

He couldn't believe his ears when she said, "Thank you for last night. I never thought anyone would be able to touch me the way James did, and there were so many times when I thought I was with him again. It's not that I was pretending, I wasn't. It's just that I'd never felt that way with anyone else. My heart kept saying it has to be him."

"He never talked about that part of your life together. He always spoke of you with respect," Fiddler said, quickly not wanting Lily to think he knew secrets.

She held up her hand. "I know he wouldn't do that, and I know you weren't touching me with your mind but genuinely from your heart. I can see your soul when I look into your eyes and sense love from your fingertips. Still, I have a problem right now. Whom am I loving?"

"Believe it or not, I have the same problem," Fiddler replied. "Did I make love to you or to the picture of the woman my friend painted for me? I never came here expecting this to happen."

"Had I thought it would happen, you would have never made it in the door!" Lily said with a smile. "I need time to sort this out, and it's too soon after James's death for me to be in a relationship with anyone, much less his best friend. And it's too soon for the children to go through still another change. I also don't know if I want to subject myself to another relationship with a man so connected to danger as part of his life. I know I'm attracted to that type of man for some reason. Maybe it's all those stories my father would tell me about the First Nation braves who grabbed their horses by the mane and rode off to save the village. Perhaps I will need to sacrifice my passion for an accountant who will be home at five for dinner every night." By then Lily was hardly aware Fiddler was still in the room. She was just thinking out loud, confused and still deeply grieving her husband.

Soon after that exchange, Fiddler's tour of duty ended with the Seals, and he did not reenlist as he had planned. Instead, he started visiting reservations and learning from the elders. He learned the flute and fiddle and began telling stories. He found he had the ability to bring music and stories to life. He had the gift, as the elders would say.

CHAPTER **13**

AFTER SHE RETURNED LILY TO the powwow, Lucy Teller got a call from an old friend.

"Bill and I have been attending a lot of Narcotics Anonymous meetings," Dawn Blackhawk said, "and we've been hearing some interesting things that I think you'd like to know about. Could you stop by and have a cup of coffee?"

"Sure I could," said Lucy. "I will be there as soon as I can get there!"

"Look," said Dawn, "It's important. It's about Doc Meany."

Lucy didn't need the added incentive; she would have stopped by under any circumstances. She had a long history with Dawn, and their lives paralleled each other in a number of ways. They had first met through Dawn's daughter, Lisa. Lucy found Lisa out on the highway in the middle of a snowstorm. When she found out that Lisa was one of Scott Brandt's students before his tragic death, Lucy was interested in the little girl. When she found out that Lisa was trying to find a way to save her little brother, Michael, who had been kidnapped by Ezra. Ezra had thought of himself as a sort of savior, sweeping in and rescuing an infant from a neglectful, drug-addicted mother. It was true: the little girl's mother, Dawn, was near death herself when Lucy brought Lisa back to the house. Dawn might not have survived if Lucy hadn't called the paramedics and prepared them for what they would find. Dawn had taken an overdose and was almost comatose. She needed medication to counteract the heroin that was racing through her veins.

Lucy didn't just save her life; she helped to save Dawn's family. With the help of the Brandts, she found Michael, got Dawn into treatment, took care of the children when Dawn was in treatment, and finally even stood up as a bridesmaid for her wedding to her long-time boyfriend. She and her husband Bill had embraced their sobriety together. Thus far they had beaten the odds, but they didn't take their success for granted; they were grateful every day for just being alive. And they were enduringly grateful to everyone who had helped them. Dawn especially would have done anything for Lucy.

When Lucy arrived at Dawn's house on Bear Trap Road, a steaming cup of coffee was waiting for her just the way she always liked it. They hugged briefly, but Lucy could tell that Dawn was anxious to talk, so they skipped the pleasantries.

"What's up?" Lucy asked.

Dawn took a deep breath. "You know," she said, "this is going to be hard. Maybe one of the hardest things I've done in a long time."

Lucy smiled. "I know you too well to think you're going to be scared off from doing what's right by any sort of challenge."

"Well," said Dawn, "you may think differently when you hear what I have to say. First off, I have to say that I have the utmost respect for the sacred trust of what goes on at an AA meeting. I'm not going to use any names. But what I'm hearing about lately...I just can't ignore this stuff, Lucy, because I believe lives are at stake. And not just any lives but lives of people that you and I care deeply about. Perhaps some of it is just gossip, but I'm also convinced there is enough truth that I can't ignore it. Remember at my wedding when the priest talked about seeds and weeds and how every word from your mouth is either a seed or a weed, and you need to pay attention to what you sew?"

"Yes," Lucy said. She remembered it well and still thought of it frequently, especially when she was about to say something nasty to Ray, her kids, or her mother.

"Well, it made a huge impression on me," Dawn continued, "and I think about it all the time. Usually when I'm about to say something to my daughter or my husband, it is very clear to me what is a seed and what is a weed. But this time I just don't know."

"I understand," Lucy said. She had learned to be patient and listen when someone had a story to tell—even when she was anxious for someone to get to the point. That day she was especially patient, because the confidentiality of what went on at a meeting was critical to her as well.

"This first part I wouldn't even bother you with if it weren't important to the rest of the story and may well just be gossip, but word is Dr. Meany's wife has developed a gambling problem. And it's said that she's having an affair with a professional gambler—a guy who's been hanging around town a lot longer than he normally would. I've heard it several times, but last night at a meeting, this guy who's had some serious drug problems talked to me on the side. He was a mess—I won't tell you his name. But he talked about the gambler a lot. Turns out this guy—the guy who's having an affair with Dr. Meany's wife—is connected to the mob and has hired a hit man to get Meany out of the way. As it turns out, this hit man has backed out of the deal after finding out what kind of man he was supposed to kill. Now this gambler has put a hit out on both of them. Meany's death should look like an accident, but the hit man's doesn't need to look that way because of his background."

"I know I'm skating on thin ice here," said Lucy, "but do you think this is fairly reliable?"

"I've heard it more than once. And last night…well, I won't lie, Lucy, it scared me. I'm not particularly concerned about the hit man, but I'm worried for Dr. Meany. We just can't afford to lose him."

"I agree." Then Lucy frowned, her forehead furrowed in thought. "Dawn, did he say who the original hit man was?"

Dawn frowned too and shook her head. "I don't think he knew who it was."

But Lucy knew; and knew it with a strange certainty—a moment of intuition that would have disgusted her Lieutenant. Fiddler. Who else could it be than Fiddler? A man of mystery. A man who, she felt sure, was more than capable of killing anyone. A hardened man, the son of an abuser. A trained fighter. A trained killer. Lucy's stomach churned, but, in a startling moment, she realized that she was not surprised. Her gut had been telling her who the hit man was all along.

"I don't know how much you are willing to confide in me here," said Lucy. "Like you, I have great respect for keeping what is said at meetings confidential, sacred, but I know you are trying to weigh that against protecting Dr. Meany. Is there a particular person who is planning to kill one or both of them?" Lucy asked the question, though she knew she might be placing her friend in danger.

"That's where I get off easy," Dawn answered, "but you have a huge problem. I can't identify a specific person because there isn't one. The guy at the meeting said that the gambler just put out the word and offered a blanket reward—so there could be dozens of guys out there. I think the guy at the meeting had thought about being one of them. Then he got scared— that's why he came to the meeting. At least that's what I thought when he was talking. Whoever kills either one gets twenty thousand dollars, but with the stipulation that Dr. Meany's death must look like an accident."

So, thought Lucy, the most immediate problem is Fiddler. Doc had some protection, but Fiddler might as well have a bull's-eye on his back with an order to shoot on sight. It hadn't taken her long to figure out the assassin's identity—and his fellow hit-men might be able to figure it out even more quickly.

She shook herself. "Thanks, Dawn. This is really helpful. Really helpful. I appreciate how hard it was for you to talk to me about this—but I think you were right to do it."

Dawn looked relieved when Lucy left, but neither woman was naïve enough to think that everything would be easy from then on. Lucy especially knew exactly how big a problem she was facing.

She knew the usual suspects in her own community, but the powwow would bring in hundreds of strangers. She still had some time since the powwow was not starting for a number of hours, but the setup had already begun. The small local police force was busy directing traffic and policing the grounds. And the powwow would be the perfect setting.

Why was it, she asked herself, that she was so concerned about a killer? He was a killer—he had set out to kill Dr. Meany. But she didn't even resent him for it. Was she just so dedicated a police officer that she couldn't bear the thought of someone being killed on her watch? Was it just because of Lily?

She began trying to think like a killer. Why wait for the powwow to start? Once it started, people would be more focused. All the police would be in one area, and there would be many more potential witnesses. She thought of the sights and sounds of setting up. People throwing things off trucks and hammers pounding in tent pegs sounded too much like gunshots. So there was ample opportunity to get the job done among the hustle and bustle of setting up the huge event.

She didn't think even a drug addict who needed his next fix would be desperate enough to shoot Fiddler at close range in the crowded powwow. But woods surrounded the bowl, and suddenly a scenario flashed in her mind that tied her stomach in knots.

CHAPTER **14**

THE EAGLE SOARED OVER THE Menominee bowl and again surveyed all that was transpiring below. The edges of dawn were creeping forward in the sky on a cold Thursday morning when Fiddler went to the site for the powwow. He stood silently, hoping to feel an emotion, any emotion. He slowly took in the scene. It could have been from a movie. Few would know this place was located on the opposite side of the Wolf River from Keshena. Fiddler crossed a bridge off Route 47 and drove a short distance through a wooded area to the grounds surrounded by small hills and marked by large old pine trees. These trees had witnessed so much. If they could only talk, he thought. Fiddler believed he too had witnessed much in his lifetime. He was just like the old trees, detached yet ever present. He was still fairly young but felt ancient like the pines that loomed over him. Hidden among the trees was a deep and very large gash cut out of Mother Earth. The circle cut into the dirt and created a bowl with bleachers built into three sides, creating the look of a coliseum. He stood in the middle of the circle for a very long time. He could hear and feel the spirits of the grandfathers and grandmothers. They were speaking to him often, and yet he did not understand what they were saying.

Fiddler stood in awe as the sun started to break through the morning clouds, exposing an entry to the circle. It was an arbor covered in cedar, the cedar wrapping completely around the saplings that were bent and shaped to make a large doorway. It marked the east door, the entry of the day and the entry of the dancers. In Native American culture and teachings, the east represents new beginnings, opportunities, and fresh starts. This doorway is always marked with cedar. He wondered if this day could be his fresh start. The cedar teachings were for the women, but he knew the story well.

The cedar that glistened with fresh dew was very powerful. The straight middle part of the cedar leaf is like a red road. We have many temptations to desert the right path. Cedar has many crooked and winding shoots, and they can represent making wrong choices or taking the wrong path in life. Fiddler hoped and prayed that he could find the right path again. Many of his choices could be viewed negatively, but he believed he had learned from them and, therefore, perhaps the path was not necessarily wrong. I can learn many lessons from my many journeys down different paths, he thought. But the Red Road or the center of the cedar branch was at his core. If he embraced a centered and spiritual way of living, he traveled on the Red Road. This road, the path of the Indian way, was indeed the right passageway. Fiddler's life had taken many turns. From his birth, Fiddler thought he was already off the straight middle part of the stem that was spiritual and wise. He suffered an abusive existence at home at the hands of his father. He was made cold and hard by all the abuses that were forced upon him. That was why he was willing to take the job to kill Doc.

So it was that Fiddler had been hired to kill Doc. But John Wolf was a good man and one of his own kind. Doc walked the Red Road. He worked hard to save people and remove the evil, destructive behaviors of alcohol and drug addiction from the Menominee Nation. As anaddictionologist, he tried to save the souls of many, and he was successful more often than not.

Where was Doc when his father was destroying him? Why didn't anyone notice when Fiddler stopped attending school? Suddenly he was standing in a place of painful memories. He could remember and still feel the physical pain his father inflicted upon him. He was a big man and would use his fists with full force against his small son. He would kick and push him down. Fiddler could still smell the rancid smell of alcohol and cigarettes on his father's breath as he screamed into his bleeding face. He would use vulgar words the boy did not understand until he was older. He would tell him that he hated him and wished he had never been born. It was his fault that his mother was gone. She should still be here and not him.

Fiddler was no longer standing in the woods of Keshena but instead in the woods of his childhood. He survived at first by hiding in the woods and then later in life by using drugs and alcohol. Now he endured through his music and storytelling. He hid from most relationships. While offering the potential of healing, there was also the potential of more pain. He no longer feared that anyone could hurt him physically as his father did. He learned skills to prevent bodily harm, but he didn't know how to protect the child he still carried inside from rejection. In his youth, alone and scared, he spent many hours in the woods until late into the bitter night; he would talk to the trees and black sky. Though they were wonderful listeners, they didn't provide him with the answers he needed.

Streaming through the east doorway, he wondered why he was suddenly consumed by his childhood memories. He tried very hard through all his military training to forget those painful abuses. Fiddler was a man, and he desperately wanted to feel, to be alive, to trust someone.

As the morning light streaked his shoes, he started to silently cry. He thought of Lily, who awoke stirrings inside him that he never had felt before meeting her. He wanted to know her and be known by her. This was foreign to him. His usual pattern was to flee intimacy. The survival technique was always to never be known. He worked so hard his whole life to be invisible. He wanted to learn the stories of others, not tell someone his. How would he explain his life? How could he make himself be understood? How would he attempt to start his story?

Fiddler, the storyteller, strove to journey back to the Red Road he traveled as a Native American man. He traveled the country and listened to others' tales and told the people's stories with his words but mostly with his music. Everyone had a story. Each had unique and memorable experiences. We all have the same dreams and similar heartaches, he thought. Yet, each is on a unique path with a beginning and an end. But my story, he thought, has a beginning and no end.

Fiddler thought of his physical presence. He stood tall and lean with his jet-black hair, long like his legs, pulled straight back. He surveyed everyone at once while holding people's pain in his dark, sad, and piercing eyes, and he soothed them with his melodic voice. His songs evoked many deep emotions. He could hear the music playing inside his head, and his response was emotional, spiritual, and physical. He heard his fiddle moan in agony, scream in pain and ecstasy. All the sounds deepened his trance.

Fiddler pictured the women he'd been with. They were attracted to him and he enjoyed their bodies, but he never entered their souls. They would feel a need, an automatic response, to reach out and offer comfort to him. Many beautiful women offered themselves to him, and he enjoyed the physical pleasure, but the little boy still ran and hid in the woods from any commitment. Usually he dressed in the middle of the night after sex and left without a word. But still in his mind he listened to their plea: "Let me love you. I could offer you the comfort you give to so many."

"I can't," was all he could say as he left them.

His gratification came by releasing the soul through his music—through a musical composition of a person's life story in which the notes paint a picture of the unique nuances of one's life experience. Fiddler traveled the country for years believing everyone had a story that is told in this life or in the next eternal life.

He met only one person for whom he could not tell a story. In fact, he was not given the privilege to determine whether her story was worth his music. That lady, Lily, did not share her entire story. While she talked about her deceased husband and her children, she spoke nothing of her life before she met James. Oh, her eyes certainly had much to tell. And after that time they had met, after James' death, Lily was constantly in his thoughts. And now she was here at the powwow.

She was very young the first time they met—tall, thin, and the mother of a son and a daughter. This willowy woman with sad eyes appeared to be happy and helpful. Fiddler could always see into a person's soul through his eyes. He had never before met anyone who could hide a story from him. Everyone opened up to his magnetism and told a story, a personal story. But she did not. Lily shared the pain of losing her husband, but it was a loss they both shared. She shared her heart and body with him for a short time.

She exhibited uncharacteristically faint lines around her young eyes. Her lines came from smiling, and yet her mysterious eyes were like dark pools of sadness with wounds so deep he could never hope to reach them. He found her both intriguing and challenging. He also found himself attracted to her, an attraction he had never felt before. Fiddler had never felt a strong desire or need for intimacy. If he felt this toward his mother, he did not remember. Such feelings could have been pushed so deep in his soul, they were lost forever. He was even more compelled to find out more about her. She had his mother's sad eyes. He often wondered over the years what else she carried and possessed that was not hers. What had she suffered in her life that caused such a heavy burden? Would he ever find out? It burned his soul at times. Wanting and longing to get close to this woman, he wondered if he would really let her in if she accepted his invitation. Fiddler longed to open up and sing to her his personal life story.

Silently, as if watching a movie about someone else's life, Fiddler recognized the sad truth. The motion picture was the story of his path off the Red Road. The lonely Fiddler let the movie describing his path continue to play in his mind. Everyone deserves to have his or her story told. Even as he ends someone's life, others might feel almost sorry for him. He believes he is doing the right thing. He calls it releasing the soul, and he is both judge and jury in his world. As he listens to a story, he decides whether the storyteller is good enough to stay alive. Should he deem them bad when a strong need arises to make things good again? Everything is based on the story told to Fiddler. Fiddler believes and feels it is his responsibility to end their suffering. Being trapped in a "bad" body is a terrible torture to endure. Starting at a very young age, Fiddler believed it was his responsibility to help all those in need, including those, like his father, who were trapped in a bad body. His soul could not be kind or do the right thing.

His father was the first soul set free. The second was an evil man who took the life of his best friend, Lily's husband. The third planned victim was a good man with a good story. He did not follow through with taking his life. Fiddler had taken many lives in his military experience, but he saw that as a job. Such duty was not a pleasant act but his responsibility, and he always took his responsibility seriously.

A loud clap like a gunshot brought him back to the powwow. The bright sun streamed through the east doorway and felt warm upon his skin. Fiddler wasn't sure how long he had been standing there.

Why did he remember so much of his past? Did the powerful spirits of this place want him to have all these thoughts and memories? Trembling, Fiddler silently cried again as he looked up. Lily stood at the top of the bleachers. Alone, she watched him but showed no facial expression or emotion. Slowly as he gazed into her eyes, he saw understanding. As he wiped the healing tears from his face, he felt achingly lonely. Fiddler had not felt this emotion since his childhood. He was remembering intense feelings for his mother. He had felt a deep aloneness when he was out in the woods talking to his mother, and he would lie on his back in the cool grass and talk to the sky. He believed wherever his mother was, she would hear him. After all, they were looking at the same stars and moon. Grandmother Moon would make sure his mom heard his pleadings and cries.

This morning no moon or stars were out, but he felt like talking to his mother. He would tell her about Lily. He would tell her that he never met another like her. She was special, and he was going to let himself love her. He believed he deserved to love and be alive without the serious responsibility of saving souls. Would Lily want him, though? He needed to know this woman, and he wanted her to know his story. They stood for endless moments with their eyes locked and spoke to each other without saying a word. He was still looking into her eyes when he was suddenly distracted by the noise of trucks, cars, campers, and shouts of welcome.

Vendors and dancers were quickly arriving. They were anxious to set up and see old friends. Even though the opening ceremony was not until the following day, they wanted to find the best parking place and get unloaded. It seemed almost surreal to Fiddler. So close to this sacred place, where the spirits roamed, were all these RVs hooking up to electric boxes. There were probably fifty electricity hookups surrounding the gravel road.

Fiddler thought he would explode. He wanted—he *needed*—to be alone with Lily.

Amid the confusion and noise, all the participants of the powwow began preparations. Natives brought out their intricately decorated attire. Regalia for the Eagle dance were laid out on top of a van. Jingle dresses sparkled in the sunlight. Sacred rattles, pipes, and feathered headpieces were kept up high, protected from the children's curious hands. Indians from the Menominee, Ojibwe, and Oneida tribes were all gathered together to celebrate heritage and history through dance and song.

It was then he saw Lily in the east door. He wondered if he was dreaming. How did she get down so quickly? Why didn't he see her walking down? His heart leapt when he saw her, and he questioned whether she was real. She walked slowly toward him, and as she got closer, he spoke: "If you are here just to tell me you are still not ready or you can't be in a relationship with me, turn around now, because I can't hold you only to let you go again. I've dreamed of this moment too many times to just let it slip through my fingers again."

She didn't turn around but continued to walk toward him.

He felt a knot in his stomach. After taking a moment to look around the sacred site, he moved slowly toward Lily. He smiled to himself. He had faced every kind of danger in complete calm, but this tiny woman made his knees feel as though they would buckle at any moment. If she were to stop and turn around, he thought he would die.

"I've tried hard to forget about you," she said as she continued to walk toward him, "but I can't, and when I saw you today, I realized I no longer want to forget but instead build new memories."

When they reached each other, they embraced for a long time.

As soon as Lucy left dawn's home, she called Ray from her squad car. He answered with the two-way radio on his belt. "Where are you?" she asked.

"I'm at the powwow directing traffic," he answered.

"I just figured out the identity of the hit man who was sent out to get Doc—it's Fiddler. And now there's a hit out on him. Have you seen him today?"

"Yes, he was one of the first on the grounds." "How about Lily?"

"She's there too. When I saw her, she asked me if Fiddler was here too."

"Where are the children?" Lucy asked with panic beginning to be audible in her voice.

"They're with Tara. I was going to drive Tara home to your mother's but she wanted to stay with the children."

"I'm sure there is someone out there trying to kill him. I'm on my way to the fairgrounds now. I will look for Fiddler and Lily. Check the woods around the arena. And Ray..." her voice became pleading, almost desperate, "find Tara! Please find Tara!"

Ray hit the road running. "I'm on my way," he said, reaching for his weapon. He reached the woods moments later, but there was so much ground to cover. As a trained sniper, he knew there was a lot of ground he could eliminate. He did not so much look into the woods as he did into the arena where the grand entrance would be held tomorrow night. A shooter would have to have a direct view of that. Ray made a triangle in his mind. He was one corner, the entrance and the dance area was another, and the third would be the spot a shooter would need to see the area but provide cover at the same time. He concentrated on three likely positions and then developed a path in his mind to reconnoiter to those spots without being observed by strangers. In moments he was on the move again, as silent as the moon moving across the sky, with his weapon held in both hands in front of him. He could afford to be a little less cautious about stepping on branches that might crack because one of the big drum groups had begun to practice.

The big drum was several feet in diameter, with a number of singers and drummers surrounding it. The sound of the drum was not the sound made in old cowboy movies; it was a heartbeat—the heartbeat of Mother Earth. It was loud, but Ray was afraid his own heart beat louder as he could sense the danger in the woods.

Lucy parked her squad car. The eagle painted on the side seemed to continue to move as she slammed the door and began to run. She looked all around her as she moved.

Soon she saw Sophie. For many years Sophie had driven a golf cart as a service to the community to bring the elders from the parking lot to the action of the powwow. Lucy hailed her down, and Sophie quickly slowed the cart.

Lucy jumped on the cart before it stopped and asked Sophie to head toward the dance area. "Have you seen Tara?" she asked. "Or Fiddler? Or Lily?"

"Tara was off with Lily's kids. She's so good with children, Lucy. You should be very proud of her." "But what about Fiddler and Lily?"

"They're here too, but I don't know if you want to disturb them. I think they are having a special sort of moment—they certainly didn't look like they wanted to be disturbed when I saw them."

"I think I'd better, or it may be their last," Lucy said. Without another word, Sophie floored the golf cart, which responded with little more speed than Lucy might do running. She thought about jumping off but decided to save her strength and her breath. She might need to talk fast and move fast, and she was struggling to get a full, deep breath into her lungs. She could not, and would not, lose her sister to some crazy scheme happening on this reservation.

Meanwhile Ray checked the first likely spot and found a crushed cigarette still smoldering on the ground. Fortunately, the boot that did such a bad job of extinguishing the cigarette left a set of clear prints that moved in a direction Ray could easily follow. Ray heaved a sigh of relief. Not only was there only one set of prints instead of two or three, but he also knew now that he was the hunter and not the hunted.

His relief lasted only long enough for him to look from that spot and clearly see Fiddler and Lily standing by the east entrance. He hoped they might be within shouting distance, but then he realized that if he shouted, he would lose his edge on the shooter and possibly force him to shoot.

Then he saw Lucy arriving at the top of the arena.

She could warn them, and it would seem more natural and hopefully not spook the shooter. He called her on the radio and spoke in a whisper. "You're right! There is someone out here! Get to Lily and Fiddler as quickly as you can, but try not to make the shooter feel desperate for a shot."

Ray followed the footprints, stepping in time with the drumbeat, though his own heart was now beating much faster and louder.

Unfortunately, Fiddler, usually totally in tune with his surroundings, now saw only one thing—Lily's eyes. He let her knock on the doors behind his eyes that he usually left closed and locked, and he invited her in to wander freely within him. He felt her hands touching every scar and felt the aches associated with them disappear.

Lucy jogged down the aisles between the benches. Heeding Ray's advice, she didn't yell. Even if she could scream out a warning, there was no place for Lily or Fiddler to hide. They were totally exposed and in the open. She reached the dance area and ran past the big drummers and the singers.

She could tell that Lily and Fiddler were absorbed in one another; she thought they would have a better chance if she broke through the magic spell that so obviously captivated them.

"Hey, Lily!" she called out. "I've been looking every-
where for you. I don't think your son's feeling well..." "Mom?" It was Tara's voice, and Lucy's heart grew cold with terror. She turned and saw Tara, with both of Lily's children beside her—and the little boy was smiling and clearly healthy."

Lily had started with alarm at Lucy's strategic white lie, but now she stood, perplexed and even annoyed, or frightened, staring at Lucy.

Before Lucy could say anything else, and before she could even shout to the children, Fiddler moved. He had emerged from his trance and felt the strange conflicting tensions between the two women. His survival instincts took over. He looked up, scanning their surroundings with an expert eye, until he saw a sight that brought him not to Keshena, Wisconsin, but straight back to Columbia, and the memory of watching James, his best friend, die, shot through the heart by a drug trafficker.

Fiddler's heart stopped for a moment. He saw a man stand up from behind a bush with a rifle pointed at him with the woman he loved standing in between them. "No, James!" he shouted, as he pushed Lily hard toward the ground. She fell toward the grass in what seemed to him to be slow motion.

In that brief second, with an instinct that would have amazed her mother if she had been able to notice it, Tara cried out, grabbed the two children, and dropped them to the ground, using her body to shelter them.

At the same time, as Lucy flew through the air in an attempt to tackle them both, Ray took the best shot he could. He knew it wasn't in time because he heard and saw the first shot fired, but he hoped he could at least prevent a second shot. The shooter staggered and fell to the ground, and Ray was on him in a moment. The force of Ray's bullet striking the shooter's shoulder had knocked him to the ground, throwing the rifle some ten feet away from where he was still lying, sprawled on the grass and blood quickly seeping through his shirt. With a quick search, Ray found a pistol in the man's jacket pocket and flung it out of reach. He then looked up to see Lily and Fiddler lying on the ground, Lucy on top of them.

And there was Tara, holding the two children and comforting them, though the tears were streaming down her own face.

Ray's heart sank when he saw blood everywhere, and nobody moved. The men from the big drum ran toward them. People began to scream or run the other way or stop and stare. Ray immediately pulled out his radio.

"This is Ray. We've had a shooting at the powwow. We need at least three ambulances, and I mean right now!"

CHAPTER 16

Lucy, lily, and fiddler Were all rushed to the hospital, but only Fiddler took a bullet. Lucy had never seen anyone move so quickly. Fiddler seemed to move Lily more with his mind than with his body. He reacted with almost animal-like instinct.

At the hospital, Lucy and Lily were checked for concussions. They had collided and had been knocked unconscious. Fiddler was in surgery, and the admitting nurse believed the wound was serious. Hearing the news, Lily realized how lives can come full circle. She and Fiddler had met after her husband took a bullet for Fiddler, and now Lily feared Fiddler was dying too because he had taken a bullet for her. What had she done to deserve such a fate? James had been taken from her; now another man was being taken too. Why couldn't she love and be loved by someone who would not leave her? As her mind raced, her heart ached. She was longing to be held by the man she loved.

Lily and Lucy both waited at the hospital even though they were told the surgery would last for many hours. It was evening before Fiddler was out of surgery and the doctor cautioned the next twenty-four hours would be critical. Lily could not bear to leave him, and decided to stay at the hospital, while Lucy went home to help her mother with the four kids. She wanted to hold Tara, and to comfort her even as she knew her daughter would be holding and comforting the smaller children.

Lucy felt an actual pain in her chest, and her heart ached badly for her friend. She wondered if she was just overreacting. It wasn't as if he were dead. He would be fine. Maybe she just needed some sleep or some food. He would be fine, he would be fine, she thought. Lucy left her friend at the hospital reluctantly, but knew in order really to be there for her friend, she had to leave.

In most circumstances, we have to take care of ourselves in order to be strong enough to help others. Lucy had thought this was selfish and self-centered until she got sober. This was one of the most important lessons she learned. She always thought of the story she heard in treatment. It came from someone whom she disliked, from a woman she felt had nothing of value to offer her. But you never know who and where someone might teach you an important life lesson. She smiled as she thought of her arrogant cleverness. Lucy was very glad she listened to the words of this disdained lady in treatment. The woman spoke of being on an airplane. In an emergency, you have to put your oxygen mask on first, and then you can help your children with their masks. If you try to help them first, you might become weak and find yourself unable to help anyone including yourself. She looked Lucy right in the eyes as if they were the only two people in the room. On that day it clicked—the light bulb went on. If she wanted to help others, she had to meet her own needs first.

On her way home, she got a brainstorm and called her old friend Cliff in Shawano on his cell phone. Cliff had been a suspect in Scott Brandt's murder for a while, but he turned out to be a good guy who just happened to be loud, obnoxious, and hot tempered. In addition to Ray, he was actually partly responsible for saving Lucy and Kathy from the real killers. Cliff gathered friends to come to their rescue—and did they need rescue! But that seemed like a lifetime ago. As she suspected, Friday evening found Cliff in a bar with his friends, but he had worked late and was only on his second beer. She asked him if he'd go to the hospital and park himself in front of Fiddler's room. He was happy to oblige as long as he had time for one more beer and a brat.

"There is only one person in the world that could take me away from a night of drinking with my friends, and that's you, babe. However, you could sweeten the deal if you told me you were ready to dump Ray and be with me."

Lucy smiled. "I think we are better off as friends, Cliff, but if something were to happen between Ray and me, I might come running to you right after you have your last drink."

"Well, as I said, babe, there is only one person who could take me away from drinking, and that's you."

Cliff, after three beers, was better in Lucy's mind than a number of other men completely sober, and it was his substantial physical presence she needed most. He was over six feet tall and around two hundred pounds. Not only that, but he could look plenty mean to people who didn't know his heart. Lucy felt a little guilty taking advantage of Cliff's obvious feelings for her, but maybe she was saving him from a hangover in the morning. And besides, she really did like Cliff and thought of him as a friend, and she wasn't asking him anything she wouldn't ask any other friend.

Her next stop was the tribal police station. Luck was finally on her side as Agent Scruggs was working and might be able to save her from an endless computer search. Agent Scruggs had gained enormous respect for Lucy when she had followed a little girl's bizarre story of a kidnapping instead of the obvious leads in the case. It turned out she was right, and he was wrong. But what impressed him most was that she never once rubbed it in.

So to her question whether he had a minute to talk to her, he said: "You bet. What's up?"

"I'm concerned about a gambler who's been hanging around town a lot longer than he usually would. Word is he has mob connections, and he may have gotten them to send a hit man to town to get rid of a husband who is keeping him from a love interest."

"Say no more," Scruggs said. "We're already looking into him but with much bigger fish to fry. He was maybe part of a scandal in Washington regarding some Native American tribes and a certain lobbyist who is buying political clout. They are throwing around big money to get things to go in their favor. He is connected to some very powerful people and could probably get anything he wants. Do me a favor; don't let him know you are onto him. He cannot know we are watching him. This is the first chance we've had in a long time to have him stay still in one place—and standing still somewhere in the United States too. He spends a lot of time in Europe and the Caribbean."

"I've read a little about that in the paper. They talk about some mysterious gambler involved in the scandal. Could this be the guy?"

"You didn't hear that from me," Scruggs answered with a wink.

"Thanks, Agent Scruggs. I will let you take care of him; I can approach this from another direction. I'll let you take care of this one—gladly!" Lucy left the station and headed home, hoping she could last the three blocks without falling asleep.

She arrived home to help her mother with the kids; once they were in bed, she fell into bed, exhausted. How did I survive insomnia for all those years, she thought. She then smiled as she reflected on how much better she'd been sleeping since Ray was in her life. She had pleasant dreams in spite of the violence earlier in the day—pleasant dreams of being safe in Ray's loving arms.

Reflecting the summer solstice, the morning dawned just after five a.m.

Lucy reluctantly left the comfort of her warm bed to put on her shorts, t-shirt, and running shoes, and slip out the door to run. Jogging gave her time to review the events of the previous day and plan the events for the day ahead. Lucy cherished this quiet, undisturbed time alone with the Creator. She needed to renew herself and sort through all the details of this complicated situation. She decided it was time to shake things up. Her respect for Doc and Gayle's privacy was now trumped by the urgency of the situation, and she could wait no longer. Although she knew Doc better, she decided to speak with Gayle first. She wanted to give her the opportunity to confess to Doc what had been going on in her life. Though she had been lying to her husband, she didn't believe that Gayle knew Slade was trying to kill Doc. How could she know and not turn to someone for help?

She stopped near her favorite tree, put tobacco down, and lit her sage and sweet grasses.

"O Great Spirit, grant me another day," she murmured.

As always, it relaxed her and helped to keep her priorities straight. She found daily comfort in this ritual of offering prayers. She would take out her medicine pouch, reverently remove the items, and place them onto a large rock. She did not carry a shell that was traditionally used to burn sage. Each day she watched the match quickly light the dried sage and sweet grass, and she prayed for her sobriety and for so much more. Lucy always felt better as the sweet smell of sage filled her nostrils.

She ran on, giving thanks for the glorious day that dawned before her. She loved the early morning with the birds singing. She saw a great blue heron fishing near the shore as she ran on the causeway with Legend Lake on one side and a small pond on the other. A little waterfall that connected the two flowed underneath the road. Once she returned home she tiptoed quietly in and took a shower, not wanting to wake her children or her mother. She dressed and left with them all still asleep.

She was pretty sure what she needed to do, but she still needed one more confirmation. That was why she stopped at the little house next to Saint Michael's Church.

She was a bit nervous as she rang the doorbell, but dcided to face the situation squarely.

"Hello, Father Dan," she said as he opened the door. "I know I haven't been coming to church and that my mother isn't happy about it. And I don't want to go to confession or anything. But I have something confidential I want to discuss with you and…"

"If I say no, am I under arrest?" he answered with a smile.

She grinned back. "No, not quite."

"Well, come on in then," he said. "We'll talk as friend to friend. And it will be strictly confidential, even without the confessional seal."

They went into his little sitting room. Lucy told him of her dilemma with Doc and Gayle—how she had promised Doc not to say anything to his wife, but that she now felt the need to confront Gayle.

Father Dan listened intently. "From what you've told me," he said, "I think you are doing the right thing. If you failed to do it, and risked your friend's life, knowing what you do…"

"I couldn't bear that," said Lucy.

"I know you couldn't. You have to decide to do the best you can for everyone. And that's what I think you're doing." "You've just said what I was hoping you'd say," said Lucy with a smile. "I trust your judgment on so many levels more than anyone else's. I think you are the smartest man I know, and I wanted your blessing."

"Well," said Father Dan, "you have it. Now go out there and do your job, Officer Teller!"

Lucy smiled. "That's just what I'm going to do, Father."

CHAPTER 17

WHILE NEVER EMPTY, THE EARLY morning hours after daybreak were the quietest at the casino. The air was heavy with the smell of stale smoke and spilled alcohol. People sat in dimly lit corners and drank and smoked and vacantly dropped coins into the slot machines. They lacked the enthusiasm you might expect when someone was anticipating that next big win. They looked dazed and almost robotic in their movements. Sadness seemed to fill this time of morning. The people looked tired and unhappy. They demonstrated an automatic response: pick up a coin, drop in a slot, pick up a coin, drop in a slot. Most didn't even pull the one arm bandit but just pushed a button next to the slot.

Lucy had mixed feelings about the casino. On the one hand, she liked what the tribe had done with the majority of the revenue from the casino. Most of it went to supporting social services for the tribe, and only a tiny portion was paid to members of the tribe. The Menominee would often kid each other about splurging with their share of the money. She also liked the entertainment the casino brought in and that it provided enjoyment for the majority of people who visited. But then there were people who became addicted like Gayle. And worst of all, the casino attracted hustlers like Slade.

Gayle started a pattern of getting up early after Doc left for his training. She quickly showered, dressed, and left before he returned home. She would eat breakfast at the casino and start work early, which provided her with the opportunity to gamble in the evening. The restaurant was off a corridor between the noise and smoke of the casino and the relative quiet of the attached hotel. Since Slade would be sleeping, Gayle usually ate alone. They avoided meeting in public.

Lucy would often meet Ray there for breakfast so they would have some time together. It was a good way for each of them to start the day, offering them a connection without interruptions that they both needed.

Phones didn't ring, nor could children ask questions. Even though it was a very public place, they both felt they had some privacy. She would often see Gayle there and began to observe her patterns.

This morning Lucy asked Gayle if she could join her, and Gayle gladly agreed.

"How are you?" Gayle asked. Without waiting for an answer, she continued. "Where is Ray this morning?" She could tell by Lucy's tone and look that she was not just looking for a breakfast partner, and she wanted to avoid whatever it was on Lucy's mind for as long as possible.

Getting right to business, Lucy started. "I think he is probably still sleeping. I don't know if you heard, but there was a man shot at the powwow yesterday. Ray shot the assailant, and I would imagine he was up late filling out paperwork and talking to the FBI." Lucy knew when Gayle's eyes widened and her eyebrows raised that she was legitimately surprised and hadn't heard.

"I thought the powwow didn't start until today," she answered, not knowing what else to say.

"You're right, it doesn't. But one of the men shot was setting up a booth."

"Someone was shot around here during the day, out in broad daylight?" Gayle asked with a surprised and somewhat sarcastic tone in her voice. "Come on." Having worked at the clinic, she was used to seeing knife and gun wounds, but the ones that weren't accidents usually happened at night and involved alcohol. Though the reservation was not immune to violence, most of it happened because of passion or alcohol or both. Rarely was it a planned event.

Lucy knew what she meant and immediately saw her opening to confront Gayle. "Yes, and I think you might be even more surprised to find out that you are connected to it."

Gayle appeared shocked and said nothing in return. She shifted her eyes away from Lucy and tried to think of a way to escape, but she wasn't sure of what she would be escaping from. She squirmed in her chair and hoped this was some sort of joke.

Lucy took advantage of the silence, something against her Indian nature, and attacked. "Let me start off by telling you two things we both already know. And please save me the time and energy of fighting through your denial of them so we can get busy with preventing some more violence." Lucy tried to sound completely confident of herself even though she operated on rumors and limited evidence. "I know you've had a gambling problem for a couple of years now, and I know that for the past six months you've been having an affair with a professional gambler."

Gayle gasped and started to protest, but Lucy rapidly raised her hand in front of Gayle's face. She almost touched her nose before pulling back her hand. Gayle flinched. "I've checked your bank records and interviewed people who have seen you entering his room both day and night. They can tell when you leave that your makeup has been reapplied, and don't make me tell you about the sounds that have been reported coming from his room." Even Lucy was surprised at her performance, and she had never taken a single acting class.

"What you may find the most surprising is that your boyfriend is connected to the mob and has put a hit out on your husband. There have been at least two failed attempts on his life already, but the main ones, I think, will come during the upcoming race he's bound and determined to compete in."

Gayle looked as if she had seen a ghost. All color drained from her face, and her mouth was open, but she made no attempt to speak.

"Take some time. Once this begins to sink in, I need you to speak to your husband and your boyfriend. You need to come clean with your husband and probably enter treatment. But before that, you need to speak with your boyfriend and ask him to call off the hits. Either that or you need to run away with him so he no longer feels the need to kill your husband. I will let the FBI worry about catching the two of you because by that time you will have become an accomplice. Right now I will settle for keeping Doc alive. Even though he may no longer matter to you, he is important to many people in this community, including me. So to use language you have become very familiar with, right now his safety trumps justice for you or your boyfriend."

Gayle had now regained some of her composure and attempted a little bravado. "For the moment, let's pretend you know what you are talking about regarding items one and two. How do I know this isn't just your attempt to recreate a happy home for your hero? You know, the one you think is totally without fault in all of this." Gayle now sounded like a defense attorney in her own trial. She was very angry.

"I have no idea what goes on in your marriage," Lucy shot back, "but I know a couple of things. First, I know I've been involved in enough relationships to know that no person is without fault. Second, I know that there is nothing going on between you two at the moment or you would have seen or felt the scratches and stitches on your husband's back from where a weed cutter tried to run him over in Legend Lake a month ago now."

The shock returned to Gayle's face, and the defense attorney retreated. Her voice changed from defense to concern. "You said there were two incidents. What else happened?"

"After the first attempt at Legend Lake, I tried to get him to tell you about it, but he wouldn't. Though it definitely seemed deliberate, and he told me about a few more suspicious things that had happened to him, he still wasn't convinced. He did agree, however, to begin training with a group I introduced to him. One day he was out mountain biking in the woods with his training partner and somebody tried to run them down, not once but several times. Luckily, Ezra ran the guy off."

"You know that my husband has several people who don't like him. Why do you think this is connected with me?"

"For one thing, some of the incidents Doc described happened when he was waiting for you down in Sanibel. And I'm convinced that the man shot yesterday was a hit man arranged by your boyfriend. The other people who might want to see your husband dead don't have that kind of range, money, or power."

Gayle sat quietly for a long time. Lucy could tell she was thinking about all that had been said, and Lucy gave her some space and time. She could tell that Gayle was sorting out all the information. Lucy was hopeful now that she had made an impact. She need only remember all the people who tried to tell her that she had a problem and how quickly she discounted them before she finally got help. She could only thank the Creator for his help on this one because most people would have simply walked away.

"I will tell you this," Gayle said finally. "I know a lot of what you are saying is true. Doc and I have grown apart over the years, and there is a lot I haven't been telling him about my life. I didn't know there was so much going on in his life that he wasn't telling me. I'm hurt and embarrassed that you know more than I do. I'd like you to give me some time to straighten this out. I'd like to talk with him to see if I can convince him to go away for a while, but I doubt I can. You may be right. Perhaps I have a gambling problem, but he has a competition problem. He has his mind set on this race so much that if Legend Lake were to freeze over tomorrow, he'd still try to do the swimming event, and then he'd try to paddle his kayak down the frozen Wolf River. You may think he didn't tell me all this to keep me from worrying, but I think he didn't want me interfering."

"I'm on your side with that," Lucy said, patting Gayle's hand. "This may be one of those doctor-heal-thyself situations. I'd like to go with you when you talk with Doc. I will be honest. Part of my concern is that you will minimize your part in this, but, also, I might have more luck convincing him to drop out of the race."

Gayle again grew quiet and thought for a long time. "I know you're right. I just think it's sad that I've lived with this man, committed to him at the altar, and borne his children, and we need a third party to help us communicate. What happens in life, Lucy? How do people grow so far apart?"

Lucy thought of her own relationships before she responded. "I guess life is what happens when you're planning something else, but we will have time to think about all that when we get old, or if we get old. Right now we need to act quickly before someone else doesn't have the chance to grow old."

Gayle left money for their check, a generous tip, and they hurried from the restaurant. They were walking through the corridor to their cars when they heard his voice.

"Where are you hurrying off to in such a hurry, Gayle?" Slade was careful to sound as if it were a casual question in a casual relationship, but there was an undertone of disapproval. He could tell from the reaction of both Gayle and Lucy that something was up.

"Officer Teller is arresting me," Gayle replied with nervous laughter and a smile. "She was trying to be discreet, but what the hell, Lucy, you might as well throw the cuffs on." Gayle held her hands together out in front of her, then she continued out the door, as if no further explanation was needed. Lucy followed her, and they both laughed loudly in a way they hoped was convincing.

Lucy wanted to take the opportunity to confront Slade with what he was doing, but she knew she had no real evidence, and even if she did, she knew he had people that could turn her evidence to dust. But still she desperately wanted to slam him on the ground and throw cuffs on him. Stifling her angry emotions, she remembered her promise to Scruggs. Right now she had to concentrate on saving Doc.

Slade stood by the door waiting for Gayle to return. He hoped that maybe she was simply walking Lucy to her car, but no such luck. They climbed into Lucy's truck and left. He suddenly realized that he might never see her again. Slade didn't like the odds. He loved Gayle and hoped they would have a life together, but she wasn't worth dying for. He knew Fiddler had survived the attempt on his life, and once he left the hospital, Slade would be dead if he was still hanging around Keshena. Fiddler was a real threat and was more than capable of killing someone who had tried to kill him. Even distance couldn't ensure his safety, but it would give him time. He'd be in the Caribbean by the morning. There were casinos all over the world, and he would just have to go back to his earlier life and not stay in one place too long. Damn, he thought, do not get too attached!

GAYLE KNEW WHERE TO FIND doc. He'd be in his office by now, probably reading over a chart of a new patient or poring over an old one, wondering if he missed anything helpful. When Gayle and Lucy arrived, that is exactly where they found him. He was pedaling his exercise bike slowly while reading a chart. He must have found something he missed because he stopped pedaling. Gayle walked in first. When Doc saw her, he got off the bike to give her a peck on the cheek. This was about the only affection they showed each other and done mostly for show to others.

Lucy closed the door. Gayle began to loosen his tie and for just a brief moment, he was aroused by this uncharacteristic action. Where it came from he would never know. Once it left his mind, however, he studied the reality of the situation and knew differently. The look on Gayle's face didn't show lust. As he looked into her eyes, he saw fear and a deep sadness.

She was already crying when she started to unbutton his shirt. She was breathing hard and almost gasping to get her words out. Gayle was focusing on only one thing: she wanted to prove Lucy wrong and prove none of this was really happening.

"What's going on?" he finally asked when he realized pretending wasn't going to provide him with an answer. His words seemed to get Gayle's attention. The realization that Lucy was a former patient and a cop made him uncomfortable. Why was she here watching his wife take off his clothes?

"I have so much to tell you, John, but first I need to confirm how out of touch I have become with you. I know about what happened at Legend Lake, but I want to see for myself." It suddenly became very clear to him now.

Doc shot a look at Lucy, and she saw an angry side of him she had never witnessed before. Even with all the crap that she and other patients give him during detox, she had never seen such fire in his eyes. He was livid and wanted to push his wife away. Gayle caught the intense anger too.

"Lucy had to tell me for reasons you will understand soon enough," Gayle said as she examined his back. Tears ran down her face, and she lightly ran her hand over wounds mostly healed and stitches long-since removed. She cried for so many reasons that she knew she would never have time to express them all. His wounds were clearly a metaphor. She cried because he was a good man who deserved better; she cried because her behavior was partly to blame; she cried because the wounds made visible the pain of their relationship; she cried for all the secrets they had kept from one another; she cried for fear of what she was about to tell him and how that might affect them both. Gayle cried because she could not hold it in any longer.

"This isn't about you and what you've done; it's about me and what I've done," she admitted, turning him around and looking him straight in the face.

Gayle didn't just start lying when she began to gamble. She had been lying to herself for as long as she could remember. She played at life as if it were a game, and everyone was a pawn on her chessboard. Now she finally understood and saw things clearly for the first time in her life. For the first time she realized she truly loved this man, and she was terrified she was about to lose him. She looked at him deeply, and he didn't look away. His eyes began to fill with tears. Neither was even aware that Lucy was in the room with them.

For her part, Lucy suddenly realized she needed to be anywhere other than Doc's office, and she quietly slipped out the door and stood in front of it so they wouldn't be disturbed. As she blocked the entry, she began offering prayers for the healing to begin.

"For the last two years, I've been gambling and probably for a year and a half, it's been out of control." The floodgate in Gayle opened, and it wouldn't close until all that had been straining against it flowed through. She felt enormous pressure in her chest and head along with a lump in her throat the size of a tennis ball. She painfully forced her words out.

Then there was a long pause, and Doc realized with dread that she was not done yet.

"When I had lost nearly everything," she finally started again, her voice at a whisper, "a man came along who promised to help me get the money back." Gayle looked away again, wishing she could somehow escape. Her tears flowed harder now, and the words came out in sobs. "But it came at a terrible price to our relationship." That was as close as she could come to the truth.

Doc listened intently though so many of the words pierced his heart, and the pain in his gut was agonizing. He suddenly had a hard time filling up his lungs. For a brief moment, he was struggling again on the bottom of the lake, fearing for his life. He didn't think he was capable of hurting so badly anymore. This felt like the pain of adolescence, the kind that you get before the mature adult takes over in your mind and helps you put things into perspective.

He had known for a long time that their love was dying, but he thought it was on his end also. Doc thought he had grieved and accepted the loss of his wife. So why now did this hurt so very badly? Why couldn't he catch his breath?

At some point, he stopped listening. He was suddenly finding answers to questions that had long plagued his mind— and he knew who it was that had been behind the attempts on his life. The image of Gayle in the arms of a man who wanted him dead burned in his brain. He could feel rage start to boil in his gut. This man could take his life, but how could he steal the intimate response from his wife that he had been searching for these many years? This man took her passion and her body. The anger he felt was almost primal, kicking in for survival. He knew he didn't satisfy Gayle and that she only went through the motions no matter how hard he tried. They both tried many things in bed early in the relationship, experimenting and searching for something, anything, that evoked passion. This man had captured the elusiveness he had been chasing since he had met Gayle. He knew it. He could sense it. She didn't sleep with him for what he could offer her. Instead, she slept with him because she wanted him. She slept with him because she wanted to. This other man had awakened something that had been dormant inside her and found it instantly, something he was incapable of doing after years of trying. His mind was racing, his imagination vivid.

Gayle's voice suddenly brought him back to reality. "You've got to drop out of the race; you need to go away somewhere."

Now the look that Lucy experienced moments earlier was fiercely turned on Gayle. She remembered it, but she had not seen it since he became sober.

"So now you also want to take from me the only things I feel I have left. I should run away from the race and my job and what? Focus all my attention on some sleazy gambler who gets a response from you that I waited for my whole life."

Gayle was stunned with his intensity, but she pressed on. "I'm not asking you to do this because I want you to feel more pain," she said. "I'm asking you because I now know how much you mean to me, and I want to have a chance to show you that, but I can't if you are dead."

Lucy heard their voices rise and knew now they were talking about the race, and she reluctantly stepped back in the room.

"Please, Doc. I know you are mad at Gayle right now, but if you can't find it in your heart to do it for her, do it for all of us who love you and can't imagine what it would be like to go on without you," Lucy pleaded. At the same time, she wondered what on earth she would tell the Brandts after all of their work and planning if Doc did withdraw from the race.

"Look," said Doc, "I know I'm out of control with this race, but this is about so much more than just me. This is something for our community, and I can't let people down who are counting on me to be in it. Besides, I need it right now. I wouldn't ask someone to give up heroin five minutes after their heart has been ripped from their chest. Right now death would be a welcome thing, but dealing with all this without my favorite way of coping is just beyond me."

He took a deep breath and went on: "I know I've been a disappointment to you, Gayle. I think that part of this is some kind of revenge to get back at me for ruining your dream. You never got the fancy house and the country club, and in a hundred subtle and not so subtle ways you've let me know that. Well, now you have a choice. Hang around the rez and support me, or go with your gambler and have the life you've dreamed of!"

"I should do that even if it means watching you die?" asked Gayle.

"Well, to put it in terms you've been accustomed to lately—one last hand, all or nothing," Doc offered. "I'm anteing my life. Are you in?"

Gayle stood in silence and gazed at her husband. She wondered what had happened to them, and why she let it happen. She wondered if she had ever really seen him and loved him for who he was and not for what he could do. Then, all of a sudden Gayle's imagination caught fire.

"I'm in, and that's not all—so are the kids!" She turned, as if she were about to leave, but instead began making plans with Lucy, continuing on her train of thought. "I just know the kids will want to be a part of this! I'll call them now and tell them to come right home. I'll call all of our family and friends too. I'll go to the powwow tonight and talk to all of your former patients that I know; we will have the race route so crowded with people tomorrow that no one would dare try to harm you."

At first, Lucy thought that Gayle was trying a new tactic to get her husband's attention and talk some sense into him, but then she realized that she was serious. This was her last and most reckless game of chance. She was playing her hand and taking the risk. And Lucy was right there with her. The idea really began to take hold. They had one more day, and both women would make the most of it to protect a crazy man from himself.

Meanwhile Doc looked on in shock. He just stood there with his mouth open, no words coming out. It really wasn't like either woman gave him a chance to speak anyway.

"Okay, let's get started," Lucy said. "First, let's get the staff in here and ask them to use their breaks and lunch hours to call former patients who are in recovery. We can tell them to make announcements at meetings between here and Milwaukee. I'll get Sophie on the phone. She knows everybody. Then I'll call the Brandts. They can contact everyone they know between here and Antigo. Then I'll call Cliff. I'm sure he can get his friends to come with their four-wheelers to patrol the mountain-bike route."

Doc tried to protest, but it was like being hit by a freight train rolling downhill. He felt like a loser, deflated and depressed. He really didn't believe people would respond just because his life might be in danger. Maybe all the positive responses he had received in his life were just pretend. What value did he hold?

THE GRAND ENTRANCE OF THE powwow was always powerful. Handmade wares abounded at the powwow, and traditional and innovative foods were a special treat, including wild rice stew, fry bread, venison stew, Indian tacos (taco filling on fry bread), and wild berries. But not even the delicious foods could outdo the wonderful outfits. The master of ceremonies opened it by telling the story of each dance that was about to begin. Great pride was taken in native heritage and in the individual regalia. Each outfit had beautiful beadwork with a pattern, an intricate web that wove a story. Seemingly endless hours were spent to create the details of the stunning beadwork.

All the outfits were worn proudly. Eagle feathers were attached to a headdress. Native Americans were the only people who could possess these precious feathers. It was illegal for the White Man to own them unless he was given the feather as a gift by an Indian. An eagle feather was highly respected and valued as very powerful medicine. Each bead, feather, skin, or ribbon painted a picture just like the dance that would be performed. Each one told a story.

Many people traveled long distances to attend because powwows were a family social event. Many people gathered to show how much their children or grandchildren have grown. Some people saw each other only at these reunions. It was common to see small children having important conversations with an elder. From young to old, they worked together to set up, dress, and dance.

The opening dance started the ceremony to showcase the dancers. As they danced in the middle of the bowl, they performed as one. Each dancer was individual, yet together they represented, moved, and danced as one. Then they split up into expeditions. Each dancer had a traditional story to tell. In this way the history and legends were passed down from generation to generation.

Warriors and royalty led the grand entrance. Only those of high status could be in the front of the line. It was their responsibility to lead all the other dancers. They were symbolically presenting the dancers to participants of the powwow. Occasionally, a male and female leader would follow the greatly respected openers of the grand entrance. Male traditional dancers followed, and next in line were the male fancy dancers, and after that, the male grass dancers. Each dance told a story. The movements contributed another line to the various stories that have been told over the years.

The story Lily liked best was that of a more recent dance—the grass dance. It told the story of a boy who was born with a birth defect that caused him to limp. One leg was shorter than the other, and he was usually in pain. He practiced every day to fulfill his dream to be a dancer. Many of his peers thoughtlessly made fun of him. The little boy could not run and keep up with the other children. As much as he tried, he could not dance as well as they could. His dance was rough and his body would turn crooked as he tried to turn. The little boy would try to ignore the pain caused by forcing his body to stand and move straight like the others. As much as he tried, his body would not move the way he hoped. His heart grew heavy.

One day when he was very sad, he slowly struggled up a hill covered with very tall grass. When he reached the top he was out of breath. The heartbeat of the drums being played down below entered his heart.

He stood and started to sway with the tall grass, and his heart became lighter. The grass bowed down, as it were dancing with him. The little boy smiled inside as well as outside. Not only was his face smiling but also his heart as he felt stronger and gained all of his confidence back. The little boy made it easily back down to the powwow and started dancing. He took the feeling of the tall grass along with him. The little boy felt the joy in his heart and let it flow to his legs and feet. People began to notice. Before very long, all the boys and girls wanted to dance like him. His movement was very uneven and interesting, and he certainly created a unique dance. Although this was a dance for the boys, the girls were seen off the stage dancing it as well. It soon became accepted and a regular part of a powwow.

In the opening ceremony, the grass dancer was followed by women traditional dancers. They stood tall knowing they carried with them a long history of past dancers. This and the jingle dance represented a very old story. These were the only two dances performed by women—they had been performed with pride by women since the dances first began.

The fancy shawl was the most recent addition and the last dance—a fast-moving sequence with complex footwork and fast spins. The outfit for this dance was colorful and bright, and the dance commonly showed off the brightest and most colorful shawl of all the dancers. Each group was lined up by age or size, oldest to youngest or tallest to shortest. Everyone continued dancing clockwise until the drums stopped. The big drums were used at the powwows, and men and women sang along with the drum. Only the men were allowed to drum. When the drums stopped, all present could still feel the beat in their hearts, in their ears, and in their very being. It was then that the opening dancers led the rest out of the entrance, and the individual dances began.

The dawn on the day of the race was everything the promoters of Experience the Rez hoped it would be. There was plenty of blue sky and no wind, but a huge black cloud hung over it all in Lucy's mind. Would Doc survive? Great Spirit, please be with my friend, was a thought that would not leave her. The Brandts, Kathy, and Brad had met at Pine Hills for dinner on Friday, the night before the race. They ate out on the deck and discussed strategy. Later that evening, they met at the Legend Lake Lodge with the participants to go over the route and give assignments to the now massive and growing group of volunteers. After that, Lucy met with all the people who showed up to support Doc. She tried to give them ideas about suspicious behaviors, but there really wasn't much she could tell them. Mostly she told them to keep an eye on Doc and be supportive. Cliff had called a group of his friends from Shawano, who showed up with their cars and four-wheelers in tow. As much as he hated it, Cliff stayed back to protect Fiddler. He cared little about Fiddler but greatly for Doc and, of course, he would do just about anything for his friend Lucy.

The first event of the race would be the half-mile swim in Legend Lake. Participants would then get on their road bikes and cycle about thirty miles to the Wild Wolf Inn, where they would switch to mountain bikes and ride on the cross-country ski trails across the street for about six miles and then return to the Inn. After that, participants would enter whitewater canoes and follow the Wolf River to Shotgun Eddy's, a raft rental place that had been around since before whitewater rafting had become popular. Then they would switch to kayaks and paddle through the Wolf River Dells and Big Smokey Falls to Highway 50. The Smokey/Keshena route had been closed by the tribe to paddling since the mid-1970s, but the tribe opened this route for this race. On Highway 50, they would in-line skate to Legend Lake Lodge; finally, if still able, they would run a 10K on South

Branch Road, 3.1 miles out and 3.1 miles back. The entire distance was nearly seventy-five miles of self-propelled agony. The leaders and teams would probably finish in three to four hours, but the stragglers could take up to eight hours; the course would officially close after nine hours. Doc expected to be somewhere in between the leaders and the stragglers; he hoped to complete the race in five hours.

Cliff sat bored and jealous outside Fiddler's room. Lily was nice, and looking at her was a joy, but he wanted to be where the action was. Lily had been kind enough to buy him a deck of cards at the gift shop, and he found an empty room where he appropriated a table used to feed the bedridden patients. If he couldn't be in on the action, he could at least play solitaire. Lily had also bought him a Sun Drop soda along with the deck of cards. And now that his bladder was full, duty called him to the restroom.

He wanted to wait because Lily was in the cafeteria having lunch, but still some things can't wait, and the men's room was just down the hall. Cliff would be quick and get back before Lily even knew he was gone. Fiddler wouldn't mind if he left; he hadn't moved all day.

Slade couldn't believe his good fortune. He had decided to stop on his way to the airport to see if he could prevent having to look over his shoulder for the rest of his life. He had been waiting down the hall only a few minutes when that woman left his room, and now the big guy playing cards outside his door was heading down the hall. Slade thought things could not get any better than this. His luck was beginning to change. He could feel it in the air. Wait, he cautioned himself, don't get excited, don't feel any emotion. He started to lecture himself about the weakness of emotions. If he just waited for the big ugly guy to hit the men's room, all he had to do was go into Fiddler's room and empty the contents of the syringe he had in his pocket into his sorry body, and he'd be gone. He was smiling when he entered the room and saw the limp and motionless body under the covers. The smile immediately left when he pulled back the covers and saw a pile of rumpled pillows. Fiddler was gone!

He was leaving the room just as Cliff was leaving the men's room. "Hey, you, what are you doing in there?" he bellowed.

"I'm a friend of his, and I was just going to check on him, but he's gone," Slade replied, after almost getting knocked down when Cliff bumped into him and charged into the room to check. Slade retreated in a hurry. The critic in his head started screaming about how very bad this situation was. Very bad indeed!

Fiddler had awakened only an hour earlier. Though he was shot in the stomach, the wound was not as severe as first thought. The bullet was deflected by his belt buckle and somehow missed all of his major organs. Still, he had lost a lot of blood, and his skipping out the window was definitely against doctor's orders and the protocols of the AMA. But he somehow convinced Lily that he had to get back and help Doc. So after she got his clothes and helped him out the window, she told Cliff she was going to lunch, but instead met Fiddler in the parking lot. When she arrived, she saw him waiting by the car with a strange expression on his face. He gazed at her with a look she did not recognize—like there was a fire burning behind his eyes. Fiddler looked like he was someplace else, someplace far away.

"What's wrong?" she asked.

"I just saw Slade go inside," he responded flatly. "He's the man who tried to have me killed. My guess is he's on his way to my room to try and finish the job."

"Well, let's get out of here before he finishes it in the parking lot. I am not going to lose you!"

"No, he couldn't do that—even with me hurt. He was planning on me being unconscious. It's the only way a weasel like that would ever have the nerve to do anything himself. My guess is he's on his way out of town and was hoping he could do it without having to look over his shoulder."

"What do you mean?" Lily asked.

"He knows I'll come after him, and there are not enough places in this world for him to hide from me. Eventually, I will catch up with him and rid the world of another evil." Fiddler was thinking out loud. Normally his filters would have kept him from saying such things out loud, but the pain medication had put the filters to sleep.

Lily shivered, not just because of what he said but how he said it. "What are you talking about? We're on our way to help save a life, not take one."

"He's evil, Lily. He wanted me to kill Doc so he could get to Gayle, and once he tired of her, he would have discarded her, too. He would then easily move on to his next victim with a smile on his face."

After a moment of silence, she turned to the man she loved and said. "If you want a relationship with me, you need to concentrate on protecting lives and not taking them. I want life and energy with you and not death. I want to make a life with you."

With tears in her eyes, Lily climbed into her car and started it without saying another word. Fiddler was still standing outside.

She would not, could not, look back.

CHAPTER 20

THE SWIMMERS WERE BEGINNING TO line up on the shore of Legend Lake. The start would be in waves, with the pros and older participants starting first and younger age groups following. Each group would be identified by a different color, and a swim cap of the group's color was provided in the well-stocked race packet of each participant. Each of the contestants would also have his or her number written on his body with a marker. Zack and Ryan took the yellow cap of the forty-to fifty-year-olds since they would be swimming with Doc. Lucy would also enter the water with Doc even though she should have started with the women her age. The four of them were standing together when Gayle came up and subtly pointed to a man also wearing a yellow swim cap even though he looked younger than forty. "I saw that man talking to Slade more than once," she stated with a knowing look on her face.

"Have you ever seen a swimmer with elbow pads like that before, Ryan?"

"No, I haven't," Ryan answered suspiciously.

The man wore the black rubber pads often seen on wrestlers. They also looked a little bulky underneath.

"My guess is he has something underneath them to make his elbows sharper and harder," Lucy suggested. "Let's watch where he lines up, but I bet it's right behind Doc."

It was not unusual in events like this for a faster swimmer to go right over the top of a slower swimmer accidently since most swimmers do the crawl and can't see in front of them. If this man were to swim over the top of Doc and hit him in the head, Doc could be knocked unconscious and sink to the bottom. With all of the commotion, he might not be missed for quite some time. Was that what the man with the elbow pads had in mind? Legend Lake is very clear first thing in the morning, but once swimmers and boats kick up the bottom, it gets murky until the sediment has a chance to settle to the bottom again overnight. If Doc were to sink to the bottom during all the confusion in the water, the volunteers on Wave-Runners and canoes lining the course wouldn't see him, and he'd drown. When the swimmers lined up for their start, Ryan stood in front of Doc, and Zack lined up behind him. And sure enough, right behind Zack was the man with the elbow pads.

"Oh, excuse me," Lucy apologized. She bumped into the man from behind and purposely hit his elbow as she lined up next to Doc. Bang! The group in front of them scurried into the water with the starting pistol, so participants in Doc's group had five minutes to their start.

"Come on, group," Lucy said, "let's do one of those huddles like the Packers do." She put her arms around Ryan, Doc, and Zack. "He is packing something. Okay, we know what to expect, so let's do it!"

The next five minutes seemed like an eternity to the group, and the butterflies of normal competition were compounded by the life-and-death struggle that they all faced.

When the gun sounded, they ran into the water and began swimming. Just as they had practiced, Ryan went first and did the breaststroke and sometimes the butterfly if he felt Doc on his heels. Doc and Lucy did the freestyle so they could watch each side, and Zack did the backstroke from behind. The man with the elbow pads stayed a few feet behind him for the first one hundred yards.

In spite of all that faced him, soon Doc was thinking of Gayle and Slade. He wondered if he could ever recover from the betrayal. The thought began to surface that, like him, Gayle had an addiction and perhaps needed to be forgiven as she had forgiven him for his addiction. He understood that gambling could fog the mind as much as drugs and alcohol, and he certainly appreciated the effort she had given since her disclosure. He knew for sure that she had not slept all night; in fact, she never came to bed. She was up with the kids, who had returned home earlier, talking and planning. He heard muffled voices until he finally drifted off to sleep. He dreamed he and another man were chasing a rabbit. They both caught it at the same time, but the other man wrestled it away from him and stole away with the rabbit, laughing and petting its soft fur. He tried to tell himself to focus on the competition since that had been about all he could focus on for the last two months—at least until yesterday.

As for Zack, he had no trouble focusing. The swimmer with the elbow pads began to make his move. At first his hands brushed against Zack's feet; then he grabbed Zack's ankles to pull himself forward, dragging Zack underwater. Zack was certain that the hard surface of the elbows pads had left bruises on his thighs. Whatever this guy had in there sure hurt.

Zack then did a flip turn that a swimmer usually does at the end of the pool and kicked his would-be assailant hard in the jaw. With that move, he was behind and climbing on top of the swimmer. He had to fight to get better leverage. When he finally reached the man's waist, he pulled his Speedos down around his ankles. Not surprisingly, the man stopped swimming. Zack stopped next to him, daring him with his eyes. By then he was pissed and would have loved nothing more than to rip the man's head off; he was just waiting for him to try something more. But Zack controlled his anger and instead motioned to the tribal police who were watching from Wave-Runners to come and pick him up. They were soon on him and pulled him out of the water.

"Check the creep's elbows," Zack said. Then he dived back in and caught up with the group. The rest of the swim continued without incident.

As Doc left the water, he was shocked to see a large crowd cheering for him. Perhaps people were sincerely interested in him. But he had many more surprises to come and he needed to get moving. The next event was a thirty-mile bike ride on a curvy, hilly road. He needed to keep moving.

The day warmed up to nearly eighty degrees by the time they left the water. Doc sat on the grass and put on his biking cleats, slipped a pair of light shorts over his Speedos, took off his swim goggles, and pulled on a half t-shirt, leaving the muscles of his stomach exposed to help keep him cool. Hank and Molly anxiously waited for him on the road by the lodge.

They biked about a half mile on South Branch Road, turned right onto County VV for a block or so, and then turned right again onto 47/55 and biked through Keshena. At each intersection, volunteers directed traffic and many onlookers shouted out to him: "We've got your back, Doc."

Doc was not surprised to see some small groups along the road cheering on the bikers, but he was surprised to hear each of them single him out with: "Go, Doc, go! We're rooting for you."

They passed the gas station on their left and the government buildings and police stations. Down in the valley, they followed Route 47 and crossed the bridge toward Neopit and Route 55 as it followed the Wolf River. They turned right on 55 and left Keshena behind. Doc figured he had seen the last of the crowds until they got to the Wild Wolf Inn, but he noticed small groups of bystanders scattered every mile or so. Occasionally, one person would run along beside them for a while and yell encouragement. One guy yelled, "You saved my life, Doc. Now we're going to save yours!"

"Why are these groups lined where they are?" asked Doc. "There's no rhyme or reason for them to be here."

"They're guarding all the dirt road entrances so no one can sideswipe us with a car or a four-wheeler," Hank responded.

"This is the most amazing thing I've ever seen," cried Molly. "I love it!"

"I know some of these people, but most of them I've never seen before. They're human barricades."

"You know I've felt the power of fellowship at meetings," said Hank, "but this is the first time I've seen the magnitude of its power. Lucy and Gayle had us call our friends and asked them to call their friends, but this is amazing. We are so grateful."

In between each group, cyclists would ride along with them. The rules of the race would not allow drafting, so no one was allowed to ride in front of Doc and thereby reduce the wind resistance. Otherwise, he was surrounded. Sometimes along the way even little kids would ride with them on their dirt bikes.

"Thanks for saving my mom, Doc," one of them called out.

"Thanks for bringing my daddy back," another said. "You gave me back my family. You rock, Doc," came from still another.

Doc wiped his eyes. "These people who are trying to save me are going to kill me," he said. "My eyes are so blurry, I'm going to run into a tree. Must be dust or something causing my eyes to water."

The Brandts laughed. "I don't think Lance Armstrong could have felt this good riding into Paris on any of his Tour de France victories," said Hank.

"How fast are we going?" Doc asked. He had his road bike stripped down for aerodynamics, but Hank and Molly had a speedometer on their tandem.

"We've been doing between fifteen and twenty the whole way, and so far we've already done twenty miles," Hank answered.

"It seems effortless," Doc said.

"Well, that's probably good at this point. You've still got a long way to go," Molly said.

You don't know how true that is, Doc thought to himself as his family situation came crashing back. I have a long way to go even after I cross the finish line. Then an ugly thought flashed into his mind—if I ever cross the finish line.

CHAPTER 21

BACK AT THE LODGE, LUCY roughly interrogated the man with the elbow pads who had been pulled from the water.

"Tell me who else you know of that is involved in this," she demanded. "And where do they plan to strike next?" She was angry that Zack was hurt even though it was only very minor abrasions and bruising on his thighs.

"I don't know what you are talking about. I was just participating in a race when some crazy kid kicks me in the jaw and pulls my trunks down. What the hell was that about? I want to press charges against him. Why isn't he in here?"

"You always swim with a rock in each elbow?"

"Yeah, it stabilizes me in the water. What do you think?" "What was your conversation with Slade all about?"

"I don't know who you are talking about."

Lucy turned to Lieutenant Moon, also in the room. "I don't have time to waste on this creep. Let's just lock him up and book him for attempted murder. We have plenty of evidence."

"Let's go to jail, pal," Lieutenant Moon barked. "I want a lawyer."

"You don't need one now. We're done talking. But you will find out that you have that right when I read you your rights."

"Okay, okay, maybe I did talk with some guy who offered me money, and I can tell you more, but I need some incentive."

"I will see what I can find out here, Officer Teller," said the lieutenant. "You get back out on the course. If he gives me anything worthwhile, I will radio you." Then he turned his attention to the prisoner: "You wouldn't have gotten a dime for what you tried to do anyway because the guy who offered you money is on his way out of town."

"Stupid, stupid people!" Lucy complained, shaking her head as she walked out of the lodge. She stopped dead in her tracks when she saw her friend Lily pacing back and forth near her patrol car. Lily's arms were folded around herself protectively, and Lucy thought she seemed troubled and very sad. It looked like she had been crying.

"Lily, what are you doing here? Who's watching Fiddler? Please tell me Cliff stayed there!" Lucy asked with some panic in her voice.

"It's more like who he is watching. He woke up a couple of hours ago and convinced me that he had to get back here, but when I saw him in the parking lot, he looked different. He had seen Slade who evidently had come to the hospital to kill him on his way out of town. I gave him an ultimatum. I said we needed to concentrate on saving lives rather than taking them, but he didn't get in my car, so I assume he's stalking Slade. I guess he chooses killing. Oh, Lucy, I don't like any of this."

"Well, I must get back to the course. Do you want to come with me, Lily?"

"I need to go rescue your mother from my kids. She has had them since yesterday morning. I just want to hold my kids, Lucy."

"They're fine. Jerrod and Tara are helping. There is nothing that Tara likes more than to have little people around to control. They actually listen to her more than Jerrod does. Come with me."

"I'm sure that's true, but I need to see them," Lily begged. "I feel like I lost my love all over again. Right now I just want to take them home. We're going home now."

When Slade returned to his car, Fiddler had been silently and patiently waiting for him. Slade sat down in the driver's seat and closed the door when he heard the voice from the back seat. "I bet you came to visit me in the hospital. So sorry to disappoint you by not being in my room."

"I heard you'd been shot, so I wanted to check on you," Slade said, trying to sound convincing. Gamblers never sweat, but this gambler's clothes were now damp with perspiration.

"Tell me the plans to kill Doc, and I will let you live awhile longer," Fiddler said, changing his tone of voice to one of menace that froze Slade's spine.

"I don't know the plans, honest. I just offered the money to anyone who could get it done."

"Then you're of no use to me, and I can kill you right now."

"I don't know, honest to God!" Slade said fearfully. "I did hear somewhere that they were going to try while he was in the river."

Just then Fiddler saw Cliff getting into his car. "You can leave town now, but I will find you. You're scum, and you deserve to die."

Suddenly Fiddler vanished—as if into thin air. Slade didn't move for a long time. He sat and cursed Fiddler as he continued to sweat profusely.

Fiddler had seen Cliff come in and out of his room and talk with Lily. He reached him before he drove away. "Cliff, can you operate a canoe in whitewater?"

"Done it many times," Cliff said, only slightly exaggerating. "What the hell are you doing out here? What is going on?"

"I heard your disappointment at not being part of the action. How would you like to be right in the middle of it?" Fiddler asked.

"What are we waiting for?" Cliff demanded, his mood changing to excitement. "Get in!" They sped off toward the river, both determined to help Doc. Fiddler briefly filled in Cliff about what had played out that morning. If Cliff thought he was fired up before this, his anger and adrenaline were really kicking in now. The fire was spreading quickly, and he pushed down on the accelerator even harder.

Cliff called Lucy and told her to have a canoe waiting at Wild Wolf Inn for him and Fiddler.

She was just leaving the lodge with Lily. She turned to her as she hung up the phone. "I need your help. I have to get a whitewater canoe to the Wild Wolf for Cliff and Fiddler."

Immediately Lily's mood changed. She had fire in her eyes now too, along with a very big smile.

Doc made it to the Wild Wolf with no further attempts on his life. They were all starting to relax a little. Hank and Molly kept up well, but Molly was tired by the time they made it to the inn. She became unnerved once again when she saw Paul waiting with Doc's mountain bike, and she thought of him all alone with Doc in the Nicolet National Forest, facing any number of potential killers. She did not want her son alone protecting or defending anyone.

The cross-country trails were divided up into a number of loops. Molly had skied them with Hank a number of times. The first loop was called the Inn Loop. The trail led out through meadows and a few gentle hills. They would be able to see a four-wheeler coming from a distance. It was not a very likely place to be attacked at any time, but it was even more unlikely that day—Molly noticed a large group of Cliff's four-wheeler buddies waiting to escort Doc and Paul through the course. She immediately felt better just knowing that there would be others to help out. The next loop was Pine Loop, and it was mostly flat with a few gentle downhill runs.

Then there was Oak Loop, a treacherous trail with large boulders and a long steep downhill, and finally Birch Loop, which included some of the prettiest country in that part of Wisconsin. Molly always liked Birch Loop the best, except today. There were a number of hills, and the trail was narrow with deep ravines on either side. If I were a murderer, Molly thought, that's where I'd attack.

When they reached Paul, she asked him to describe the guy who had previously attacked them.

"Helmet, reflecting glass, green Yamaha," he said as he and Doc pedaled across the street.

Ryan and Zack had dressed and driven out to the Wild Wolf to meet them. Molly hurried over toward them.

"I need some rope," she yelled to the crowd.

One man had some in the back of his truck. Molly had never seen this man before and yet he brought it over and handed it to her without asking any questions.

She and Hank rode their tandem to Birch Loop. Ryan and Zack hitched a ride on one of the four-wheelers. They had some time because Birch Loop was actually next to the Inn Loop that Paul and Doc would ride on their way back. All they had to do at the end of Inn Loop was ride up the steep hill that the Doc and Paul would be riding down, and they'd be at the very spot Molly was worried about.

They covered the half-mile distance in minutes but needed to walk their bikes partly up the steep hill. When they arrived on top, Molly looked down in the ravine. That's when she had her first surprise.

CHAPTER **22**

PREVIOUSLY MOLLY HAD ONLY VISITED these trails during the winter. Without the under brush, she could look all the way to the bottom of the canyon, but now in the summer she could only see a couple of feet in front of her. The trees were thick with old and new growth. She then asked everyone to be quiet, and she listened carefully. She thought she heard an engine idling, but it could have been the others in the distance. She yelled anyway. "Hey buddy, we're on to you." But if the rider with the reflecting visor heard, he didn't seem. He certainly didn't move. They began stringing the rope between the trees to cordon off the trail from the hillside. They tried to stretch it in the most likely places, but there wasn't enough rope to cover all the exposed spots. Within twenty minutes, Doc and Paul arrived at the spot. The group of four-wheelers rode behind and Doc pedaled on the trail first and Paul followed.

That's when Molly heard an engine roar to life. Holding a deep breath, she held back a scream. The killer for hire broke free of the underbrush but saw the rope, slowed down, and swerved. He raced along the rope and found an open spot and headed toward Doc, but because of the rope and the people, he couldn't get the speed he wanted as he headed down the trail toward his victim. Suddenly Ryan appeared, as if out of nowhere, and jumped on a boulder. He only spared a fleeting thought for his mother, wondering what she was going to say about this adventurous display, then he hit his target. He leaped at the man feet first and kicked him from the four-wheeler.

The four-wheeler continued on for a few yards but did no damage to anyone before a large tree stopped the driverless machine. Several other men on four-wheelers quickly surrounded the angry fallen man. They used the rope to tie him up and carried him off to the tribal police. They were whooping and hollering as they dragged their prize off to be arrested. Some even got in a few hits and kicks before they turned him over to the authorities. They later learned that he was an abusive husband whose wife had left him after being in treatment with Doc. He was looking for revenge.

Ryan had hit his head when he landed and was a little woozy when he stood up and came to his senses. He had just reacted spontaneously, and it took him a moment to realize what he had just done. He looked at his mother and shrugged his shoulders with a sheepish grin on his face. It was the kind of look he had when she caught him going off a ramp on his dirt bike. Molly realized she was still holding her breath. She was feeling the fatigue right down to her bones, but she breathed in deeply and ran to hug her son. He was alive. With surprise, she realized she was more proud than angry, especially when she looked to see Doc continue down the hill and make it back to the inn safely.

Hank put his arm around Ryan. "Nice move, son. You were amazing. I didn't know you could do that."

"Neither did I," Ryan answered. "Man, I sure couldn't do it now. My knees are shaking too bad." They both laughed, releasing some of the pent-up tension and fear.

Then Molly reminded Hank they were due on the river with Doc. After affectionately punching his son in the arm, Hank moved toward his wife. He was bursting with pride over his caring and competent children and friends. He felt he must be one of the most blessed people in the world. The Brandts jumped on the tandem and quickly headed downhill. Ignoring their exhausted bodies, they moved toward their next job.

It was now just Bobbie waiting for Doc in the water. While waiting anxiously for her turn to help, Bobbie also wished someone else would be with her. Her heart was pounding so loudly that she was sure Doc would hear it. Her breathing was fast and shallow. Well, she thought, if I pass out, at least I would have a doctor around. Bobbie was athletic, as was her whole family, but she rarely took risks. She would kayak the whole way while Doc switched from a whitewater canoe to a kayak at Shotgun Eddy's.

They headed down Gilmore's Mistake, and the large crowd applauded when they reached the bottom of the rapid. They paddled downriver and were out of sight when Cliff and Fiddler arrived. The two men jumped in their canoe just as Hank and Molly headed down Gilmore's Mistake. Fiddler's gut hurt with each forward stroke, and the pry and draw strokes were even more painful. Each stroke caused him to wince even though he never made a sound or complained. He took the stern of the canoe and

Cliff the bow. Cliff was almost as good as he had promised, and soon they had passed Hank and Molly. Momentarily, they had Bobbie and Doc in sight. Both canoes quickly caught up, and other than the challenges the river provided, they canoed without incident to Shotgun Eddy's.

Rapids are categorized on a scale of one to seven depending on their difficulty. Many whitewater passages don't get classified, so anything above a one is difficult. There were at least two class two rapids on the stretch that Doc and his three canoe escorts were paddling, including one fairly long one just above Shotgun Eddy's, where a number of canoes had been destroyed over the years. Molly and Hank's skills were severely tested in this stretch, so they had to stop at Shotgun Eddy's. The river ahead was beyond their skill, and what had gone on previously had totally exhausted them.

There was a water stop set up at Shotgun Eddy's for the competitors, and the group stopped long enough to get a long, cool drink. The Wolf River Dells were much smaller and less dramatic than the famous tourist attraction at the Wisconsin Dells. There were no fancy hotels or fancy people, and it was missing streetlights and cement sidewalks. There were no water parks here either, just a small concession stand that sold snacks for weary rafters seeking a break from the river. But still the dells were dramatic with high cliffs through which the Wolf River provided challenging class two and class three rapids. Several challenges included a long class two to three run called Duck's Nest just before the Dells, not to mention Sullivan's Falls, a solid class three run. The passage was lined with huge pines and birch trees, and the foliage was thick and blooming—breathtaking. The temperature was now in the mid-eighties, and the sun not only beat on them from the sky but also reflected brightly off the water wherever there were no tall pines to protect them. After the short break, Doc started out again and paddled slightly ahead of the group. Fiddler looked around in all directions and couldn't imagine how another canoeist or kayaker was going to catch them; they would have to be waiting upriver.

He would be ready for anyone who was lying in wait for Doc. There was a large crowd at the Wolf River Dells, where a cliff stood some twenty to fifty feet above the water, and Fiddler could already hear hollers and applause as Doc approached.

Still, there were no other canoes or kayaks in the immediate area. Where would they be waiting to make their move? Would they even be on the water? Cliff and Fiddler had just started from the water stop when Fiddler looked ahead to the dells, taking in the beauty he remembered from their practice runs. At the time, he was watching young Native kids jumping from the dells into the foaming Wolf River below. He remembered thinking this was their water park—Mother Earth's water park. The kids could remain slightly hidden, then run out, laughing, and launch themselves off the cliffs. The young ones would hold the hand of an older child, squealing as they flew through the air and into the water. The older kids seemed to enjoy landing close to the unsuspecting rafters, scaring them to death.

The day of the race, Fiddler's adrenaline kicked in as he anticipated what would happen next.

Swimmers here referred to this area as the bottomless pit because the water was very deep here. If a jumper were able to land on Doc and disrupt his kayak, he could easily get him underwater and finish the job. None of the bystanders would see what was happening or even know what was going on. This was a perfect location to attack, to get rid of Doc once and for all. He could smash his head on the large and jagged rocks or even get stuck underneath them. Very easily, he could be taken out. "Cliff," cried Fiddler. "Catch Doc! I think I know what's going to happen! Hurry!"

Fiddler could see Cliff's paddle digging harder into the water and his did the same. His body was now screaming at him in pain although he fought to ignore it. Now was not the time for his gut to demand attention. He felt something wet and warm on his shirt and jeans and hoped the warmth on his abdomen was not blood.

They were a length behind Doc when three jumpers hit the water. One instantly disrupted Doc's kayak, and he went down fast without even knowing what hit him. It had all happened so quickly that Fiddler had no time to read the faces of the jumpers. Were they just kids playing a prank or were they murderers? When none of the three jumpers surfaced, Fiddler dived into the dark, cold Wolf River to find Doc. Even with adrenaline and endorphins at their peak, Fiddler felt searing pain in his side as he went over the gunnels of the canoe. He tried to open his eyes, but there was zero visibility in the churning river. The swift current pushed him downstream as he frantically groped for bodies. Then he heard what sounded like a muffled scream and swam toward it.

Immediately in front of him, he dimly made out the shadows of two men in the water. One had what appeared to be a choke hold on the other. Fiddler swam up from behind and knew that in an instant he could easily break this guy's neck. Then he heard Lily's voice reminding him that we were here to save lives today, not end them. He was contemplating plan B when he realized that Cliff and Bobbie were next to him. The three surrounded the assailant and pulled, and all five of them shot quickly toward the surface. The man still had a strong hold on Doc's neck and pulled him along through the churning water. Once above the surface, the man soon let go of his neck. Then the two other jumpers surfaced as well—and the faces were friendly. They were also there to protect Doc. When they had seen a grown man on the cliffs, they quietly climbed the rocks and waited until he made his move. When he jumped, they both followed the man over the edge, hoping to stop him.

Still wet, Fiddler did not want to look at his wound, not wanting to see blood. He was starting to cramp, the result of pushing his body hard when it needed rest to heal. He longed to be in the arms of the woman he loved—warm, safe, and loved in Lily's arms. But for now he just rested in the back of the canoe and hoped Cliff would do most of the work. Other members of the crowd retrieved their canoes and kayaks, and they were once again able to continue down the river. At this point, the rest of the dangers came from nature.

They still had to negotiate Big Smokey Falls. It was at least a class three rapid and possibly more depending on the height of the river. The greater the rain or snowmelt, the deeper the river and the more water that was forced to pour through small spaces. In some cases, the smaller rapids were easier to negotiate because more rocks are covered, but the bigger rapids could become deathtraps if a canoeist or kayaker spilled and landed in the water. There was rarely a day during summer that Big Smokey didn't spit someone out. Usually, if the river was low, a capsized canoeist or kayaker would float downstream without incident. The trick was to keep feet aimed downstream so the feet would hit the rocks first instead of the back, or worse, the head.

The whole crew, all of them, made it through the rapid, but now there was still one last obstacle, and that was the flat, slow water leading to where they would take out their canoes or kayaks along Highway 50. All of this had taken a huge toll on Doc as well. He had planned to paddle hard on this part to finish it quickly, but the thought of two more events and the exhaustion of his body told him otherwise. He leaned his head forward and rested it on the front of his kayak, letting the river do the work. Bobbie, Cliff, and Fiddler looked ahead, but they weren't looking for bad guys. They, too, had the hypnotic look of fatigue.

By the time Doc and the others made it to Highway 50, a number of competitors had already passed them. Doc was nearly an hour behind his scheduled time, but he had survived three attempts on his life, which was more than most people had to deal with in a lifetime. He was thankful to all the people who supported him, even without knowing about what Ray and Ezra had been doing in the surrounding forest. They had scoured the area without a break all day. They knew the area better than most and knew what to look for. They both had Doc and all the others in their prayers, though neither one would have admitted it. Praying was not something they talked much about.

When Doc arrived at the bridge, Kathy and Brad, who had awaited him anxiously, helped him from his kayak. They approached him with their skates off so they could help, but they already had on their helmets and pads to protect their knees, elbows, and wrists, all required by the race rules. They would have plenty of time to lace their skates while Doc put on his. The transitions are all part of the race, and Doc had practiced doing these changes a hundred times, but again he was slowed by his fatigue and went through his routine on autopilot, moving without thought.

If Kathy and Brad were disappointed at his late arrival or at the slow pace he was able to blade, they didn't show it. He was too tired to talk or share with them what had happened, but he figured they probably heard most of it from Lucy or other volunteers with radios. Even though it had been five hours from the start, supporters were still there. Many had made a day of it and brought picnic baskets and shared food with one another. No one ever thought of leaving; most felt they had a debt to repay.

Even some of Doc's former patients who had relapsed cheered him on.

One man waved his whiskey bottle as Doc went by. "If you finish, I will give you another shot at me, Doc. Keep it up. You're giving me hope."

Kathy and Brad were nervous and stole glances at one another because there were so many people surrounding Doc. How could you sort out anyone who meant him harm? A real danger was a downhill skate with the trees so close to the highway that one push could send him flying into a tree at twenty miles an hour with no protection other than his helmet. An accident here could be very bad. This was not going well, and they both worried. One time Doc started falling and headed toward a tree, but Brad was able to get between Doc and the tree and right him before he crashed. The day had taken a huge toll on him, and he was not sure if he could finish this race. For the first and only time, he had serious thoughts of quitting. Not only quitting the race but also quitting it all. Maybe he was not good enough to have everything he had in his life: his wife, his children, his work.

"How will I ever be able to repay all of you?" he managed to gasp between breaths.

"It seems more that others are finally getting a chance to repay you," Kathy assured him.

But he was too tired to accept the assurance. They skated on in silence. The crowd kept up the noise with loud cheers and support. At times it was deafening.

When they finally reached the lodge, Gayle and the children were waiting for him. Doc was already seven hours into the race, and he still had the run to complete. Sally and Paul let Gayle and the children run with their father, and they kept up the pace behind him. For them, it was like walking. Doc refused to walk, but his pace was slower than many race walkers. He shuffled his feet as best he could. He hoped to do seven-minute miles during the run, but he struggled with a pace that was more like eleven-minute miles. Doc's head was hanging and he ran silently, unable to speak. Occasionally he had a weak smile for his children and onlookers. By this time, word spread that Slade had skipped town. While the threat was diminished, the volunteers stayed vigilant and kept a sharp eye. Not one of them would walk out on Doc.

It took Doc another hour to finish. Just in front of the finish line, he stopped. He turned to Gayle. "Just to show you that I will change too, I don't have to cross this," he said. This was the first full sentence he had said in a long time.

Gayle smiled. "Over my dead body," she said. "You're doing this!" Weeping with exhaustion and happiness, she pushed him across the finish line, delighting the cheering crowd.

SHORTLY AFTER THE SUCCESSFUL CONCLUSION of the race, Gayle, as well as Doc and the kids, left for Hazelden in Minnesota for treatment. The whole family would have to make changes. They knew it was going to be difficult, yet they all affirmed that, to use gambling jargon, they were all in. Doc would need to take over the finances and Gayle would quit her job at the casino. The tribal clinic was only too happy to have her back as a nurse, and they promised to hold a position open for her. Doc would have to cut back on his exercise and work schedule to spend more time with the family. If he was unable or unwilling to do that, perhaps he needed to consider treatment for exercise addiction. Most of all, the marriage needed work, and even at the end of treatment, its survival would be in question.

But there were many things on their side. After seeing that money and power actually were not rewarding, Gayle was not nearly as interested in them as she had been. She was willing to give up her empty lifelong goal. Seeing the outpouring of love and concern from the community, she decided she wanted to make her life on the rez, no matter what happened to their marriage. The kids agreed and were willing to come home for some family therapy. Family counseling was incorporated once a week with all those who were able to be there. After almost losing both their father and mother, the children developed a new appreciation for their parents. Sometimes it takes a crisis for people to realize what they have and to be aware that they do not have their loved ones forever.

As for Gayle's gambling addiction, the good news was that it was caught early enough that she hadn't lost everything, nor accumulated a huge and unmanageable debt. One of the major reasons for relapse is to attempt that one last big killing just to break even. She knew enough about the odds at the casino to understand that she wasn't going to win that next big game. Gayle had to admit she just wasn't that great a card player. The gambling had been an excuse to avoid her emptiness inside. This void had to be filled by her and her alone, and nothing on the outside could fix it. She was finally ready to take an honest look to discover who she was, what she liked and felt, and even what made her giggle. So many hours, days, and years had passed, with her unaware of her own true feelings. Gayle needed to find what was really important to her in this life.

Gayle and Doc rented a house in St. Croix Falls, Wisconsin, during the thirty days of Gayle's outpatient treatment. The house was near Hazelden, and the St. Croix River reminded them of the Wolf.

Doc spent the first week just recovering physically. Other than stretching and walking, he did not exercise at all. After that he did some running and biking and even canoeing, either with Gayle or with the children. Once word spread that Slade had left town and probably would never come back, nobody else seemed interested in killing him.

He had been so devastated and so insecure that the thought of making love was more frightening than exciting. One of the counselors at Hazelden suggested that he and Gayle forget about having sex and practice just being close again and having affection toward one another. He gave them a series of exercises and some guidelines that forbid intercourse, suggesting instead that they simply give and receive pleasure. Once the threat of performance was out of the way, Gayle became more eager to show him how much she cared. Things then began to progress, and in time they made love. Gayle couldn't pretend to have the passion and excitement of the affair, but they responded as a loving couple with intimate knowledge of each other, with tenderness and devotion. This was a deeper and richer experience than they ever had before, and Gayle surrendered to new feelings she had never experienced.

Still, they had a huge hurdle to overcome, and only time would tell if they could succeed.

Sometime after Gayle had completed her treatment at Hazelden, the whole group got together again for Tara's naming ceremony, which was held at her uncle's place on the Ojibwe Reservation, north and west of the Menominee Reservation. Her uncle had built a replica of the Ojibwe villages of the past, including a sweat lodge and longhouse. It was on a piece of land that included a small lake and woods with trails and a campground so people could sleep overnight. Tara had given Lily a pouch of tobacco and asked her to find a traditional name. She carried the tobacco everywhere for a year, and during that time she hoped the spirits would inspire her with a name for Tara. Following the Red Road, she finally found Tara's name and was ready to offer it to her friend's daughter. It took Doc at least three weeks to develop any interest thick and jet-black, her eyes dark and kind, her smile spread across her whole face. She looked very much like her mom. She was less demanding as she grew and showed much greater respect for her elders. It was another story with the boys in the neighborhood—but that would come soon enough, and Lucy wasn't in too big a hurry for Tara to change her feelings toward boys. Tara loved the water and all the birds of the water. She loved the herons, egrets, seagulls, and loons. And though they were rare in northern Wisconsin, she loved swans and could watch them for hours. Lucy thought Tara was like a mother hen when it came to younger children. Lucy even sometimes called Tara a mother hen to her face when she was caught bossing kids around.

The entire Brandt family came to the naming ceremony. With a deep and growing respect for Lucy, her traditions, and spirituality, they wanted to know more about the Menominee culturally, and Tara's uncle was a great teacher. Hank, Molly, and their children arrived at the village and were anxious to see Doc and Gayle and hear how their treatment had gone. They all just wanted to rest and to enjoy camping and the naming ceremony. But the whole Brandt family looked uncomfortable after they arrived and seemed uncertain about how they would fit in. Lucy approached them and welcomed them to the rez. They chatted a short time and decided to set up their camping gear. Lucy pointed out a spot near the lake, far from the teaching lodge where the naming ceremony would take place. As Paul and Ryan began to unload the van, Hank looked up and saw Fiddler. Fiddler had lived with Lily and the children since leaving Keshena, and had accompanied them to the ceremony.

Usually Hank was pretty good at reading people. Years of AA helped him trust his instincts and his intuition. Yet Fiddler was an enigma. He saw and heard about all he had done to help Doc. He respected his contributions but still was apprehensive around this man who was so very different than he was.

Or was he?

Fiddler had healed from his gunshot wound, and though he loved living as part of a family for the first time in his life, he was having a hard time letting go of his desire to pursue Slade. He would fight this immeasurable urge to leave by touching Lily. He was worried that if he didn't go after him, Slade would take the offensive and again start sending people to kill him. That could put Lily and her children at risk. He felt he could lose his family by leaving, but he also could lose them by staying. Still, he was trying a new life that he had never known, and he had to expect to be restless. Since he was a boy, he had thrived on danger, and now he was trying to find peace. He wanted to stop judging people, but he didn't know if he could ever stop these thoughts. Fiddler was confused about how much responsibility he had for the new people he thought were in his charge.

Hank struggled with many of the same thoughts and feelings. He blamed himself for the death of his son Scott on a regular basis. He felt responsible for all the problems and struggles of his children, feelings that usually became exacerbated when he was hungry, angry, or tired.

Hank was deep in thought as he turned around with his arms full of firewood and literally bumped into Fiddler, who was coming over to say hello. He dropped his armful of wood in front of Fiddler's feet, and they stood in silence eyeing each other. The awkwardness ended when they started to laugh together while picking up the wood. Fiddler, who had been at the camp for a few days, offered to show Hank around. As they walked the grounds, Lily joined them. Hank and Molly had many questions about the traditional ways of the Indians. Lily had spent most of her life around Native Americans but still felt a great thirst for learning more, and she wanted to instill the spirituality she had learned from her friends in her children.

Lily, Hank, and Fiddler felt something other than the pleasing smells in the air. As they headed back to gather together on the grass and watch the children, they noticed that Doc had arrived. They were glad to see him but were disappointed to see him alone. Their disappointment did not last for long. Doc greeted the group briefly and explained that Gayle had dropped him off and was at the reservation gas station and grocery store, buying tobacco for a gift. They planned to spend the weekend camping as well.

After Gayle arrived, the group showed her around the grounds as well. Leaving as quickly as he came, Doc made his way up the dirt and wooden steps. Doc had never really spent time there before, and he was already wondering if he could get volunteers for a community service project. Maybe a group of his patients could give back by cleaning and preserving this site. He believed it was an integral part of the healing process. If someone was hurting and struggling to stay clean and sober, it helped to give back. Doc suddenly realized how much he and Hank had in common.

They both practiced the twelve steps of AA and believed in reaching out and helping others in need. He wondered how he could repay the Brandt family for all they had given up to help a stranger.

Soon Ray arrived and decided to have dinner with the Brandt family, Fiddler, Lucy, Lily, and the children. As the women cooked dinner over an open fire, they all enjoyed the relaxing star-filled night. The Aurora borealis was faint but could be seen—red and green lights dancing near the horizon of the wide sky. The elders in the group began teaching the children beliefs of their ancestors. Some First Nations believed the northern lights were their ancestors' spirits dancing before the Great Spirit. Many Native American cultures thought the sky people were playing ball. The children laughed when Fiddler told of the Makah tribe, which thought the lights were the fires in the north over which a tribe of dwarfs steamed whale blubber.

The children were all particularly intent when the Menominee legends were explained. The Menominee of Wisconsin thought of the lights as torches used by gracious giants of the north while they spearfished at night. The whistling and crackling sound that occasionally accompanied the lights was thought to be voices of spirits trying to talk to the people of earth. It was believed that one should answer in a whispering voice.

At this point, Ray and Fiddler started whispering to each other. Smiling, they stated that the spirits foretold that it was time for the children to go to sleep.

Ray said the sky spirits told him they could stay up until they were done eating. Then each child needed to quietly go into his tent without argument.

The children strained to hear the spirits talking. After eating everything on their plates, the children brushed their teeth and climbed into sleeping bags. The women just smiled and were grateful the two men could easily influence the children to mind the rules.

Everyone pitched in to clean up, and they enjoyed lighthearted conversation. Preparation for the naming ceremony would start very early the next day. Tara needed to wear a skirt, be prayerful, and prepare the feast for everyone after the naming was completed. She also needed to present gifts to her new guardians. Tara had asked Hank, Molly, Fiddler, her grandmother, and Ray to be her *we'ehs* although Tara's grandmother was not a strong believer in the old ways.

A *we'eh* was like a godparent or confirmation sponsor, although there is no clear way to translate it into English. It was a respected person who was to provide wisdom and guidance from the time of the naming ceremony onward, particularly in spiritual matters. While most of her spirituality was centered on her Catholic faith, Tara's grandmother loved her granddaughter and would do anything for her. Through this experience with Tara, she actually had gained a new appreciation for her ancestors. This also helped Lucy's relationship with her mother because they would often argue about Lucy's participation in traditional ceremonies. It was a great honor to be asked and an even greater honor to be accepted. The role they agreed to play in this young lady's life carried a big responsibility. If Tara needed guidance, support, encouragement or help in any way, they agreed to step up and support and nurture her. She could go to them for ideas, teachings, spiritual guidance, and so much more. This was a serious responsibility that demanded accountability. When someone was asked, they were encouraged to reflect carefully before accepting.

The men in the group took a walk around the grounds, smoking and bonding as only men can do. Tara was still awake and checking her gifts for her naming ceremony. She was so excited that the nervousness would not let her relax. Hank sat quietly with her after deciding to stay behind at the campsite with the women and sleeping children.

The sun and birds woke everyone up early. Tara had been up in preparation for some time already. She started to cook the feast for later that day—a venison stew with wild rice. Other woman on the rez brought pies. The berries were mixed. Tara only still had to make the cornbread.

Many people were moving around slowly and quietly as Lily crawled out of her tent. She was careful not to wake her children. She had not slept well and was looking forward to a few minutes alone. Fiddler had awakened early and made coffee for Lily. He never developed a taste for coffee himself, but he handed a steaming cup of coffee to her just the way she liked it. They smiled at each other and sat in comfortable silence. They both were completely lost in their own thoughts. It felt more right than they could remember.

He had already smudged and offered his prayers down by the lake. His sleep had been disturbed by violent dreams. That morning, he talked with Lily about his dreams, and she was comforting as always. He rarely had the chance to talk about himself, but he always seemed to feel better after explaining his troubling dreams and talking briefly about his family life.

Their time together was interrupted as Lucy and Ray came toward them. Up before the sun, they felt the need to patrol the area.

Fiddler felt the need to touch Lily. He stood by her, holding his breath. He could feel an electric energy that seemed to have a life of its own. He wondered if she was feeling it. Then Lucy's son joined them. All the kids were awake now and laughing and demanded hugs and tickles from all of them. The kids were well rested and full of energy, with empty stomachs. Fiddler smiled from ear to ear, welcoming the attention and affection from his future stepchildren—at least he hoped they would be his stepchildren someday. Fiddler had hoped for some more quiet time with Lily, but hungry children were a higher priority.

Anxiously waiting for the naming ceremony to begin, the guests felt the anticipation in the air. Finally an elder called attention, and women were asked to put on skirts before entering the teaching lodge. It was time to learn the name that was found for Tara. Quietly they entered the east door of the lodge. Each person was asked to take sama into his or her left hand and offer up a prayer while tossing it into the fire burning in the middle of the lodge. After everyone had entered and been seated, the traditional songs began. Old songs were sung to honor and welcome ancestors.

Tara was asked to stand. She was excited and very nervous. Tara had been to a naming ceremony only once in the past and that was her brother's. She did not remember all that took place. At the time Tara was more interested in the fire and the songs than in paying attention to the important steps in receiving a new name. Tara had a beautiful voice and loved to hear her own singing woven together with others. She was lost in thought when Lily took her by the arm. After gazing affectionately into each other's eyes, they both walked around the fire three times. The nervous young lady was being described to the Great Spirit and the guests, and Tara heard some wonderful, loving words to explain who she was during this rite of passage. The two ladies stopped in front of the west door of the teaching lodge. Her *we'ehs* were asked to surround her. Each person was asked to describe Tara, tell a story about her, or simply tell the guests what they liked or admired about the young lady. The important responsibilities were described and all were asked if they would take the duty seriously. Many people present were crying or trying to stifle their tears. It was a great honor to be present during this significant rite of passage for a young woman, who in her short life had suffered so much. As they spoke, Tara presented each *we'eh* with a gift made of wood, which demonstrated her deep appreciation. Tara choked back tears as she described what each one meant to her.

Lily then stood to give Tara her new name. She spoke clearly the cherished name: *Waabiziikwe*, meaning White Swan Woman. Lily walked across to take Tara by the arm; she told Tara why the name found her. Tara loved the water; she was beautiful and graceful like a swan. Like the maternal swan, she could be very protective of the young. Lily walked her three times around the lodge. As they were walking past, each person present spoke her new name. *Waabiziikwe* was spoken with great respect. Tara's bright mind raced forward, worrying that she did not know how to spell her new name and that she might forget it. Trying to make sure this beautiful new name stayed in her long-term memory, she silently mouthed the unfamiliar words. Tara felt very grown up and emotional. She was honored and very proud of the name she was given.

After the ceremony, everyone was ready for the delicious feast. Tara had been concerned about how the stew would taste. She was not allowed to taste the food while she was cooking it. She was to be prayerful and trust that she would add just the right spices. That night, *Waabiziikwe* was very happy because everything tasted just right. First she served the women on their moon time. These loving ladies stood outside the lodge for the ceremony, able to hear all that went on inside the lodge. Women in their moon time, or during their periods, were considered very powerful, and their power could take away from the ceremony. Tara received many hugs and kind words as the people ate her gift of venison. She was finally feeling that things would turn out to be just fine after all. Everyone enjoyed the ceremony and the feast. Tara was now a lady with many people who would be watching out for her best interests. It was as if her family grew in just a short time. Tara felt very proud to be a part of such loving and caring people. She also loved her new name very much. It seemed to fit her just right.

During the dinner that followed the naming ceremony, Fiddler looked at the people eating and laughing around him.

He looked over at the Brandts. He saw them talking and laughing with Lucy and Ray, and he remembered the struggles they told him about when he had joined them in workouts, and the camaraderie they shared afterward, having coffee. There is hope, he thought to himself. Perhaps I can learn to be part of a community of people and be loved and accepted by them. Fiddler had to believe there was hope.

After dinner, Tara took a walk with her grandmother. Although she wouldn't admit it out loud, she was beginning to see the wisdom of the old ways and the value of preserving them. As they neared the lake and the sun was setting, she put her arm around her granddaughter.

"You are going to be a fine woman, *Waabiziikwe.*"

Tara looked up at her grandmother. "I come from good stock, and I have great *we'ehs*—especially you, Grandmother."

OTHER BOOKS OF INTEREST FROM

Sober
Spring

Sober Spring tells the compelling story of the Brandt family's struggle with the tragic uncertainties of alcoholism. The book brings to life the torment of a father's addiction, the pain of a family's recovery, and the healing of a community's deep inner trauma.

Flight of the
Loon

This sequel to Robert Bollendorf's *Sober Spring* chronicles the rebuilding of the wounded Brandt family, and shows how events, even tragic ones, can hasten the family's healing.

Autumn
Snow

Autumn Snow, written with Donna Gluck, is the third novel in Robert Bollendorf's addiction and recovery series. The Brandt family faces its greatest crisis when Scott, their eldest son, is involved in a terrible car accident and drug use is suspected. Officer Lucy Teller feels there is more to the story and sets out on an investigation that uncovers disquieting facts about the accident and truths about herself.

Witch of
Winter

Witch of Winter, written with Donna Gluck, is the fourth novel in Robert Bollendorf's addiction and recovery series. It continues the story of the Brandt family and Officer Lucy Teller. Involved in a harrowing investigation set in deep Wisconsin winter, Lucy learns a great deal about relationships, recovery, and the true meaning of love.

PROCESS ADDICTIONS

As noted in *Witch of Winter (2017)* and *Summer Heat (2017)*, research on heroin addiction discovered that one of the reasons an extract from the poppy plant has such a powerful effect on the human body is that it is similar in chemical makeup to a peptide already present in the body, which we call endorphins. Endorphins and other chemicals such as dopamine play a strong role in our experience of pleasure, and are found in greater amounts when we are engaging in eating, laughing, and sex, but also when we are experiencing pain, according to the American Society of Addiction Medicine. This may partially explain why some people don't seem to need to ingest a chemical to reach a desired state of pleasure.

For these people, simply engaging in a behavior brings them such a profound reward that they may spend the rest of their lives pursuing that behavior to obtain that same level of pleasure they initially discovered. And just like their brothers and sisters who do the same thing by ingesting a chemical, it can lead to the same negative consequences and the same vicious cycles, which lead to addiction. The only difference is instead of a chemical addiction, we refer to this as a process or behavioral addiction.

Process or behavioral addictions include sexual addiction, gambling, eating, and exercise. Research has found that people with these addictions have endorphins in greater amounts when engaged in these activities than people who don't suffer from these addictions when engaged in the same activities.

There are other reasons why people develop process addictions. One of these reasons is how these addicts experience anxiety and how they define anxiety. First, addicts experience higher levels of anxiety than non-addicts. Anxiety is similar to fear, but where fear has a specific cause, anxiety is more general.

For example, if you walk into a grocery store and notice a robbery in progress, you will probably feel fear, but some people can simply walk into a grocery store under normal circumstances and feel anxiety. Often, if you ask that person why they are anxious, they cannot give an answer.

There are also a number of ways in which a person can relieve anxiety. We often describe these methods of relieving anxiety as coping mechanisms. Some people cope with feelings of anxiety through various means, based on the particular situation. This might include taking a bubble bath, taking a walk, treating themselves to ice cream, calling a friend, or a number of other activities. In the case of an addict, they tend to describe all anxiety as the same, and they identify only one way to relieve it.

In the book *Out of the Shadows: Understanding Sexual Addition* (2001), Patrick Carnes says sexual addicts describe all anxiety as sexual anxiety and therefore the only way to relieve it through sex. Again, we can find the same symptom maintaining sequence that Haley and others have used in Strategic Family Therapy.

Carnes describes this cycle with the following sequence: The addict feels anxiety and engages in his favorite form of sexual activity. After engaging in the activity, he feels guilty, and in order to relieve the guilt, promises never to do that again. The promise never to do it again leads to obsessing in doing it again, which then leads to anxiety. For this type of addict, all anxiety is described as sexual anxiety, and therefore the only way to relieve it is to engage in sex.

Another symptom often found in process addictions is distortion of reality. The gambler can be convinced they will win the next big jackpot, even though the odds may be millions to one. The food addict may see food as looking better than it is and have a number of distortions about why they won't gain weight. The diet and supplement industry makes a fortune on these distortions and even creates new ones. The sexual addict whose primary outlet is having affairs may believe all women find him attractive and want to have sex as much as he does (Carnes 2001).

Like their chemical counterparts, all these addictions lead to both physical, emotional, and relationship consequences. Gayle, in the book *Summer Heat*, was one such example, despite the fact that her husband worked in an addiction treatment center. Gayle ended up in a dangerous affair that could have gotten her or her husband killed. She lost all her family's savings and put her children's education and careers in jeopardy. And, as is almost always the case in addiction, she lost a great deal of self-esteem.

Finally, the treatment for process addiction is similar in many respects to chemical addiction. Most are best treated by beginning with an inpatient or outpatient treatment, with some sort of recovery program that includes 12 steps often following the inpatient treatment. In the case of gambling, it is Gamblers Anonymous; in eating, it is Overeaters Anonymous; in sex it is either Sex Addicts Anonymous or Sexaholics Anonymous. Each group describes certain triggers which must be avoided: for overeaters, it is sugar; in gambling, any kind of wager; in sex, it is any kind of dishonest sex, sometimes described as any sex that is not part of a committed relationship.

Most of these programs also include turning one's life over to a higher power. This is often difficult for the atheist or someone who really questions the existence of a god. As was suggested in *A Rose by Any Other Name (2017)*, one answer to this is that the higher power could be turning one's life over to a set of values. No one can be successful in recovery without honesty to self and others. All 12-step programs include helping others, which might be referred to as love or spirituality, and not necessarily include God. Some other values may include respect and understanding.

In any case, we hope everyone who reads these books will benefit in some way. Whether you are addicted yourself or love someone with a problem, or if you are a counselor or an aspiring counselor, or just someone who wants to understand people better, thank you for taking the time to read these stories, and good luck in your personal recovery. Because as stated in *Flight of the Loon*, life itself is a terminal illness from which we are all struggling to recover.

<u>Assignment</u>

"Why don't they just quit?" is often a question we hear when people are talking about addiction. Identify a behavior of your own that you have trouble giving up, even though you know it is not good for you. Try to answer the question, "Why don't you just quit?"

BIBLIOGRAPHY

1. Malenka, RC; Nestler, EJ; Hyman, SE (2009). "Chapter 15: Reinforcement and Addictive Disorders." In Sydor A, Brown RY. "Molecular Neuropharmacology: A Foundation for Clinical Neuroscience" (2nd ed.). New York: McGraw-Hill Medical. pp. 364-375. ISBN 9780071481274

2. "Glossary of Terms" (http://neuroscience.mssm.edu/nestler/glossary.html). "Mount Sinai School of Medicine. Department of Neuroscience." Retrieved 9 February 2015

3. Volkow, ND; Koob, GF; McLellan, AT (January 2016). Neurobiologic Advances from the Brain Disease Model of Addiction." N. Engl. J. Med. 374 (4): 363-371

4. Albrecht, U; Kirschner, NE; Grusser, SM (2007). "Diagnostic Instruments for Behavioural Addiction: An Overview"

5. Potenza, MN (September 2006). "Should Addictive Disorders Include Non-Substance-Related Conditions?" Addiction.101 Suppl 1: 142-51.

6. Shaffer, Howard J. (1966). "Understanding the Means and Objects of Addiction: Technology, the Internet, and Gambling." Journal of Gambling Studies. 12 (4): 461-9

7. Olsen, CM (December 2011). "Natural Rewards, Neuroplasticity, and Non-Drug Addictions" Neuropharmacology. 61 (7): 1109-22

8. Blum, K; Werner, T; Carnes, S; Carnes, P; Bowirrat, A; Giordano, J; Oscar-Berman, M; Gold, M (2012). "Sex, Drugs, and Rock 'n' Roll: Hypothesizing Common Mesolimbic Activation as a Function of Reward Gene Polymorphisms" J. Psychoactive Drugs. 44 (1): 38-55

9. Brewer, Judson A.; Potenza, Marc N. (2008). "The Neurobiology and Genetics of Impulse Control Disorders: Relationships to Drug Addictions" Biochemical Pharmacology 75 (1): 63-75

10. Dichiara, G; Bassareo, V (2007). "Reward System and Addiction: What Dopamine Does and Doesn't Do." Current Opinion in Pharmacology. 7 (1) 69-76

11. Kuss, Daria (2013). "Internet Gaming Addiction: Current Perspectives Psychological Research and Behavior Management. 6 (6): 125-137

12. Grant, Jon: Impulse Control Disorders: A Clinician's Guide to Understanding and Treating Behavioral Addictions

13. American Society of Addiction Medicine. Public Policy Statement Definition of Addiction. https://www.asam.org/resources/definition-of-addiction

14. Grant JE; Potenza MN; Weinstein, A; Gorelick, DA (September 2010). "Introduction to Behavioral Addictions" Am. J. Drug Alcohol Abuse. 36 (5): 233-241

15. Carnes, Patrick. "Out of the Shadows" (2001) Hazelden

CHAPTER 6

BINGE DRINKING ON COLLEGE CAMPUS

By Kimberly Groll LCPC, CADC, CAMT

UNDERAGE DRINKING IS A CONCERN whether your child is at home or going off to college. Dealing with a DUI for underage drinking and driving is a bigger concern. I have seen the affects of young adolescents who have been charged with underage drinking and getting their first DUI. When I hear their stories and how sorry they are for making a bad decision for one night of drinking with getting behind the wheel of an automobile, it truly is heartbreaking knowing their lives have changed forever.

First of all they are inexperienced drivers with only a few years of driving on the road. Add alcohol to the inexperience and now their overall perception is compromised. Adolescents don't have the reasoning skills in place and don't always make good decisions. They believe they will never get caught or it will never happen to them. Too often it does happen and they are left with the consequences that follow.

I know of individuals who were accepted to the college of their choice. After getting a DUI this changed their plans to attend that college because they feared they would not be able to drink the way they attended when they entered their first year on campus. There are a few things wrong with this type of thinking. First of all, it appears the drinking is a priority, and secondly their choice of college is now compromised with making plans to attend a community college. Don't get me wrong; there is nothing wrong with attending a community college. What I find troublesome is not following through with their original plans with attending the college of their choice due to worrying about fitting into the drinking crowd and not being able to drink as they planned due to getting a DUI.

What are the chances of your child drinking too much when they go off to college? When our children leave home for the first time and experience life on their own, we hope they use their better judgment and make good choices. Many do; however, many will experiment and will want to fit in with going along with the rest of the crowd.

When parents bring their adolescents in to see me prior to leaving for college with concerns of drinking and smoking marijuana in which they know has taken place, they want to know what to do. They are concerned about their child leaving for college with continuing use of alcohol and drugs and getting into trouble. These are good kids, making good grades, and when I meet them they state their use is minimal. They all have good intentions on keeping their grades up, and they all claim to not overdo it with drinking or smoking marijuana. As a counselor I need to bring awareness to their using patterns and to make them aware of when they are minimizing, rationalizing or justifying their behaviors.

Counselor Tip: If a person is **minimizing** their use, he or she would play down the amount they are drinking or using drugs.

If a person is **rationalizing** their behavior he or she would be convincing themselves it was okay to drink or use drugs because they are doing well in school and keeping up with their grades.

If a person is **justifying** their behavior he or she would accept their pattern of drinking or using drugs because that is what all their friends are doing and they want to fit in and be like everyone else.

It is important for the individual to understand when he or she is using these patterns of thinking.

I inform my clients about these three cognitive distortions and to be aware if they are indeed using any of the patterns of thinking when drinking or using drugs.

If a student has entered into their college years and starts to fall behind with his/her assignments, this could be the first signs of alarm. I know students have good intentions to study and to write papers that are needed to fulfill their obligations; however, if a night of drinking interferes with their original plans, and they put their studies off, they need to take a deeper look at themselves and realize this can be the beginning stages of losing control.

Newspaper Column written on Binge Drinking on College Campus

With many adolescents graduating from high school and planning to attend college, awareness about binge drinking on college campuses needs to be addressed. Many adolescents will be leaving their home for the first time and many of them will have and feel a new sense of freedom. They will be away from the everyday rules and regulations set forth by their parents. They will need to learn to balance their time, manage their studies, and of course they will be meeting new friends while experiencing the college lifestyle. For some this means buckling down and applying themselves. For others this means time to party without being told what to do and how to do it.

As an addictions counselor for drugs and alcohol, I have counseled many adolescents who started partying in high school and carry this with them into their college years. What concerns me as a counselor is the amount of drinking that occurs on a college campus. I hear stories of all sorts; I also am called when the reality of drinking or drug use turns into trouble.

Some of the things I've heard are, "I can't wait until I get into college, then I am going to do what I want to do." "I will be able to smoke my dope or drink anytime I want without my parent's drug testing me." "I thought I would be able to keep up with my studies after a night of partying; however, I just kept getting further and further behind in my classes."

This is scary to hear as a parent/counselor, and I have to wonder how many parents would be willing to pay for their children's education if they knew their child's first interest in going off to college is partying, and secondly trying to keep up with his/her studies.

A parent wrote to me this month with this same concern and I thought it would be important to bring information about college binge drinking to this month's column.

Dear C. W.

I would be concerned in how much your son is drinking, especially since he is underage. I would want to know his pattern of drinking and how much he is drinking during the week or on weekends. At what age did he first start to drink? Does he go on binges? Has he experienced blackouts?

When a person starts to drink at an early age he builds a tolerance. He will need to drink more in able to reach the same affects he is seeking. The earlier he starts the more dangerous this can become for an individual.

It would be important to discuss how alcohol abuse affects him and the family. You may want to sit down with him prior to leaving for college and have a family meeting. You may want to discuss your concerns for his safety and educate him about the seriousness of alcohol and the possible trouble that can follow him for the rest of his life if he is caught doing something under the influence of alcohol. If he is open to speaking with you, perhaps you may be able to identify his needs and issues.

I see so many cases after the damage has been done. If you recognize any unusual behavior, it is important to address the issues right away. Sending your child off to college, or just off for the day with knowing things are not right with your child, would be sweeping the problem under the carpet.

Having a child see a counselor can sometimes help to regain balance. It would be cheaper in the long run to have your child speak to someone about his issues rather than getting into trouble later on with having legal fees, a possible record which would follow him for the rest of his life, or court-mandated counseling ordered.

Sincerely,

Counselor Kimberly

I would also like to address the secondhand victims of college binge drinking:

44% of college students binge drink at least once every two weeks. Binge drinking equals 5 or more drinks in a row for a male; 4 or more drinks in a row for a female.

87% of college students have suffered from "Secondary Binge Effects" caused by other's drinking.

68% had studying/sleeping interrupted

54% had to take care of a drunken student

34% been insulted or humiliated

26% experienced unwanted sexual advances

20% had a serious argument or quarrel

15% had property damaged

13% have been pushed, hit, or assaulted

2% have been a victim of sexual assault or date rape

College drinking not only affects the person drinking but it also affects the ones who choose not to drink. It is important to realize the seriousness of underage drinking and the effects it has on everyone.

College kids do have a choice to request alcohol free dorms to avoid these problems.

THE CHALLENGER

I'm not an addictions counselor or student, nor am I an alcoholic or co-dependent, but I am an avid reader and I love Bollendorf's books. When I read I want to learn something. With Bollendorf I get that and more — stories that hold my interest from beginning to end. The Challenger *not only gives one insight into Post Traumatic Stress Disorder (PTSD), it is wrapped around political intrigue, one of my favorite subjects. Now that we have lost author Tony Hillerman I'm glad I have Rob Bollendorf to help fill the void.*

—Bill Vlasek, trial lawyer

To our grandchildren.
Ones we have now and the ones to come.
May they live in peace.

ACKNOWLEDGMENTS

As of right now i'm thinking this will be my last book, at least as a part of this series. So I want to recognize several people who helped me along the way. First, I'd like to thank Greg Pierce of Acta, the people at Augsburg Press, and Joe Barillari at College of DuPage Press who all have taken a chance on one or more of the books, starting with *Sober Spring* through *Summer Heat*, book five.

I'd like to thank Donna Gluck. She came along before *Autumn Snow* was published. There was a version of *Autumn Snow* and *Witch of Winter* already completed but I lacked the confidence to give them to anyone because of the strong Native American presence in the book. She not only read the books and gave me confidence that they were worthwhile, but also added her expertise, especially to the ceremonies in the books. Thanks again to Joe Barillari for encouraging me to spilt *Autumn Snow* and *Witch of Winter* into two books and keep the shorter format I am comfortable with and many people seem to enjoy. Thanks to Jim Tipton and April Hanstad for editing and to April for her constant advocacy and advice. Thanks to my friends Billl Vlasek and Alan Bergeson for help with the military and political aspects of the book. Both of these guys are news junkies and read several newspapers and blogs a day. Thanks to Kathy Quinn Reyes for her research. I'd also like to thank Mike and Ashley Rutcosky for their technical support.

In this last book I also hit what may be the third rail with several of my loyal readers and that is politics. I was happily able to avoid this subject in my previous books, but in this book a major issue is Post Traumatic Stress Disorder (PTSD) among war veterans. Post Traumatic Stress Disorder can occur from any trauma, not just war, and the major factor is the trauma and how it is dealt with, but I can't help but think that in war politics plays a part. I have never been in a war but I have lived through several now, and the homecoming has to be part of the problem. Here is a man or woman coming home from war having difficulty finding a job, and fighting with the Veteran's Administration for services as well.

And, after putting their life on the line for their country, learning that the people who sent them there are using their power for their own personal gain. Imagine being a vet coming home from war and hearing about rich Americans complaining about paying higher taxes when you just saw your best friend pay with his life—his body spattered in a million pieces by a roadside bomb. I can no longer stand the state of politics in this country and I didn't have to defend this Country with my life. If this book serves a purpose besides teaching something about PTSD, I hope it helps people with different beliefs and views to begin talking again. It used to be religion was something you didn't bring up without knowing the beliefs of who you are talking to, now it is politics. I tried to bring up the views of both sides but I'm sure my own bias will show through.

On a more positive note, though the characters in this book are fictional, many of the events and background data are true. Billy Mills, besides the great Jim Thorp won the 800 meters in the '64 Olympics and is the spokesperson for Running Strong, an organization which works to improve the physical health of Native American youth through nutrion and exercise. Ada Deer, a Menominee, was the first Native American to head the Bureau of Indian Affairs and Winona La Duke was a Vice Presidential candidate for the Green Party. The Menominee High School in Keshena has increased their graduation rate to over 90%. Also Historically Native Americans have the highest record of service per capita when compared to other ethnic groups, with over 40,000 in both World War II and Vietnam alone. Yet they often come back to homes without heat or plumbing, have double the poverty level of the general population, and unemployment from 35 to 85%.

Finally, I would like to thank the students of the College of DuPage where I taught for forty years. They have been a constant source of inspiration and support to me.

CHAPTER 1

TWO NIGHTS BEFORE THE POWWOW

A RIVER OF STARS FLOWED BETWEEN the canyon of trees through which Highway 55 ran as Lucy Teller drove her squad car and tried desperately to keep her eyes open. The night was warm, and the air did little to keep her awake as it rushed in her driver's side window. The Menominee tribal policewoman was working the midnight shift from twelve to eight. She hated the shift, particularly in the summer. It was difficult to sleep in the heat of the day, and her kids were off school. She had been staying up late with her daughter, Tara, putting the finishing touches on the dresses and moccasins they would be wearing for the dances at the powwow. The kids were old enough now that they didn't need—or in most cases even want—her attention, but they and their friends were often running in and out of their house on Rabbit Ridge Road and letting the screen door slam behind them. She also tried in spite of their objections to stay involved in their lives.

She called the dispatcher to tell her she was a danger on the highway and needed to pull over briefly to close her eyes. She pulled over by Spirit Rock at a small turnout that allowed people to pull off the road and read the story of Spirit Rock, a rock that had eternal life. Lucy thought that the rock needed eternal life because legend had it that if the rock ceased to exist, so would the Menominee.

Lucy's exhaustion was probably responsible for her skipping the crazy thoughts that lie between wake and sleep and went right to dreaming. Spirit Rock, at least the one inside her dream, had exploded and become a mountain. Like the tribe, it was an old mountain whose sharp rocks and edges had been worn down by centuries of wind and rain. Now, there were paths that twisted and turned their way up the mountain used by travelers to reach the top and beyond. She and Ray Waupuse were running along the paths, trying to catch someone running ahead of them. She had a vague feeling that this was not someone they were trying to apprehend but instead trying to protect.

The undeniable truth, however, was that in either case they were losing him. She could feel herself gasping for breath. Suddenly, Ray, who was slightly ahead of her, stopped and bent down to catch his breath—she thought at first—but she soon discovered he was throwing up. What came out, though, was some sort of demon with whom Ray immediately began to wrestle.

"You're losing focus!" she yelled as she passed Ray on her way up the mountain. The object of their pursuit was now well ahead of her and reaching the top of the mountain, which she realized for the first time was a volcano, and the man she was chasing was standing at the edge. All of a sudden Lucy realized she could no longer move, and the words "Don't jump!" came out at too slow a speed to recognize.

Soon the man was gone and it took her what seemed like forever to reach the edge of the volcano. All the while she was running with what seemed like an abnormal amount of lactic acid in her legs, she was asking herself what good it would do to dive after him when all it would mean is that two people would die in the hot lava. When she reached the side and looked in the deep hole, at first she saw nothing. No sign of the man, no hot lava, only darkness. But as she continued to peer into the hole, she saw a gravestone several feet down. A name was written on the stone, and as she strained to see the name, the ground underneath her began to give way.

That is when she awoke in a cold sweat. The sleep and dream/vision had accomplished one thing: She was wide-awake and had plenty of thoughts to keep her occupied for the rest of her shift. Lucy first wondered whether it was a vision or a dream and second, whether it foretold what was coming next in her life.

CHAPTER 2

TWO DAYS BEFORE THE POWWOW

"We need him assassinated, and preferably by his own people, Agent Scruggs," the Egg vowed from behind his large walnut desk. Egg was nicknamed by the president himself, who gave nicknames to just about everybody he crossed paths with regardless of political affiliation. Scruggs felt his stomach and chest tighten. He was confused and hoped that he heard wrong; this must be some sort of joke. He looked warily around for hidden cameras as the words slowly sank into his overwhelmed consciousness.

"What would my role be in this if you want an Indian to be the assassin?" Scruggs asked as he crossed his fingers now hidden from view by Egg's desk. He was hoping that he was being included in this plot simply because he was knowledgeable of the culture and the area of Egg's political enemy. In his lawyer's mind, he might already be an accessory to murder if this crazy plan succeeded.

"We need you to investigate the death threats against Alex Fish. He has received several since he announced his candidacy for president and has asked for a Secret Service detail. This will make points for the president when word gets out that he is sending you to head up the investigation. In reality, however, you will be our eyes and ears near him."

When he was first notified of his new assignment at the White House, Scruggs couldn't believe his good luck and was floating on cloud nine. He hoped for the Secret Service, but he scored an even better assignment—what his supervisor identified as Special Agent to the President of the United States. Who would have believed that a man coming from his roots would guard the president? He would no longer report to the FBI but instead directly to the Special Counsel of the President. Agent Scruggs truly believed that he was being rewarded for all his hard work and dedication.

When he arrived at the White House, however, he suffered his first big disappointment. He had hoped to have more direct contact with the president—a man he deeply admired. He not only admired the president for his policies, but he truly believed he was a good man who made decisions based on his strong moral convictions. Political truth can be an oxymoron as he learned from years of government work. Finding a man of great power that held to high standards was refreshing.

The special counsel, to whom Agent Scruggs reported, was another matter. Being new on the job, he searched to find something admirable about his new superior but found that a very difficult task. After all, the special counsel held a high position; he had to have some integrity. Maybe Jim was just being judgmental of the arrogant Egg who in personality and appearance did remind Scruggs of an egg. But Agent Scruggs was intuitive, and his intense training assisted him in feeling people out rather quickly. How could someone rise to such a high position being a snake? Actually, Egg earned both his lofty position and his nickname because he was a brilliant political strategist. If you put all the different groups that had voted for the president in one room, they would barely speak to one another. The one thing they had in common was loyalty to President Howard Barker. This strange coalition was largely due to the political instincts of Robert Brooder, alias the Egg.

The Egg had never served in the military, nor did he ever run for political office. He was born into money and attended the best schools. He looked like a guy who was bullied in school and perhaps because of that distrusted everybody. He was incredibly powerful because of whom he knew and the favors he could parcel out. The Egg and Scruggs clearly had nothing in common. Nothing brought that more to a head than when Brooder tried to create commonality. "Imagine this Fish trying to keep sportsmen like you and I from saving farm animals from vicious killers." Scruggs wanted to dive over the desk and choke the fat bastard to death. To keep from doing that, he began to wonder whether Brooder actually believed the spin that he was so good at creating.

Fish had introduced a bill that would make the hunting of wolves from aircraft unlawful. This was the only hunting that the fat ass, Brooder, was capable of doing. Brooder developed a campaign against Fish, saying he was against hunting and gun ownership, which was not true. Scruggs loved hunting but had no problem with keeping people from shooting animals from aircraft.

Scruggs found Robert Brooder annoying, shallow, self-centered, and myopic. And to make it worse, he thought, I have to answer to him. The Egg appeared to be the antithesis of all Scruggs had learned about himself through years of struggle from his modest upbringing. He was surprised at how fast the serenity that he had learned while in the North Woods of Wisconsin had abandoned him. What a dichotomy, he thought. His nickname said it all. Robert was just a kid, and he was brilliant, but spent most of his life in his head, and his pale skin, unfit body, and bald head also made him look like an egg. Brooder didn't have the looks or the personality of a politician; yet he had the intuitive instincts of a mastermind political strategist.

"Assassinate? Does the president know these orders, Robert?"

"No, of course not. And he can't. He cannot and will not ever know. Do you understand me?" Robert Brooder demanded, giving Scruggs a look that was both threatening and scrutinizing at the same time.

"You were handpicked for this assignment for a number of reasons. You are very knowledgeable about this Indian man in question and the culture he comes from. You have also shown a great deal of loyalty to the Bureau and your country. You have made no secret of your admiration for the president and his party. You aren't going to disappoint us on this, are you Jim?"

Jim Scruggs hoped the pause was not too obvious. "No, no, I understand why it needs to be done. I was just surprised for a moment, that's all. Would you give me some additional information?"

"Good," Brooder replied while quickly standing up from behind the large desk in his office and ignoring his last question. "Now, this has to be our little secret. Hire whomever you need to get this job done and done fast. But make sure of them before they are brought up to speed. You know, the less they know, the better; and the better for all of us. Remember, they can never know that I'm involved because I am too close to the president. All the money you need to remove this presidential candidate will come from offshore accounts. As much money as you need will be made available when you need it. And just as soon as you need it. From now on, you will talk to someone else regarding this matter. Not me. You will not talk to me about this ever again. You will contact him by cell phone. Here is his number."

Robert handed Scruggs a small piece of paper. "Make sure you have the number memorized, and then shred it. It's an international number because he moves around a lot. He also has your number and will be contacting you for updates."

"Who is he?" Scruggs asked.

"Damn it, Jim, you don't need to know that!"

"Well, how do I refer to him? How can I check that I'm talking to the right guy?"

"You will refer to him as Dealer. And that's all."

"Got it." Scruggs decided he needed to sound totally convinced that this was the right thing to do. If Brooder were willing to have a candidate killed, he sure as heck would not blink an eye about killing Scruggs. One thing he knew was for sure; he'd either do this or be dead.

The main subject of conversation since he had arrived at the White House was how to deal with the up and coming star of the opposite party. He posed a threat in so many ways. First the president was running for re-election, and it was beginning to look like Alex Fish would be his opposition in the national election. Not only that, but Fish was currently way ahead of the president in the polls. There was so much more involved here than the average citizen might be aware. Then there was the whole First Nation issue, which Robert Brooder criticized with the utmost disdain.

"That's the problem with these minorities. Nobody even knows what to call them anymore. Are they Blacks, African-Americans, or Negroes, or are they Indians, Native Americans, or First Nation people? If Alex Fish were elected president, what if he forced America to honor all the treaties it had broken? What would happen then? What if he started asking the government and private corporations to pay the billions of dollars that were promised the Indians but never paid? What the hell would happen then? And if that was not enough, there's this ridiculous scandal rumor."

This was the most important political challenge to Brooder, though not even Scruggs knew about it. Not yet anyway. There was a current lobbyist who had been paying off congressmen to recognize tribes. Interestingly, these same Indian tribes were paying the lobbyist big dollars to represent them. If they paid handsomely, the tribe could have a voice and be heard clearly. Representation was a direct reflection of the amount paid to the lobbyist. In addition, this political con artist was also paying the congressmen not to recognize other tribes that had refused to give him money to represent them. Big money was moving around very swiftly, and it was easy to lose track of what went where.

The congressmen were mostly from the current president's party. This was a very sensitive and messy situation. And if this was not enough,

Robert Brooder, one of the president's closest advisers, was dead center in the middle of the ugly scandal.

The powerful Egg had looked Scruggs straight in the eye with a look implying that the lobbyist was a good man. He even suggested that Fish was having him investigated for political gain to embarrass the current president.

But this was one area where Brooder was in the dark! Agent Scruggs had been investigating a certain "Gambler" who was involved in this very scandal while he was still on duty in Wisconsin. Having the powerful, intimate experience on the reservation, Jim Scruggs had a clear advantage here. Who would have thought his time on a poor Indian reservation would affect things this far removed. He shook his head while thinking; it really is a very small world, a very small world indeed. Though they were not able to come up with enough evidence on the Rez for arresting anyone, Scruggs did not believe the lobbyist was quite as innocent as Brooder wanted him to believe.

The two men said their goodbyes. Scruggs's feet were soundless on the plush carpeting, and he glanced one last time at the paintings and sculptures in Egg's office. He passed the Secret Service office and walked down the long corridors of the White House and out onto the hot streets of Washington where the tourists pushed and shoved their way through the museums and monuments. This is where Jim Scruggs always thought he wanted to be, but now he longed for the cool green trees of Wisconsin although he dreaded the reason he was returning to the Rez.

CHAPTER 3

THE NAME FISH WAS WELL known on the Menominee Reservation. Members of this large extended family frequently ran for almost every office from sheriff to tribal council; but now the Fish family was on the national stage. Alex Fish was the talk of political pundits for quite some time. He grew up relatively poor on the Menominee Indian Reservation in northern Wisconsin. He proudly attended the University of Wisconsin on a track scholarship, and his name was first spread across the headlines when he won the 800 meter race at the Olympics. It was a thrilling race where he charged out of the pack in the last three hundred yards and roared past three world-class runners on the way to the finish line. America really embraced him when they discovered that he went to the Olympics as an alternate and had to borrow a pair of track shoes for the race. That fame was short lived, however, when he unexpectedly gave up more lucrative offers to return to his old high school to teach and coach. Alex wanted to return to his home, to his people. He became very dedicated to improving the lives of Native Americans and soon became principal of the high school in Keshena and, later, the superintendent.

He recognized early that there were no magic bullets to improve the education of Native Americans who traditionally have the highest dropout rate of any group in the country. He worked very hard on all the challenges he faced. Fish made himself available at lunch in order to know the kids personally, and he spent a lot of time instilling hope in them. He promptly threw out programs that didn't work and researched the ones that were successful, encouraging the teachers to implement them. As the teachers began to achieve more success, they also began to work harder and collaborate with one another. The energy to reach out and up grew quickly. Alex instituted core values that emphasized the balance and harmony with nature that had been valued by tribes long before the White Man ever came to America. He encouraged all staff to operate from those values, and in time, a group of teachers and community members also added values of humility, respect, honesty, empathy, and concern. Working tirelessly to incorporate these into his own dealings with staff and students, Fish ultimately encouraged everyone from administrators to teachers to custodians and staff to do the same. He endlessly met with members of the community and instituted their ideas and encouraged them to work with their kids on their homework.

It was a rewarding experience for teachers and community members when they spent time after school working with low-achieving students. He encouraged everyone to expect success instead of looking for failure. Reading and math scores began to rise, and the dropout rate declined at every level. He was careful to give credit to all who helped. Alex was very aware that without the help of many dedicated people, success could not be achieved. This assistance included the elders of the Menominee Tribe who built the new high school in Keshena and started the College of Menominee Nation right across the street. Walking out of school, the young people of the community could see the college and respond with pride. Going to college was literally within their grasp and gave them an incentive to understand the advantage of staying in school.

After fulfilling his important goals for the students of Keshena, he decided to pursue a political career and was elected to the Wisconsin State Legislature. Alex Fish believed he could achieve greater influence for his people if he ran for political office, but his true passion was to help people become successful. The sitting president at the time, Bob Clark, remembered him from his Olympic success and read about the progress he made with the school system. Clark appointed Alex Fish to his first national office— head of the Bureau of Indian Affairs. Most of the Bureau and others in Washington soon recognized his intelligence and savvy political skills. After a term in that position, Alex Fish was asked by none other than President Bob Clark himself to head up the Environmental Protection Agency. This is where Alex began to truly shine. Using the same core values and motivational skills he had honed as a superintendent of schools, he motivated a large segment of the American people to move from a rather apathetic position regarding the environment to being energized and interested in doing their part. It was largely on this issue that he was elected to the U.S. Congress as a representative from Wisconsin.

Over the years of public speaking, he was able to shed some of his quiet and shy mannerisms and he became a dynamic speaker with a charismatic personality. He watched Bob Clark engage audiences and learned much from him. Soon people in the audience would respond to him more like a rock star than a politician. Alex Fish was able to point to his ancestors and show he had white, red, and black blood running through his veins and therefore was uniquely qualified to represent all Americans.

"I'm practically a medicine wheel all by myself," he would jokingly suggest. "Maybe I can find a running mate who is yellow and brown, and we will represent everyone."

He was smart enough to downplay his Native American background since that group is among the smallest minorities in America; yet he was able to assist his people through his efforts in the U.S. Congress. His honest sincerity in wanting what was best for all citizens made him a favorite of many Americans. Yet, there was no doubt that his popularity was tempered by a large contingent that was scared to death he would get elected.

There were definitely groups willing to work against him. The candidates debated before members of the so-called national Religious Right. All the other candidates paraded in front of them and affirmed a private and deep love for the Lord Jesus Christ. Alex admitted that he was very spiritual but not very religious. His spiritual practices had more to do with a personal relationship than with any organized religion. He even went on to criticize all of the world religions for being myopic. He was particularly hard on the groups that seemed hell-bent on making sure all women carried their children to term but didn't seem to give a damn what happened to those children after birth. He criticized those who seemed to care little for the soldiers and civilians who were dying in senseless wars based on fear and revenge.

Alex clearly lost a number of conservative voters in that debate but also gained a number of votes from the people who were looking for a candidate who was willing to speak the truth. Here was clearly someone who wanted to either be elected or defeated for who he was rather than winning by pretending to be who he was not. Many Americans saw his honesty as refreshing and much needed in the country.

Another group lined up against Fish included the powerful energy companies that had cheated the Navahos and many other tribes out of millions of dollars from oil and natural gas rights in the Southwest. They absolutely did not want to see Alex Fish elected. Luckily, both of these groups were in favor of the sitting president, and as any one watching TV around election time can tell you, being the lapdog of energy companies does not necessarily translate into an advantage on election day.

It reminded Scruggs of going to Comiskey Park in Chicago to watch the White Sox when he was a kid. He often wore a t-shirt that read: my two favorite teams are the Sox and whoever is playing the Cubs today. Funny the things we remember. Here Scruggs was definitely having a dilemma. Though he leaned toward the president and his political views, he did truly respect what Fish had accomplished. Actually, Jim Scruggs was growing to admire Alex Fish more and more. He decided it was time to find out more information about this Alex Fish.

ONE DAY BEFORE THE POWWOW

NO MATTER WHAT ANYONE THOUGHT of Howard Barker personally or as president, he was, at fifty years old, undeniably in better physical condition than many thirty year olds. In spite of his election to one of the most demanding and certainly important jobs in the world, he always exercised vigorously at 5 p.m. each afternoon. His presidency consumed him from 7 a.m. to 5 p.m. After a workout for an hour and a half followed by dinner, Barker then frequently returned to the Oval Office for several more hours of conducting the nation's business.

He was usually awake by 5 a.m. and started his day with a half hour of spiritual reading to keep his priorities in order. After a shower at 5:30, the president would enjoy a relaxed breakfast at 6:00 with his wife, and when they were at the White House, his two children—a son, twenty-three years old, and a daughter, twenty. Both kids still attended college. The son was pursuing his MBA and the daughter her bachelor's degree at small colleges with religious affiliation. To both the president's pride and relief, both son and daughter were good kids who gave neither him nor the Secret Service details any grief or concern. Howard and his wife Lynne had agreed to keep the kids out of the limelight as much as possible. They did no campaigning for him in the last election, and there were no plans to use them in the next election either. Both parents were relieved that their children had no political ambitions.

Agents Scruggs hoped to meet with the president in his office— alone and without the Egg present. But since the president's schedule was full, suddenly a better opportunity presented itself; he miraculously received an invitation to join the president during his daily workout. With the ever-present Secret Service agent posted at the door and the president's personal trainer ready to spot Barker on weights, Agent

Scruggs stepped briskly on the elliptical machine while the president ran on the treadmill. Scruggs observed the president closely as he finished a circuit of weights and punched vigorously on a heavy bag. The president was an informal man not hung up on protocol, and they talked about their mutual enjoyment of exercise and wondered how so many people were able to get through their days without some type of physical activity.

Scruggs was shocked—and nearly exploded in laughter— when the Egg, in tight gray sweatpants and sweatshirt, suddenly waddled into the gym. Utterly out of shape, the Egg was beyond a doubt sorely out of place. Scruggs bravely tried to keep his mouth shut and his amusement to himself. The president started in immediately.

"Hey, Egg, did you take a wrong turn at the library? Are you afraid you might have to actually track those wolves to kill them?" Then turning to one of his Secret Service agents, he said with a smile, "Hey Johnny, run up to the library and get the Egg some books to curl. Maybe you could bring a couple of Vanity Fairs for single arm curls and the unabridged dictionary for double arm."

The room, including Brooder, broke into loud unbridled laughter. Obviously not trusting Scruggs to be alone with the president, the Egg looked around the room for something he could do that wouldn't add to his humiliation. Robert finally decided on the stationary bike next to the president. He began pushing the pedals slowly around, and perspiration and heavy breathing commenced immediately. The tight sweatsuit appeared to be painted on his fat body. He had bulges in unimaginable places and rolls of fat on top of rolls of fat. The Pillsbury doughboy and the Egg were twins, thought Scruggs.

"The object here is to get that little needle on the speedometer to move, Egg," the president observed, bringing peals of laughter to the room. With that, the president pushed a button on the panel in front of him, and the tread beneath him hummed with greater intensity as he became absorbed in keeping up with the speed. Jim Scruggs also pushed harder on his machine even as Robert Brooder eased off even more on his cycling. After fifteen minutes of silence, the president again pushed a button and slowed down to a slow jog as Scruggs began his cool-down, and Brooder began to coast on the stationary bike. Self-consciously, the Egg was trying very hard to hide his huffing and puffing from everyone, but he could not hide the sweat stains that spread across his sweat suit.

"I just want to tell you, Mr. President, that it is an honor to serve you," Scruggs said. The president, not used to compliments lately, smiled broadly.

"Thank you, Agent Scruggs, and I want to wish you the best with your new assignment."

Brooder looked sharply at the president, and the two looked at each other for a tense moment. Brooder nearly imperceptibly shook his head. After stuttering briefly, the president added, "Whatever that may be." instantly no longer so proud to serve this man. He saw with crystal clarity what was actually going down here. He felt distaste toward the man who just a few moments ago he admired. Luckily, Agent Scruggs was good at masking his feelings. He was certain that neither man read his thoughts or feelings of great disappointment or even the bad taste he suddenly had in his mouth.

The following day, Agent Scruggs booked a flight to O'Hare International Airport in Chicago with a connecting flight to Austin Straubel Airport in Green Bay. He was waiting impatiently in the Dulles Airport in Washington when his cell phone suddenly rang. It was the Dealer. His mind raced, but he decided he needed to concentrate on the conversation.

"There is a man I'm sure you met during your assignment with the Green Bay office who visited all the powwows and had a cover as a storyteller and musician. He is actually a hit man, and he calls himself Fiddler. I want you to hire him to do the job."

Scruggs was silent for what seemed an eternity. He was still trying to regroup and gather his racing thoughts during the pause. Agent Jim Scruggs could not decide whom he hated more at this moment. Was it the Egg or this man on the phone?

"I don't think he will. . . ." Scruggs started to say.

"He only kills bad people, I know that already. Trust me on this, he will do it," was the terse reply.

CHAPTER 5

THE FIRST NIGHT OF THE POWWOW

THE TALL PINES THAT COVERED the Keshena bowl like the dome of a covered stadium looked like daggers with serrated edges stabbing the blood-red sky bleeding the last bit of daylight from it. Underneath the pines, the women old and young seemed to be dancing on the breast of Mother Earth, bouncing up and down to the rhythm of her heart. The big drum provid- ed the sound of her heartbeat, and the singers that surrounded the drum provided her a voice to her pain and pleasure.

Fiddler traveled to Keshena with Lily and her children for the powwow. It was their first visit here since the previous summer when they met by accident after Lily had told him she needed more time to mourn her husband, who had also been Fiddler's friend, before she could start a relationship with him. This had been the very place where they had reconnected just before Fiddler had been shot. As his wound healed and he regained his strength, so did their relationship strengthen. Both Kaitlyn and Tyler, Lily's children, became attached to Fiddler long before Fiddler was able to let them inside. He still diligently and unknowingly guarded his heart. Many times he was not even aware of the tall, thick, unshakable wall that surrounded his vulnerability. Lily helped him thaw his emotions and start trusting.

It seemed to him that her children found it easier to love him in a nonjudgmental way. Even though they had lost their father, they rarely worried about the price it cost to love Fiddler. In turn, Fiddler made a conscious effort to love them openly and completely. Unfortunately, the children had lost a great deal in their short lives. They still talked about their beloved dad, but Fiddler harbored no jealousy since he had loved their father too. He was the first person he trusted, and they had become like brothers. They openly cried and honestly stated painful real emotions. So these two little kids were teaching Fiddler much about loving another and the precious gift of life.

Kaitlyn was now five and still talked a mile a minute. She was already beginning to read well and was quite the budding artist. Kaitlyn also loved to dance with her mother, which is where she was now, while Fiddler stayed in his booth and sold music.

He still loved to make and play music. His music was soft and soothing and often accompanied by a flute—his escape for many years. Fiddler knew all too well how to hide himself in music. Many things had changed dramatically in Fiddler's life. There was so much for him to learn and feel with these three precious people. Music was now something the whole family could enjoy together. They would all sing and dance at every opportunity.

Lily's son became very attached to Fiddler after his daddy was killed. Since he was very young when his dad died, many of his memories were already fading. Today Tyler, now three, decided to remain near Fiddler as he often did. The boy had developed the habit of following Fiddler everywhere he went, and there was little that pleased either of them more. Fiddler saw in Tyler the characteristics of his deceased best friend, Tyler's father. But he could also see Tyler imitating his very own behavior. He would walk into the deep woods near their house and Tyler would follow. He would toss a rock into a stream, and Tyler faithfully would imitate his every move.

Slowly and gently, Fiddler was beginning to heal from his own horrific and painful childhood. Being loving and kind to these children helped him to heal his own little boy inside. He treated Tyler as he wished his own father had cared for him. Fiddler was loved by his mother; he knew this in his heart. But she was not strong enough to leave his terribly abusive father. Maybe she believed that she didn't deserve any better treatment. He was unsure, but he did know he needed to forgive both of them. Fiddler knew he could never forget, but he did need to forgive. There was still a part deep inside of him that silently cried out to Grandmother Moon. A hidden part of his soul still talked to his mother through the stars.

Tyler played with a flute that Fiddler had given him in the back of his booth while Fiddler spoke to some customers. Fiddler smiled; he loved to listen to Tyler play. He recognized the pride he felt and wondered whether it was just his perception or whether Tyler was quite talented for a three year old. A woman asked him a succession of quick questions, and Fiddler didn't even notice if Tyler had stopped playing or if his music was simply overpowered by the big drum and the singers. When the drumming and singing had stopped long enough for another group to begin, he did notice the flute was quiet, he quickly turned around. Tyler was gone! His flute lay silently on the ground alone and abandoned.

Like any three year old, he may have dropped his flute on the ground, Fiddler tried to tell himself to quiet the dread and fear growing inside of him. It took Fiddler a few seconds to comprehend, to wrap his mind around the situation. He was definitely confused and thrown into a tailspin. Hurriedly, he deserted his customers and left his wares unattended. Shaking his head, Fiddler immediately ran to the back of his booth and out the back of the tent. His eyes frantically searched the area behind his booth. There were a few people around, and he asked if anyone had seen a little boy. Had anyone seen his little boy! Fiddler's throat began to swell. He choked out his words.

It had been many years since he was this frightened. Panic quickly spread through his whole body, and his pulse raced. He felt nauseated, his mind turning to unimaginable, unthinkable thoughts. He had to find to him right now! He wanted to see him and to touch him.

He yelled at the confused people around him. What was wrong with these people? Why weren't they helping him? Finally, someone said yes, they had seen a young boy asleep in what appeared to be his father's arms heading off toward the parking lot. Knowing there was something very wrong, Fiddler sprinted in the direction they pointed. He felt as though he was living one of his crazy nightmares where he tried to run, but his legs were like clay. He struggled to make them move faster, but they seemed frozen.

As he reached the parking lot, he saw a man placing a boy, wrapped in a blanket, in the back of a car. "No!" was all he could scream, and even then the words seemed to stick in his throat. When the man saw him approaching, he quickly jumped in the passenger side, and the car sped off. Fiddler ran toward the car, but it roared out of the lot and onto the road that led to the bridge across the Wolf River and Highway 47 and was soon out of sight. He wasn't close enough in the dusk to get a description of the automobile or see its license number.

As he was desperately thinking about what to do next, his eyes searched his surroundings like a cornered animal. Every nerve in his body was taut, awake, and alert. Fiddler's cell phone rang. The sound made him literally jump—both feet were off the ground. Still shocked, he fumbled to get the phone from his pocket. Fiddler wanted to scream. He felt such a heavy burden right now. How could this happen? Especially, how could this happen to a sweet and innocent boy like Tyler?

Suddenly, he heard a familiar voice on the line, and his mood rapidly changed. The sound started deep in his belly and came out more like a growl than a word "YOU!"

FIDDLER RECOGNIZED A VOICE FROM his past, one that made his blood boil. *Why didn't I kill him when I had the chance?* He thought to himself.

"If you want to see that cute little boy—Tyler, isn't it?

—If you want to see him alive again, I have a job for you." "You touch one hair on his head, I won't rest until I've torn your body into little pieces and fed them to the dogs. Give me my boy back!"

"You're not in a position to be making threats," the Gambler said coldly, secure in the distance between them and in the wild card that he held. Had that not been the case, the Gambler would have been terrified. The last time their paths had crossed, it was Fiddler who could have killed him, and he would have gladly done so except it would have meant losing Lily forever. Normally just the sound of Fiddler's voice frightened the Gambler. The thought of him out there alive and possibly still on the prowl for him prompted the Gambler to sleep with one eye open and never feel completely safe.

He was always dreaming up plans to rid himself of Fiddler for good. The bloody and dramatic fantasies played out in most of his waking hours— it was almost a terrifying hobby. Gambler was code named Dealer by Egg, the cunning and brilliant political operative in Washington, D.C. His ties to the mob and politicians meant police and jail were less of a threat to him than to Fiddler, but Fish and his investigations were becoming a thorn in his side. This was just too good to be true. But it was true, and he would enjoy every minute of this as it played out. It was as if the Gambler was holding all the aces while his opponent was nearly out of money.

If he could get rid of Alex Fish and frame Fiddler to take the rap—or better yet, be killed while attempting to escape— life would be good again. It would be very good indeed.

Confidently he made the call to his hated enemy.

"You may not believe this, but I abhor violence and have no interest in any harm coming to an innocent child." A deadly pause from Fiddler unnerved the Gambler, but he continued.

"So, as long as you follow orders, stay away from the police, and don't even think about coming after me, no harm will come to him. I promise."

"And I'm supposed to trust you? You won't ever let him go, because you know as soon as you do, I will start looking. I will hunt you night and day to the ends of the earth. I will never give up! And I will find you! So help me God!" By this time, Fiddler was in a rage.

Interrupting Fiddler, the Gambler continued. "You let me take care of that part. All you need to do is wait for further instructions. Nothing else! Do you hear me?"

Then the phone went dead. A sickening silence fell over his heart. Fiddler's next thought was of Lily. He wanted to vomit the evil from his body. He dreaded being the one to break the news to the woman he loved.

At this point, he felt exhausted and desperate, and he quickly ran to the bowl where Lily and Kaitlyn were dancing. He stopped and looked at her for a moment. He hated to steal her joy. He hated to know she would be devastated shortly. There was little that Lily enjoyed more than dancing, and she looked so beautiful out there lost in the rhythm of the drums and the chanting of the singers. She also loved to dance with her daughter. She was serene and at peace because dancing was spiritual for her. She was in tune with Great Spirit and Mother Earth. Her long dark hair moved as she moved. He remembered her saying, "This would be a good day to die." By this she meant that everything was good, nothing was left undone. The world was the way it was supposed to be. He knew this would be her last moment of peace until Tyler was found—one way or the other.

Fiddler reflected for a moment; he had heard the word *kidnapping* thousands of times, and he even participated in them with covert operations; but those victims were grown men. I know the meaning of that word, he thought. Kidnapping is to take someone against his or her will. And then he went on with life. He also heard the words *innocent child* or *frightened mother*. But then . . . when it happened to him, when he was living the words, he realized the word meant nothing. It told him nothing. It does naught to convey the horror a parent feels when his or her own child is taken. The emotional fear and pain overwhelmed him. The physical and emotional anguish nearly knocked him to his knees as he stood gazing at Lily. There was a deep longing to touch his missing child, as if a part of him was suddenly ripped from his own body, leaving a huge gaping, bleeding, hole.

Everyone at the powwow was going on with his or her business as if nothing changed. The drummers continued to drum. The singers sang. The vendors bargained. Even Lily and Kaitlyn continued as if the world was still turning, but the Fiddler's mind and emotions were colliding violently inside him.

Lily stopped in her tracks the moment she saw Fiddler. Never breaking eye contact, she sensed something was very, very wrong. She walked slowly over to him, trying to prepare herself for the dread she knew was coming. She stared at him blankly; her eyes grew cold, as he shared with her what had happened. Other than her eyes, there was no apparent emotion. But deep in her eyes, he quickly saw confusion, terror, and then coldness. Her warm gentle eyes appeared to turn to ice, and all the warmth quickly evaporated as he stood in front of Lily. He saw that an invisible veil covered her eyes, blocking the unthinkable from her bleeding heart.

"Where's Tyler?" she asked, fearing she already knew the unthinkable answer. Fiddler could not speak; all of his words were used up. After stating that her beloved baby boy was stolen and in the hands of strangers, what more could he say?

Closely watching his love, it was as if she pushed all her emotions down so deep even her friend, partner, and lover could not get a glimpse of them. She raised her protective wall and moved into survival mode. Lily knew all too well of the danger and loss of a loved one. She thought she knew the deepest pain imaginable. But today she learned this was not true.

When her husband was murdered serving this country, she was forced to push crippling pain away. She had two children to raise and to nurture. Lily had to push her fears and grief deep inside her. She had to survive for her children. There was no choice. Unfortunately, she was suddenly recalling the day a military car pulled up outside of her home. It was clearly an official car. The two people sat in the car for several minutes before coming to her door. She wondered what they were debating. Who would have to tell the wife the bad news? Maybe they drew straws and the white guy lost. That is why he had to speak the ugly words. Lily knew instinctively her husband and best friend was gone. Deep in her being, she knew that her first and true love was dead. By the time the bearers of bad news touched the doorbell, she had no feelings at all. Lily felt nothing. It was surreal standing there and hearing, "I am sorry to tell you this." Lily thought, no kidding. I didn't think you would like notifying people about the death of a loved one. Did you grow up hoping this would be your job and that you would get paid to say the man of your dreams is dead? Such stupid shallow words, she thought. Why did they even say them?

But really what could they say? What words could soft- en the emotional and physical blow of such news? Lily did feel nothing at that point. Effectively numb—is that what she would call it? Quickly, she stopped the racing thoughts and returned her full attention to the abduction of her son.

Standing with his mouth open, Fiddler was shocked when she simply returned to dance with Kaitlyn. She left his side without even one word to him, and returned to her dancing! Relieved, he noticed she was dancing next to Lucy Teller. Her head was bowed and not one person, not even Fiddler, could see her lips moving, but he knew what she was saying. He recognized the deep and abiding level of trust between these two women. She was trusting Lucy with her son's life.

LUCY WAS TORN ON WHAT her immediate response would be. Her thoughts and emotions screamed very different things. She knew in a kidnapping that every precious minute counted, and yet if she left too quickly after dancing next to Lily, she would raise suspicion if anyone were watching them. She steadily danced away from Lily forcing herself to dance until the drumming stopped. Then acting as if the dance and the warm summer air exhausted her, she walked to the side and grabbed a towel to dry her face. She went over to her daughter and explained she was taking a break and then tried to quiet her racing pulse as she slowly walked up the steps of the arena toward the outer rim of the bowl. From there, she hurried to her truck and called Lieutenant Moon who was the only officer at the station besides the dispatcher. By this time, not only her hands, but also her whole body trembled.

When she spoke, her voice also trembled. "I have to report a kidnapping of a child."

"Do we have a name and description of the child?" the lieutenant asked, without his usual sarcasm toward Lucy.

"Yes," Lucy said, following with Tyler's name and description.

"Let's get a child alert out ASAP," Moon barked.

"We can't do a child alert!" Lucy quickly filled him in on the rest of the story. There was a pause at the other end.

"What do we know?" the lieutenant asked, his voice cool and businesslike. She had no idea of the fear he felt deep in his soul. A matter of minutes could mean life and death in missing children cases. This was his one weak spot. He always despised the people who could harm a child. If he were dealing with men who could take a child from their parents, what else would they be capable of doing? This had been true since he first started as a rookie cop. He knew working hard was the best they could do. Sometimes he knew even that wasn't enough.

"We know who's behind the kidnapping." Lucy said, feeling some confidence because she had an idea of where to start. "I'm going to talk with Gayle Wolf," Lucy said into the phone and quickly hung up before the lieutenant could talk her out of it. Lucy switched her phone to vibrate and raced off to talk with Gayle.

When she knocked at the door of Doc and Gayle Wolf's home, a part of her hoped that Doc wouldn't be home. That was a definite possibility since he often worked late at Maehnowesekiyah the treatment center just outside Keshena where he was the director. The last thing she wanted to do was bring up an ugly subject that she knew would open wounds. Lucy was hoping some of the hurt had begun to heal. But Doc answered the door and smiled when he saw Lucy's face.

"Hey, I expected you to be dancing yourself into a frenzy by now. Did Gayle invite you to dinner and not tell me? Where is she? Gayle!" He shouted out to a silent house.

Lucy frowned. "No, I wish this was a social call, but I need to talk with Gayle if she's home. I am sorry but I need to talk to her now."

Lucy saw the look of fear cover Doc's face. Gayle had had a gambling problem a year or so back, and it had been a struggle for him to regain trust in her especially since the problem included a distasteful affair with the Gambler. Unknowingly to him, it was the same man who kidnapped Tyler. His wife had been working hard not only on her addiction but also on restoring her marriage. Doc, for his part, realized his own mistakes and was making every attempt to correct his own issues.

It would take just one careless moment or the wrong word or look for all this hard work to fall apart in an instant. Both of them decided to fight with everything they had to keep their marriage intact. They made a pledge daily to save their relationship.

Lucy recognized the look immediately and quickly added, "I need her help with a problem I'm having. Can I please talk to her? It should not take very long."

She saw relief spill over his face. But it was followed with a look of confusion as he went to retrieve Gayle.

"Come on in," he said warmly, remembering his manners. "I think she's in the bedroom. I'll get her."

Doc and Gayle lived in a two-story house on Legend Lake, just a few miles from the treatment center. It was not large by White Man standards but bigger than most of the one-story houses on the reservation.

It had a kitchen, dining room, and living room in the front of the house on the first floor and a large walkout family room in the back overlooking the lake. They enjoyed a beautiful view of a long tree line and clean, clear, welcoming water. They spent hours gazing at the lake and talking about their future. They had moved here shortly after Gayle had finished treatment in part because the old house had deteriorated much like their relationship had, and though Gayle was trying to let go of her dreams of wealth, she did want a home that was comfortable and inviting. There was a small study next to the family room, and medical journals were stacked on the desk and the floor next to it. Lucy noticed piles of paper scattered across the floor. It looked as if they spilled over from the cluttered desk reminding her of a waterfall gently tumbling down. It was the only room in the house that Doc was solely responsible for keeping neat. He wasn't doing a very good job, Lucy thought. Clearly, it was a character flaw he hadn't addressed yet.

She quickly caught herself being judgmental. After all the terrible things she disclosed to him during treatment, he never once judged her. If he did, she was never made aware of it anytime during her long, difficult battle to get clean and sober. Lucy was guilty of some pretty ugly things during her using days.

Doc asked Lucy to have a seat in the living room, and he went upstairs to get Gayle. The two of them came down the steps together a few minutes later. They held hands. Gayle wore a robe and already had removed her makeup. She looked as if she had been sleeping. Lucy looked at her watch and for the first time realized it was well after ten. Lucy thought to herself that many women would be embarrassed to be seen this way. But Gayle had no reason to be as Lucy was impressed at what a naturally beautiful woman Gayle was. Her red hair fell to her shoulders, a strong contrast against the white robe, but her freckled face came closer to the color of the robe. The robe was open at her chest just far enough to display a lighter shade of skin where her bathing suit ended, and Lucy guessed she had been spending a little time sunbathing on the deck off of the family room.

Gayle smiled warmly and sat directly across from Lucy on the couch while Doc stood uncomfortably for a moment trying to decide whether to stay or leave. He looked to Lucy, and she picked up on his dilemma.

"Doc, I am sorry. I hate to do this, but I didn't know where else to turn. It might be a good idea if both of you decide if Doc should stay or not," she suggested. "I know this is a painful subject between the two of you. It is maybe harder than I can imagine. But we have reason to believe the Gambler is involved in kidnapping Lily and Fiddler's son. I'm here looking for information, and I wanted to know if there is anything you could tell me about his whereabouts. Or maybe who he may have contacted to commit this crime?"

Suddenly frightened, Gayle moved her lips silently. Lucy could not tell if she was swearing or praying. With large misty and searching eyes she looked first at her husband and then at Lucy. She held her gaze as if looking for something, searching for something.

"Would you like me to leave?" Doc asked with a hint of resentment in his voice.

"Oh my, no. I can't stand to think of that little boy scared and alone with that man or the creeps he'd be associated with. No secrets between us, remember? I would like you to stay, if you can. Actually, I need you to stay. Please, stay."

"I know he is connected with organized crime in some fashion, but I don't know how," Gayle continued. "I can tell you one thing for sure. He is nowhere near the kidnapped child. I know he is ruthless, but he is also a coward and would never do his own dirty work." They sat in silence for a brief moment to allow Gayle to gather her thoughts and continue. Looking at her hands, she pushed back tears and continued softly.

"He would never talk about that." Then Gayle turned to Lucy. She talked slower and softer now. "He did call me once and left a message on my cell phone. He told me it wasn't too late, and if I ever wanted to get together, I should call. He left an unfamiliar phone number. He told me they would know how to get in touch with him. I don't remember the number, and I deleted it. I do remember the man's name: It was Jim Spade at the Oasis Casino in Vegas. Supposedly, he would find the Gambler for me."

Then she turned back to Doc. "I was trying to decide what I could do with that information. I did not call the phone number. Trust me, my only reason for remembering that was to see if it would be at all useful to the authorities in locating him and charging him with attempted murder—the attempted murder of you." Gayle's eyes begged her husband to believe her. No matter what she knew, she would not lie to him again.

Gayle turned back quickly to Lucy. "I think my higher power brought you to me tonight. There is still much healing that needs to take place. Healing for me and healing for us. I will do anything to bring him to justice, including trying to lure him back here if that is what you want me to do. I think I could be convincing. He really is a very shallow, narcissistic man. Lucy, just tell me what you need from me. I want to help that poor little boy!"

"I think we need to think this through and decide how best to use what we have. And I appreciate not only the information, but also your willingness to help. I'm afraid if you called him now after this has happened, he'd be suspicious. I'll get back to you." Lucy said. "I want to talk to my supervisor and maybe to Ray and see if we can come up with a plan. I want to act quickly, but not so quickly as to tip him off and get that innocent child killed."

She reached out and gently took Gayle's hand into hers. "Apparently, he wants something from Fiddler, or he wouldn't take the kid, not for money or even revenge. The last thing he wants is to give Fiddler any more reason to kill him. You are doing the right thing, and I need your continued support. This means a lot to me." Letting go of Gayle's ice-cold hands, she stood to leave.

"I had better be going now. This could be a long night." Lucy said. She thought to herself that this would be an excellent time for her old friend insomnia to visit. Instead, she could feel the rough sand already beneath her tired eyelids.

"You can call me at any time, day or night. It's not just my resentment toward him. I will do anything to help save that boy. Lucy, I mean anything," Gayle said, standing tall.

"Me too," Doc added. "Fiddler and Lily both helped save my life. You know I will never forget what all of you have done for me. The day of the race through the reservation, when I pigheadedly refused to back out, there were several attempts on my life, none of which succeeded. And there might have been more if you and others hadn't made sure the course was lined with people."

Lucy gave them both a warm hug and left. She turned to see them in the doorway. Gayle and Doc held each other and watched Lucy leave.

Doc heaved a heavy sigh. "I knew he was still lying between us at night in bed, but the image was fading. Now I feel he's back bigger than ever. You never told me he called you." "The man means nothing to me anymore, and I too can sense he is still between us. I also felt the image fading and just didn't want him back in our lives," Gayle said slowly, choosing her words with care. "Remember, I was sick when he was a part of my life, and I don't mean just with gambling. I had made some very bad decisions about men and what makes them good or bad. This started long before I had met either one of you. Since I've been recovering, I'm looking at a lot of choices I made that got me in trouble—serious trouble that I pray will be forgotten someday or at least forgiven."

"I believe now in my heart that you are a good man, and one that is a worthy companion. You bring joy to my life. He is a bad man who in the long run would have brought me pain and misery and quite possibly death. I realize now he was controlling and had no morals or conscience. He will kill anyone, and I mean anyone, who is in his way and especially those he has no further use for."

"I know it is not good for me to hold on to resentments, but the one I have the hardest time letting go of is what he tried to do to you. Again he showed his cowardice by hiring people to kill you. And the guilt I can't shake is how blind I was to what he was doing, and the kind of person he was."

Doc could feel the lump in his throat. There were days he didn't know whether he could ever get past the thought of her being with someone else, but at this moment he was glad she was with him.

Normally Lucy would have called Ray as soon as she reached the car, and it bothered her when she hesitated. But Ray had changed. And she was not the only one to notice. Her children complained that when he was watching them, he was often short and overprotective, even to the point of refusing them visits from their friends in the middle of the day. He restricted their play outside and ordered them to stay inside where he could observe them. When he was not working or watching the children, he spent more and more time alone. He was crabby and irritable with Lucy for no apparent reason. Making love became having sex. Knowing each other's body as well as they did, the mechanics and even the pleasure were still there, but even though it did not enter into their conversation, they both knew the energy and passion were sadly missing. Recently, during the rare times they spent the night together, his sleep seemed fitful, and she would often wake to find him sitting alone in another room in the dark. Calling to him, he never gave an explanation to what was going on inside of his mind or heart. Sometimes she could smell alcohol on his breath, and he had begun smoking again after quitting nearly five years before. He became a stranger in his own church. His faith and his church had been a major part of his life even before Lucy came into his life. Desperate, she even stopped in to see Father Dan about it. She was hoping his priest would be able to explain to her what had happened to change him, but Ray had not spoken to him either.

"I am glad you came here to talk with me. Matter of fact, Lucy, I was just getting ready to call you," Father Dan said with frustration and confusion in his voice. "I was so happy Ray made it back safely from Africa. And I was anxious to talk with him about his experiences over there, which I'm sure were not all pleasant. I scheduled him as a Eucharistic minister, and he didn't show. This was so unlike Ray. I had a voice message from him during Mass saying he wouldn't be attending St. Michael's anymore and please not try to contact him. I've seen him drive by in his squad and I wave, but he acts like I'm not even there. We spoke before he left, and everything appeared fine. I don't get it. Wouldn't you think if something awful happened over there, he'd want the support and forgiveness this community can offer? I really don't understand this. He won't answer my phone calls. Actually Lucy, I am almost afraid to call him. He asked me not to call. I just don't know what the right thing to do is."

"I'm beginning to think he met someone over there," Lucy replied, with the anxiety in her voice now breaking through the edges of her words. "You know how men and women work so closely together now on assignment. They are away from their families, seeing all kinds of tragedy. It seems natural that they would turn to each other for comfort in the middle of the night." Pushing down a deep sadness, she looked at her friend through tearing eyes.

"I'm sure there are temptations along that line. Many of us fall," Father Dan said as he patted Lucy's hand. "But I've rarely seen a man fall as hard for a woman as Ray fell for you, young lady. Given the conditions you describe, it may be possible that he made a mistake one night, but I'm sure he still loves you. No, Lucy, I think something happened over there that has rocked Ray to his very core. My hope and prayers are that in time he will return to his Christian family and his community. We truly do miss him."

He stood in front of Lucy and held both her hands. "Can we pray together?" She felt herself pull away slightly. Through treatment and struggling with her spirituality, Lucy prayed alone. Being a dear friend, he sensed this hesitation.

"Can we pray then silently?" They both bowed their heads and asked for God's help in their own way.

"There was a psychiatrist whom I deeply respected when I worked at the hospital years ago. I will give him a call and describe Ray's behavior. Maybe he has some suggestions."

After departing the rectory, Lucy thought of everything she and Ray shared as she picked up her cell phone. Calling Ray, she explained what had happened to Fiddler and Lily's son. She could tell that she had awakened him from a deep sleep, and at first he sounded groggy, even irritated. Sadly, she thought she detected just a slight slur in his speech. Maybe she was just getting paranoid with him. Continuing to talk, as she described what happened and in spite of the tragedy, Lucy sensed a shift in Ray's attitude. He suddenly seemed excited and engaged for the first time since he returned from Africa. She heard emotion in Ray's voice that seemed to drag him from a spot inside of himself where he had been dwelling self-ishly in pain. She heard the confidence in his voice that gave her hope, but his response also confused her.

"We are not going to lose this kid. Not on my watch, not again. We will not lose him."

Lucy thought about asking him what he meant by not again, but Ray suddenly took the lead asking her for every detail of the kidnapping. She was beginning to feel a missing partnership between them again, when he suggested that she go home, get some rest, and make sure her own kids were safe. He promised and reassured her that he would get right on it.

"Make sure you keep them safe. Do not let anything happen to those kids." Another odd comment, she thought.

Earlier that evening Ray sat at his kitchen table staring at the dinner he had prepared for himself that he couldn't eat. He was disgusted with himself and his total inability to rid himself of this endless depression and anxiety. Food no longer tasted good, relationships no longer seemed to matter, and there was nothing he looked forward to; even intimate moments with Lucy were now interrupted by the brutality in his brain. His job, putting on his uniform in the morning, and strapping on his weapon had gone from a matter of pride and satisfaction to fearful events that took all his strength to force himself to do.

Finally, he pushed himself away from the table and found the bottle he hid in the kitchen cupboard in a spot where Lucy wouldn't find it. He wasn't so afraid she'd find it and drink it as much as he knew what it said about him—that he had resorted to hiding bottles. And in spite of his knowing their relationship had deteriorated, he could not bear the thought of losing her. He took a long pull from the bottle and felt it burn all the way to his stomach, and he waited for the almost instant relief it provided. He knew Lucy was at the powwow and would go to work immediately after taking her children home and dressing in her uniform so he could drink enough to get to sleep. He knew the drug-induced sleep was less effective, but it was that or nothing. After several more long drinks from his self-medication, he stumbled to the recliner in his living room and turned on the TV to drown the noise from the powwow and once happier times in his life; he fell asleep or passed out, he didn't know or care which, as long as he could escape the pain. And for a while he did, till the dream started again and he was back in Africa. He was crawling toward a campfire where men and boys partied. Their faces were painted in ways that made them look like devils, and the fire seemed to dance all around them. He was dressed in his Guilly suit, and he pulled his sniper's rifle behind him as he had learned in sniper school. When he reached the point where he had a clear shot he wanted to take, he turned for his rifle while keeping his eye on his enemy, but what he grabbed was not his rifle but something warm and wet. His hand came back empty, but when he looked at it, it was covered in blood. He turned around and when he looked between his legs he could see that he was not dragging his rifle but the bodies of a woman and girl who had been brutally murdered and raped. When he turned back, the devil-faced men had discovered him, but they weren't after him; they were simply pointing at him and laughing their evil sardonic laughs.

Still half asleep, perhaps with his gut and brain still feeling the effects of alcohol, Ray reached for his service revolver. He stared at it for a long time and then put it to the side of his head. At the moment, none of the Catholic teaching about suicide being wrong, about the possibility of going to hell, even entered his mind; all he could think about was the pain ending. Maybe death was just endless sleep, and to Ray, at the moment, that was close to heaven.

That's when the phone rang, and Lucy took him from Africa, even took him from his own pain to someone else's. He didn't know how long he had slept or how long he had been awake, but the news she told him changed his focus.

After hearing what she had to say, Ray leapt from his recliner and immediately showered and changed his clothes. He was careful not to wear his uniform, and raced to the grounds of the powwow. There, he found Fiddler preoccupied and tensely packing up his booth. Distracted, Lily was helping him slowly, and Kaitlyn was asleep near the spot where Tyler had been stolen. Lily and Fiddler rarely let a second pass where one or the other wasn't checking to make sure she was still there. Many times Lily would quietly go to her daughter and gently touch her sleeping child. Lily really did not want to be helping. She just wanted to curl up somewhere and make all this go away.

When Ray approached Fiddler, he began a casual conversation like two friends just saying hello. Ray began to help him pack up his music to create the appearance that it was not police business that had brought Ray to the powwow. He was very cautious in case they were being watched. There were still many people around, and they could not be sure whom they could trust.

When they were finally alone, Fiddler described the woman he had talked to when Tyler was kidnapped.

"She just kept asking me so many questions and so quickly, I lost track of our boy. I still can't believe I didn't notice the flute music stop. I can't believe I let this happen."

Ray stared at him with a sad, faraway look in his eyes.

"I know," he answered as he left very quickly on a mission to find the mysterious woman. He was angry and determined to find some answers. He would make people talk! Ray knew effective ways to get someone to talk.

RAY FIGURED FROM FIDDLER'S DESCRIPTION that he had seen the woman in question in the casino. She spent a great deal of time by the slot machines. Her blond hair and a skin condition called vitiligo made her ap- pear as if someone had poured bleach on half of her face. Her build was more typically Native American, with thin legs and a barrel-shaped upper body.

As he walked down the row of slots, he found the variety of people who played them readily observable. There were those looking and finding a good time. They laughed and talked with one another and yelled and cheered even when the machine doled out only a few dollars. Some laughed the loud laugh of several drinks, and then there were those who simply stared at the machines and the steady roll of images they produced with no expression whatever. The woman he sought looked like that. He found her blindly playing slots in a row void of other gamblers. Silently, he slid onto the stool next to her.

"Do you ever win on these things?" he asked.

She never even changed her rhythm. It looked to Ray as if the machine hypnotized her; she didn't even pull the lever at the side but simply pressed the button at the top of slot machine. He'd seen a film in psychology class in which a monkey would press a lever over and over again to get a small amount of cocaine, and this woman had a similar look. He couldn't tell whether she was drunk or simply intoxicated by the machine, but in any case, she wasn't responding to him. After a number of tries with the machine refusing to pay off, she stood up from her stool and walked unsteadily down the long row of slots. He could now see she was very drunk and used the slots and stools and occasionally another person's back to help her maintain balance as she headed for the exit.

Once outside, it was obvious that she had no idea where her car was. She began stumbling up each row, clicking her car alarm in the vain hope she'd hear the beeping of the horn or see the flashing of her car's lights.

Ray decided to seize the opportunity. He pulled out his badge and approached the woman.

"Ma'am, I'm with the Menominee Tribal Police. As far as I can see, you look like you are in no condition to drive. I will give you a ride home, or if you do find your car and drive it out of the parking lot, I will gladly arrest you for DUI. Which do you prefer?"

The woman steadied herself with her hand on the hood of a car. It took a long time for the options to sink in and an even longer time to decide on one. She gave Ray a blank stare and rocked back and forth.

Suddenly, she slurred, "I will walk home."

"That's not an option," Ray said, and he took out his cuffs and slapped one to her wrist. She tried to struggle but ended up stumbling and landing face first on the hood of the car that had been supporting her. Luckily, the alarm did not go off, bringing unwanted attention to the two. Ray found her other arm and soon had both of her hands cuffed behind her back. Unfortunately, she was very unstable, and Ray nearly was forced to carry her to his car. He opened the passenger door, pushed her into the back seat, and refastened the handcuffs to the hand rest above her window. He slowly left the parking lot, with her nodding head indicating she might just pass out. A passing thought swiftly went through his mind. I hope she doesn't puke in my car. Then his mind went back to the missing child, and puke seemed like a small matter.

He drove out of town, parked at a small parking lot near Keshena Falls, pulled her out of the car and roughly laid her face inches from the flowing water on a large, flat rock that Mother Earth was kind enough to provide. Then he promptly stuck her head in the cold rushing water just long enough for her to miss a breath or two. He lifted her head up as she coughed and sputtered. Ray let her breathe for a moment and then stuck her head back in the river. He let her struggle a while before giving her another breath of air.

Breathing close to her face, he snarled, "There was a boy taken from the powwow tonight, and you were an accomplice. Tell me what you know. Tell me now!"

"I don't know what the hell you are talking about," the woman shot back, trying to look confused, but clearly frightened and unaware as to how she got here.

"I guess all the alcohol has clouded your memory," Ray responded as he roughly pushed her face back in the river. This time, he held her down hard. He heard the woman scream with her mouth closed as she tried to

raise her head for air. When he was ready—and only when he was ready—
he grabbed her hair and ripped her head up.

"How is your memory now? Are you going to talk to me? Answer my
questions now! I am losing my patience!"

He finally appeared to be getting through to her.

"Two guys came up to me and offered me a hundred bucks to go up and
ask one of the vendors questions about his music. Lots of questions 'bout
his music. While I was asking him some questions, I saw one of them take
the boy. I thought about warning him, but I needed the money. I wanted
to tell him, you know?"

"Yeah, and I can tell you turned right around and put that money to
real good use," Ray snarled.

"I was hoping to use it to make more, but those damn machines took
that too," she choked.

Ray wanted to shove her disgusting wet head under water and keep
her there forever.

"What did the men look like and how were they dressed?"

"Look, when they gave me the money, they said I should forget I ever
saw them. I know they meant it. I just want to go home. Why don't you
leave me alone? I didn't do nothing wrong."

"You didn't do anything wrong? Well, you're wrong about that too.
You're an accomplice to kidnapping and maybe murder. Listen very
carefully. I can cause you pain in ways these guys never thought about.
What did they look like?"

Shaking her head and looking away, she continued. "They wore suits.
They looked expensive. They had short hair. You could tell they lifted
weights, both over six feet tall."

"Do you have any idea where they were taking the boy?"

"No, I swear. I really don't know anything else."

"If you remember this conversation in the morning, promptly forget
it. If you tell anyone we spoke, I will kill you! Anyone! And if you don't
care about yourself, I will kill someone you love so you get a deeper
understanding of what it's like to lose someone you care about. That's a
promise! They took a little kid! A little kid," he repeated in case she hadn't
heard it the first time.

Ray angrily returned the soaking wet, crying, drunk woman to her car.
By this time, he was cold and soaking wet too. When she got in to drive
off, he gladly arrested her for DUI and took her to the tribal police jail.

It was shortly after Ray had left Fiddler that Scruggs approached his booth. Scruggs walked toward Fiddler with a great deal of trepidation. Although he worked out regularly and completed his share of self-defense classes, he knew that he was not in Fiddler's league. He could be ripped apart in a minute if Fiddler should so choose. He recognized the need to convince him quickly that he was not working for the Gambler and that he truly wanted to help. It was odd, he thought, that Fiddler was packing up his booth in the middle of the powwow. Lily was mindlessly helping him pack his things into his pickup. She kept one eye warily on her daughter.

They had never officially met, but he was quite sure Fiddler knew who he was. He decided to start with some idle chitchat.

"Packing up a little early, aren't you?" Fiddler barely looked up from his task.

"Family emergency," he replied tersely.

Scruggs was not aware of what had happened but figured that the Gambler was somehow involved, and that meant so was he. He could not explain how he knew; it was just a knowing feeling in his gut. And Jim Scruggs learned to listen to his intuition more now than ever before.

"I might be a part of that emergency somehow, and I need to speak with you about a way out."

That comment definitely targeted Fiddler's attention. He looked up as if seeing Scruggs for the first time. There was a strange mixture of fear and loathing in his eyes.

In a flash, Fiddler's hand was tightly wrapped around Scruggs throat. "Where is he?" he demanded.

Scruggs did not even see his hand coming until his viselike fingers were firmly squeezing his throat.

"I don't know. He's only contacted me by phone," Scruggs gasped through his constricted airway.

Fiddler loosened his grasp. "How can he do that? He's only three years old!"

Scruggs looked confused. "I thought you were talking about the Gambler?"

"No, I'm talking about my son. He took my son." Quickly it began to come together in Scruggs's brain.

Now he knew how the Gambler would blackmail Fiddler to kill Alex Fish and get rid of Fiddler at the same time. Scruggs reached up slowly and took Fiddler's wrist. He slowly pulled Fiddler's hand from his throat, and Fiddler didn't resist.

"We've got a lot to talk about, and it would be easier if I could breathe. First, let me tell you, though it may appear otherwise—particularly with what I'm about to share with you— that I'm on your side. Can we go somewhere and talk?"

"I'm not supposed to talk with the cops," Fiddler answered.

"Let's head toward the parking lot where it's dark."

"Lily, I'll be right back. Do not take your eyes off of Kaitlyn!" Fiddler ordered.

Lily stared blankly; she could not even respond. Silently, she wrapped her eyes around her resting child.

"I need you to listen to me carefully," Scruggs began. "Some people in very high places in Washington want Alex Fish dead. They have a connection to the Gambler that I don't understand. I have been ordered to find someone to kill Fish and my contact is called the Dealer. I believe strongly that the Gambler and the Dealer are one and the same. Actually, I know they are. The Dealer, I mean Gambler—whatever the hell his name is—called me and demanded I hire you." Stopping for a moment and rubbing his bruised neck, Scruggs continued.

"I told him that you have a rep of killing only the people who are worthy of dying. He said he knew that, but not to worry—you'd go along. I realize now why he said that."

Fiddler started to interrupt. He had so many questions that needed to be answered. Coughing, Scruggs put up his hand.

"Please, let me finish. We have to buy time. I will call the Gambler and tell him you will take care of Fish but that you absolutely need assurance that your son is still alive. You want a video of him talking, with a copy of the *Green Bay Gazette* sports section in front of him and the date clearly visible."

"How do I know what side you are really on?" Fiddler asked.

"You don't, but I have no good reason to approach you this way. I'm sure when this is all over, they will try to find a way to get rid of me as well. The people involved are too important to leave any kind of trail that can be traced back to them. You and I have both served this country for a number of years. You must know some people who can vouch for me. They will tell you that I would never be a part of this crap. This is not who I am."

"Okay, then why don't the people who hired you know that?"

"I think they thought that one set of values I have would trump another. They also think they are always the smartest guys in the room."

"What do we do next? What can I do? It's difficult for me to sit around and do nothing while my son is missing. I can't stand this. This is just killing me. I've got to do something!"

"You are a man of action. I understand that. I don't have children, so I won't pretend to understand that part. It is clear you need to let others help you. Now is the time to accept help. It is not in your boy's best interest if you go out half-cocked. Now, does anyone else know about this? Whom have you talked to?"

"Yes, Officer Lucy Teller. Lily told Lucy. I don't know who else she may have told, but we trust her."

"You made a good choice. I was thinking about talking with her myself. There is no one else in the area I trust more. I'll call her tonight. We need to develop a network of people who can work together. If we can pull together, I think we have a chance here."

"I am not taking any chances with my boy, I will get him back!" Fiddler promised.

"Yes, I believe so too. I will do all I can to make that happen."

Right after leaving Fiddler, Scruggs called the Gambler. He passed on Fiddler's demand.

OFFICER RAY WAUPUSE REALIZED HE was probably wasting his time, but he knew he couldn't sleep anyway. With racing thoughts and emotions, he spent the night driving around the reservation and circling Legend Lake several times looking for anything suspicious or out of place. He hoped to spot a car with a license plate from out of state. He had to find something that could help. A number of people with cabins on Legend Lake were from Illinois, but few cars came from the East or West Coast. He marked four places on his map pinpointing cars with license plates from those areas. He figured most were just people attending a fam- ily reunion. The lake, pristine and hauntingly beautiful, was the perfect place for families to gather, especially in the summertime. With fishing, boating, skiing, rafting, and a variety of nice restaurants, it was a perfect vacation spot.

The beaches of Legend Lake glowed in the evening with people sitting around campfires, renewing relationships and reminiscing about the good old days. With the powwow, people came from reservations all over the country to dance and sell their wares. But the woman he had interviewed said the men were white. It was almost dawn, and he still had more cottages on Legend Lake to investigate.

Legend Lake was a large housing development carved from the reservation at the time when the U.S. government convinced the Menominee to give up their reservation status. The developer turned a number of small lakes and streams into a large lake with a series of inlets and channels. The main roads of VV and South Branch circled the lake and featured several connecting roads that came to a "T" near the water and included cul-de-sacs at each end of the road. Twenty-five to fifty houses were built in each neighborhood.

Legend Lake was considered Menominee County, and jurisdiction here created tension. The tribal police, county sheriff, and the federal authorities all patrolled the area and each claimed to be the ultimate authority. Sometimes all three would show up to claim jurisdiction for something as minor as a resident cutting up the firewood left behind by the power company clearing trees too close to their power lines.

Once Ray finished observing each of the houses, he returned to places he found most suspicious and continued to stake out the visitors and their cars. While he drove, he cursed the day he ever agreed to be an officer in the Army. At the time, the extra pay seemed worth it, so he could send more money home to his mother every month. He even considered a career in the army and jumped at the opportunity to attend a ten- week Marine training program in sniper school at Quantico, Virginia. While the training would be valuable to him, it also presented a challenge. Usually Navy Seals and Army Rangers were invited to participate, but even among those elite troops, less than half of them completed the training. In addition, the fine print indicated that graduates agreed to a lifelong obliga- tion to serve. Had he not been an officer, he would have been discharged at the end of Desert Storm, and he never would have been called up to be part of that peacekeeping force in Africa. His law-enforcement skills were particularly valuable there since soldiers were not allowed to engage in combat but instead were peacekeepers. Ray had been posted there as an adviser to teach and train local police officers.

In one way, it was hard for him to be too upset about the training he received, since at one point he used it to save Lucy's life as well as Kathy's when they were being held hostage. Ultimately, he became so involved with Lucy and her family that the loneliness in Africa seemed unbearable. He longed to hold her and deeply missed the sound of her children's laughter. To help ease some of the pain, he became involved during his free time with an African family with two children of similar age to Lucy's two children.

There were some obvious differences in the lives of children in this African village. The kids' days began very early with household chores and preparation for school. Each of the children proudly wore uniforms and walked over a mile to school. The children spent four days a week in school with shorter hours compared to some of the rest of the world, but they studied what American kids learned in school. A typical day consisted of reading, writing, arithmetic, and studying different languages. Ray learned that the whole family was pleased and grateful that the children could attend school since many children did not have that privilege.

The mother and father seemed close to each other and to the children. Ray would bring the children candy from the PX and helped out the parents with food and medicine. When he could, Ray would walk the children to school if his training schedule allowed. The family took time to teach him games they all played as a family. One game reminded him of a Native American game. His newfound family called it "Zuni basket game." It consisted of five pieces and a basket. Sitting ina circle, they would toss the marked pieces into the air, catch them, and add up points assigned to each piece. The winner was the first one to reach twenty points. Somehow Ray never reached twenty points to win the game!

The children even taught Ray their greeting. They would giggle and shout *"Jambo! Habari?"* which meant, "Hello! How are you?" He saw himself teaching the greeting to Lucy's children. Ray became the brunt of many jokes played on him in Africa by the two children. Since he was unfamiliar with the games, the children would quickly change the rules in their favor. He could clearly remember the sound of these two kids as they laughed together for hours. Communication for them was difficult at times, but it was clear they all cared about each other very much. Ray found himself almost adopted into the African family, and he shared as much of their life as possible.

He spent so much of his free time with them, playing games, singing, sharing of meals, that they even gave Ray some minor household chores to complete before he could play games. He enjoyed helping the family work. Not only did it make him feel part of the family, it gave the children more time to play. It all helped to nurture a strong and lasting bond between these most unlikely friends.

They in turn were grateful to him; Ray was generous with anything he had. He taught the children and gave the hardworking parents a break once in awhile. They offered Ray some of the affection he so missed from home from Lucy and her children, who had become his family. This African family, on the other side of the world and very different from him, openly and warmly welcomed him into their family.

One day while Ray and his group were away on a mission, rebel forces brutally attacked the family's village. The father and son of the family and other innocent men and boys were roughly taken from the village at gunpoint and killed.

The rebels kidnapped small and frightened children and shot them. The mother and daughter and other women were held in the village, and the soldiers molested and raped them over several long hours. Daughters were brutally mutilated while the abusers laughed, and their mothers were forced to watch. All the captives were eventually slaughtered.

It took Ray some time to wrap his brain around the horrific scene. He was devastated and sickened; his newfound family was dead—senselessly tortured and killed. Ray witnessed his share of violence as a soldier and policeman, but this went beyond whatever mechanism Ray used to deal with those instances. What he saw in the village cut to the very core of his soul. The ungodly images haunted him from the second he laid eyes on the bloody massacre of loved and innocent friends.

Ray was a born tracker. He hunted with his father and uncles from the time he could walk. The army recognized his skills and taught him to hone them to perfection. In his ten week training at sniper school, he learned new and deadly skills to add to his natural ability and all that he learned growing up. The first three weeks of his training consisted of long hours of academics, plus further training and practice in long-range shooting as well as physical conditioning. Ray, in spite of his years in the military, never identified himself as a warrior, at least not in the Native American sense. He did what he thought needed to be done and fulfilled his duty. Now, something that stirred from deep within broke loose, and the peaceful Christian he had become vanished in the scene before him.

He easily tracked the rebel band responsible since they had little fear of retaliation from frightened villagers and the impotent peacekeeping force. When he located them, he began a long and patient vigil until nightfall. As he waited, he spent his time working on his Guilly suit. The term could be traced back to the early origins of snipers and originated in Scotland. Literally meaning "man suit," it is a camouflage uniform with a mesh and burlap material outside that allows the sniper to attach grass and twigs from the local environment onto the fabric. The sniper can blend into his surroundings and not be seen. There are documented cases of snipers so well camouflaged that enemy soldiers have literally stepped on them and not recognized they were enemy soldiers. Ray was a master of the Guilly suit.

All of his thoughts focused on planning this new mission. Someone had to avenge the death of his friends, but Ray wondered if anything or anyone ever could. As he silently moved around the perimeter of the camp in the jungle, he noticed that several of the rebels were children themselves, and the adults in the group moved among them. He watched in horror as they handed the children alcohol and drugs, and slapped them on the back for their great job of killing, burning, looting, and raping. Rage seethed in

Ray not only for the lives they had taken so savagely but also for the young men they were shaping into another generation of murderers.

He had no fear, only loathing, as he intently focused on his revenge. He carried two rifles with him as well as a handgun. He dragged his M40A1 with him in a case between his legs while he crawled for a closer look at the camp. The M40A1 was a special rifle made for snipers and designed for engaging targets at long range. He would use his service rifle for the closer shots. As he retreated, Ray would take the longer shots, targeting with his scope. His sense of smell, sight, and hearing intensified greatly as the moment of contact approached. Ray was on full alert.

During the day, he had staked out spots in the jungle where he could get clear shots. He mapped out in his mind how he would fire his weapons and move quickly to stay hidden from the enemy. He had been trained to plan his egress (exit) as part of his training. He did not eat or drink even though the day was hot and humid. During the final week of training at sniper school, he was assigned one mission after another for seventy- two straight hours. During those seventy-two hours, he went without food or sleep.

The rebels were not prepared for a counterattack after the raid; they simply did not expect one. They were all high on alcohol and drugs, and food, and sex. After dark, Ray crawled on his belly to within a hundred yards of the camp. The partying of the rebels had grown quieter, but most of the men and boys were still awake. They sat around a fire with no guards posted. He squeezed off the first shot from his rifle and part of a man's head was blown off. The effect of the headshot at first froze everyone. They were paralyzed and momentarily sat like statues.

Some rebels recognized that they were under attack and scrambled to determine the location of the sniper. By that time, Ray had moved and another shot ripped clear through a man's chest. Splattered with the blood of some of their own, they all then selfishly scrambled for cover, pushing others out of their way.

Callously, several men grabbed children and used them for human shields. Ray moved again and swiftly zeroed in on another man using his sniper rifle. He fired again just as one of the young boys was pulled in front of the hunted. Through his sight he saw the young boy fall, and from the flickering fire of the camp, Ray also saw the fear and pain in his young face. Sickened and repulsed, he could shoot no more.

The rebels cowered in fear behind whatever cover they could find. Ray sat several minutes and watched as no one came to the boy's aid. The young boy lay alone in the dirt with his lifeblood quickly draining from his body. Ray wondered where his mother was. Could she feel her child's life leaving this earth? Not one of them helped the frightened and dying child. This was not what he wanted. Should one child suffer and die to atone for the death of another innocent child? Deflated and dejected, he started his long and lonely walk back through the jungle.

The sounds of the jungle echoed differently than those of the North Woods he knew so well, but he was oblivious to all of them anyway. Ray was unaware of all the pain and turmoil he kept in a fragile place in his subconscious mind. He returned to his barracks late and tossed on his bed for hours without the escape of sleep. He was there to train the UN peacekeeping force and therefore was forbidden to use his weapons except in self-defense. By the time he woke from his tormented sleep, word had already traveled across the camp about the ambush in the night.

The corrupt local government, which was supposedly battling the rebels, had already made a protest about a suspected UN soldier who was taking the war into his own hands. As Ray awoke, his superior officer stood at the foot of his bunk, and sniffed his rifle.

"This weapon has been fired," he said with a mixture of impatience and compassion in his voice.

"I was doing some target practice to keep my skills sharp," Ray lied, not wanting to force his superior into being an accomplice.

The officer was deeply concerned at the dreadful and complex situation they were facing. He respected Ray and could fully understand why he would take things into his own hands. Ray had left his Guilly suit next to his bed and made no effort to disguise what he had done. The superior officer watched the relationship grow between Ray and the African family, but he never quite understood that, despite their differences, they found common ground to connect.

Ray showed little to no emotion at being caught, and he was immediately rotated home. That was the good news; the bad news was an extreme effort to cover up the incident. Ray was ordered not to discuss it with anyone. Actually he was ordered to observe complete silence surrounding the incident. An *incident*, he hated that word.

It was not an incident; it was a brutal bloody massacre of innocent people he loved and respected. Yet, he was expected to hold all the pain and suffering inside. His pain and guilt consumed him, as he pulled farther and farther from the ones he once loved. He tried to push the memories so far down they could no longer be felt. But it was an ugly secret that grew as it was kept in the dark. Ray understood that when you talk and put things out to the light, they could grow smaller. When we hold on to pain, it grows and unmercifully eats away at our soul.

He was left with the nightmares and the endless flashbacks. He had no worries about rebels tracking him to America to retaliate, but then again they didn't have to; unknowingly, they stalked him day and night. But the night was the worst; it was difficult to run far enough in the dark of the night. Horrifying images were imprinted in his mind and haunted him. No amount of alcohol or cigarettes killed the horror or the pain. The ugly bloody visions were as clear as if they happened yesterday. He could smell the acrid odor of flaming huts and burning flesh—a putrid smell that one never forgets. The jarring memory would forever be with him. His invisible enemies were slowly killing him without even knowing it.

And now on the other side of the world, a new group of greedy men with no regard for human life had entered his life and threatened a child. He would not stand down and let an innocent child be hurt again. This time he had to stop it before it happened, but how?

FIDDLER, LILY, AND THEIR SLEEPING daughter drove to Lucy's home to spend the night, as sleeping at the room they were staying at was simply not an option. Neither Fiddler nor Lily could stand the thought of seeing Tyler's empty room with his bed vacant and his toys he had brought with him scattered about and neglected. The fear and grief was just too much for both of them.

"I can't stand to see Tyler's pajamas laid out for him on his bed," Lily lamented.

Each evening the four of them performed a cherished evening ritual. After the children would bathe, they would find their pajamas laid out in their bedrooms. If they got themselves dressed for bed without any argument, the family would play a game before bedtime stories. Tyler's pajamas were neatly nested on his pillow waiting for the little boy to be safely tucked into bed.

"I know," Fiddler answered. "Somehow, we have to get him back."

"Where is he tonight? Lily asked the air. "Is he cold and crying? Is he hungry? Please, God, let him be alive."

"Don't even say that," Fiddler snapped. "He is alive, and we are not going to think otherwise."

Kaitlyn wanted all the children to sleep together, and Lucy agreed. So Tara and Jerrod sprawled on the living room floor in sleeping bags with Kaitlyn. Maybe they would be able to play and distract each other from all the turmoil since Tyler was kidnapped. Fiddler and Lily could then sleep in Tara's room. They felt comfortable in Lucy's home—almost as if it were their own home.

The truth of the matter was that neither Fiddler nor Lily could look at the abandoned flute. One of his first thoughts was to use it for a talking stick. But clearly he could see that just by looking at the prized instrument, they could probably not even get any words out. Fiddler decided to keep the flute in his pocket to keep Tyler close. He tried to imagine holding the boy, praying maybe he could feel loving arms wrapping his small body.

When Lucy asked if they could watch Jerrod and Tara while she worked, they both quickly agreed. Her two children and their daughter were tucked in safely for the night. Fiddler checked his phone for messages and checked the locks on all the doors and windows. Then Lily and Fiddler quietly lay down in Tara's room together. They left the bedroom door open so they could hear the sleeping children down the hall.

Lily desperately wanted to be comforted by the man she loved. For a long time, they simply lay next to each other in an intimate embrace. Neither talked as each hoped the other might get some sleep. Having lived with fear his whole life, Fiddler was able to clear his mind and drift off to sleep.

Lily, on the other hand, was wide-awake and felt like she was trapped. She struggled to catch her breath as if a vise were slowly closing in on her chest. She fervently begged to have sleep rescue her from the mayhem of emotions that weighed heavily upon her. She wanted to escape. When would this nightmare end? Lily wanted to run from reality and find some rest if only for a few minutes. Unsuccessful, she quietly slipped out of bed and stood in the doorway.

From her viewpoint, she could see the man she loved and the three dreaming children. Lily said a silent prayer that they were all enjoying rest and sweet dreams. She prayed for her stolen and lost little boy. For much of the day she surprisingly had felt little emotion. She seemed to be almost on autopilot. Now Lily slowed down long enough for her painful raw emotions to catch up with her, and they weighed heavily on her slight frame. As she stood in the silent night, she could only bear witness to her own thoughts. Her mind was racing from the past to the present, and into the future. What if this, what if that?

Lily rushed outside to relieve the swelling in her chest. She frantically wanted to be alone. The paralyzing emotions started deep in her abdomen, rumbling and growing as they quickly coursed through her shaking body. Lily would not sleep or sit still tonight. She needed to move. Outside in the darkness she paced back and forth as fear and loneliness drew closer and closer to the surface. Physically, she felt bruised and badly beaten.

Looking toward Grandmother Moon, Lily begged for help and fell hard to her knees. A deep guttural sound escaped her throat, and she wailed as only a mother who has lost a child could. Alone and in the dark, she was being torn to shreds— ripped apart. Her heart ached, and she could barely breathe. Lily sobbed so fiercely that she began to wretch but vomited nothing. It was as if her body needed to rid itself of something toxic. Exhausted, Lily crawled a short way before she could struggle to her feet. She felt more weary and helpless than at any other time in her life.

She crawled back into bed just as Lucy arrived home from work. Lily pretended she was sleeping as she did not want Lucy to be burdened by the intense pain Lily held in her thin body. She knew her friend would not hesitate to wake her immediately if there was any news about their boy.

Lily then noticed by Fiddler's breathing that he was no longer asleep. She wondered if he had purposely faked sleep so she would release some of her pain. In fact, he awoke when she left the bed but knew she needed to grieve alone. He gently slipped his arms around her and kissed her forehead. They lay silently again listening to the gentle breathing of the three children. Lily quietly and gently cried. He stroked her hair and allowed his own silent tears to fall. Pushed to their limits, they felt beaten and battered. But in the safety of each other's arms, unexpectedly, they slept deeply.

After talking with Doc and Gayle, Lucy returned home and immediately checked on her friends. Grateful that her friends had decided to stay with her, Lucy was surprised to find everyone in bed soundly sleeping. She was slightly confused yet very thankful. The house was quiet, and she was drained. It had been a very long difficult night for all of them. Lucy felt exhausted as she laid her tired body onto the bed. To be dog-tired and to crawl into your own bed was worth more than she could imagine tonight. Best yet, she thought, before drifting off to sleep, my mother must have changed and powdered my sheets.

Soon after passing out, several of the recent events invaded her dreams. She dreamed that she and Ray were ice fishing on Lake Winnebago. They were spear fishing for sturgeon and staring into the cold, dark water through the four- by-four-foot hole they had cut in the ice. It was pitch dark, and they could barely see the water. Then Lucy thought she saw something in the darkness and powerfully threw her spear.

She immediately felt a tug on the attached line and pulled the fish to the surface. To her horror, she had speared a little boy. She panicked! What had she done? The spear she threw impaled a small child. It was the face of an African boy she had seen in one of the pockets of Ray's uniform. It was one of the few times that he had been upset with her. In fact, he became livid but would not explain his anger. In her dream, Ray dove into the freezing water to rescue the boy, but they both disappeared. Then she saw Ray emerge from another hole in the ice accompanied by a white blond-haired woman in uniform. When Lucy called to him, Ray ignored her and walked off with his arm around the blond. The wounded boy was nowhere to be found.

Lucy sat in her bed and attempted to relax and recall what else she might have dreamed. Could it have any relevance to the missing boy? In the silence of the early morning, she was suddenly startled by sound of her cell phone ringing next to her bed. It was only shortly after 5 a.m.

Lucy expected it to be Ray, so she was even more surprised to hear Agent Scruggs's voice.

"I know it's early, but could I please take a minute of your time?" he asked, sounding apologetic.

Lucy smiled at his formality. "What do you think this is, the Oval Office?" she said. "I was awake anyway, but I didn't expect to hear from you. I heard you were promoted. Congratulations! By the way, you've got the wrong area code for the West Wing."

Scruggs, never one to be much of a joker even in the best of circumstances, just smiled and got to business. "I need to talk with you. Is there somewhere we can meet that is private? But be sure I will not worry Ray or you about my intentions."

Now she was really confused, and again Lucy smiled. She didn't have to know Agent Scruggs long before realizing that she might disagree with him on many issues, but he was a man of honesty and integrity. Lucy also admired his candor even when it hurt or offended others. If you asked him a question, you'd better be ready for an honest answer.

"Agent Scruggs, I hope you will take this as the compliment it is meant to be. I don't know what your intentions are, but I have no doubt that they are honorable, and I will meet with you anytime and anywhere. But since I don't know what you have in mind, can you give me more of an idea of the kind of setting you need?"

Agent Scruggs smiled much more than he did when she tried to be funny. "I need a place that appears that we meet by accident. But even then, it would be good if a few people might see us talking."

Lucy thought for a moment. "I go running every morning down Old South Branch Road. I leave my house on Rabbit Ridge Road around 6 a.m. Perhaps we could accidentally meet at 6:03 at Old South Branch and

Rabbit Ridge and run for a few miles together. Would that give you the time you need? And do you know the area?" she asked.

"It's right by the burned-out house, isn't it?" he replied. "I believe it would give me the time I need if you run slowly. That way I can talk. I get anaerobic easily, and then I can't breathe and talk at the same time. I am sure I will not be able to keep up with you."

Lucy smiled because she could tell that Scruggs was in excellent shape. He continued. "Plus, it will give me more time to say what I need to tell you. I will accidentally see you at 6:03, a little over an hour from now."

Lucy was normally not a clock-watcher. It was summer, and Lucy woke with the sun. She'd usually make herself a cup of coffee and let it perk while she dressed. This morning, however, thanks to her company, she could smell the coffee and breakfast cooking. Fiddler and Lily must have found what they needed in her kitchen and now sat staring into space with a look of exhaustion and depression.

Lucy stopped and looked into the mirror at the dark brown eyes looking back at her for a very long time. This was a morning ritual that helped her to check in with herself. She could never afford to forget who she was—more important, she thought, who she wasn't. Lucy reviewed her priorities twice a day. First and foremost came God, Great Spirit, then her sobriety, and finally herself and her children. Ray was mixed in there somewhere, but right now she was still confused about his place in her life.

After finishing in the bathroom, she went to the kitchen to visit her friends. Lily poured her a cup of coffee, and one taste told her it was made just the way she liked it. Lucy smiled and without a word sipped some of it as she walked out on her porch. Lily and Lucy could communicate so well with their eyes that they almost behaved like twins. It was that scary. The three didn't talk much but then they didn't need to. With a gentle hand on each of their shoulders, she told them she'd be back soon and she walked alone down to a picnic table near Legend Lake Lodge and drank more of her coffee.

Fiddler and Lily watched Lucy from a distance while she gazed at the sun rising majestically from behind the trees and splashing its first yellow ribbon of light over Legend Lake. They were each praying the Great Spirit would give her insight and help her find their little boy. It was the kind of morning Lucy liked the best: the wind was calm and the trees reflected in the water, creating a mirror image of the trees, sky, and birds that flew overhead. She wanted to linger and finish every drop of coffee, but today she was meeting Agent Scruggs, and she knew 6:03 meant 6:03. She left the last few swallows, the best part of her coffee, in the cup on the table. Lucy was in a hurry.

Diligently, Lucy glanced at the wristwatch, which she rarely wore, to make sure she would arrive at Old South Branch at precisely 6:03. Never had she worked so hard to be the casual person she really was. She used a bench to stretch her hamstring, quad, and calf muscles. Then she walked back on Old South Branch toward Rabbit Ridge. Sure enough, at exactly 6:03 the two runners just happened to meet on the corner near the burned-out house that had been a derelict for the last two years. Lucy waved as she saw him, and the two easily established a comfortable jogging pace, or at least at a pace at which her friend Agent Jim Scruggs could breathe and talk.

"What do you know about Alex Fish?" Scruggs started out.

"This is a small community," Lucy answered. "I know pretty much everybody even if they are not a superstar. But now you're talking about our most famous citizen. Even if he is not our next president, which I really hope he is, he has still distinguished himself beyond, I think, even his wildest dreams. I was a few years behind him in high school when I watched him win that Olympic medal. I actually stayed straight for most of that day because I knew I couldn't get any higher. Then, of course, my body told me I needed drugs. I was already addicted. But just ask any Menominee about Alex Fish and just watch his chest swell."

"I understand he's been heading up a Senate investigation on a lobbyist who has been helping certain Indian tribes. Those who pay him get casinos, while he's been blocking others who don't pay him?"

"Yes, but Alex is doing a lot more than just protecting Indians, and that particular lobbyist looks like he's guilty of a lot of other violations like bribing congressmen and Senators to vote his way," Lucy responded, sounding just a little defensive.

"Would you be as strong an advocate if he wasn't Native American and a Menominee on top of that?" Scruggs asked, trying hard to keep any accusation out of his voice.

Lucy ran a few steps before answering. "I don't think I can honestly sort that out. I've never known a presidential candidate before. I'm sure there have been some presidents who may have had Native blood in them, but they probably hid it. As far as I know, we've only had one candidate before, and she was running for vice president on the Green Party. But I can tell you I would not support anyone who I didn't believe was a decent man, a respectable man, with the good of all America as his primary goal. I've had people tell me the first two goals of any politician are to get elected number one.

And second to help his friends. I don't believe Alex Fish is like that."

They had already run a ways and Scruggs realized he had to get to his point quickly.

"I think you are right, even though I wouldn't have voted for him, before what I'm about to tell you happened. I've been sent here to have him killed, and the reason that Fiddler's stepson was kidnapped was to force Fiddler to do it."

Lucy stopped dead in her tracks. She stared right through him. If looks could kill, he would be history right now.

"Pretend you are rubbing out a cramp in case anyone is watching us."

Lucy bent down and began rubbing her calf. Now she looked at the world as if it were upside down, which seemed right since that is the way it had just become anyway. She tried to process what she had just heard. She continued to massage her calf, but the pounding was in her head. Suddenly, she realized the best option was to keep putting one foot in front of the other and see if she could come up with some questions that would begin to help her make sense of Agent Scruggs's story. When something like this happens, the best plan is to do what you would normally do. So she placed one foot in front of the other and attempted to wrap her brain around the shocking self-disclosure of someone she thought she knew.

"I've talked with Fiddler last night, explained the plot, and advised him to go along with the request. First, he needs proof that his stepson is still alive. I need to buy us some time to try and find him. I have another problem, though. As soon as they find out I'm not on their side, I'm a dead man because of what I know. Lucy, this all became so complicated quickly. I am still sorting it out."

Lucy's head continued to spin. She was as scared and confused as the time her friend Kathy had been abducted and threatened with murder by men who were now thankfully in jail. Lucy faced a scenario where so many people she cared about could die. She tried to think of questions, but each time she opened her mouth, nothing came out.

Luckily, Scruggs had more time to think of this than she did.

"I've got a plan. It's far from foolproof, and we need some luck to save Fiddler's boy. But at least it will buy us some time. That's all I have right now."

During the rest of the run, Scruggs spelled out his plan to Lucy.

She agreed that it was indeed far from foolproof, but she was sure there was little time to improve on it. Alex Fish was scheduled to visit Keshena today, and she was sure that's when the Gambler would order the hit.

CHAPTER 15

FIDDLER'S PHONE RANG EARLY, AND he didn't have to wonder who'd be calling him at that hour. He hoped it was someone with good news, but he knew better. He closed his eyes and tried to center himself before answering, but the image of him strangling the Gambler won out. Just thinking about the Gambler made him sick to his stomach. His spirituality told him every living thing deserved respect, but he did not even consider looking for anything good in Jack Slade, alias Gambler, alias Dealer. All life was to be revered and celebrated. Yet, he only had thoughts of taking Gambler's life.

"Fish will be visiting the powwow tomorrow. I don't want him leaving," Gambler said, trying to sound confident.

"I'm not doing anything till I know my son is alive." "You are not the one giving orders here, Fiddler." "Listen, for all I know he is already dead, and if that's the case, I'd rather spend my time finding, torturing, and killing you. Much rather do that, than kill a guy I hope will be president."

Gambler hoped the forced swallow wasn't audible over the phone. He felt his throat tighten up and his stomach turn over.

"I will have him call you in a half hour."

"He's only three and doesn't speak on the phone, particularly if he's scared. Besides I want to see him to make sure he hasn't been hurt. And if you hurt him, so help me. Listen, I want a videotape of him with a picture of today's *Green Bay Gazette* sports page in the picture."

There was a brief silence before Gambler spoke again. "If Fish leaves the powwow alive, that will be the last time you will see your kid. I will make sure you get his mangled dead body so you can always blame yourself."

"You know I've got friends and contacts all over the world. They will find your sorry ass. If anything happens to him, you won't finish another card game."

"You will get your pictures, and then do as you are told."

"I don't have a cell phone that receives images; I want a tape."

"You will have it," the Gambler had to use both of his trembling hands to press the off button on his cell phone to end the unsettling call. After his hands stopped shaking violently, his next call was to Scruggs. He was still running with Lucy when his cell phone rang. He knew he had to take this call. They slowed down their pace so he could answer his cell.

Gambler started talking as soon as the phone was answered.

"You are going to have to deliver a package to Fiddler." "How and where will I be receiving this package?"

"It will be at the front desk of the casino hotel today. You need to be there when it comes. We are running out of time.

He will be shooting Fish tomorrow at the powwow, so you need to move on this quickly. The package should be ready for you in a couple of hours. Get there now. Be there, waiting and ready! And after Fiddler kills Fish, you must eliminate him. And I mean kill him. No mess-ups. Do you understand me?"

"Okay, what about the boy?" Scruggs asked, afraid of the answer.

"He's not your concern. I will make sure he's taken care of. He will definitely be taken care of."

Scruggs wanted to ask what "taken care of" meant, but decided not to raise suspicion.

"How will I explain that I just happened to be at the powwow when a shooting occurs?"

"What do you think? The FBI has heard rumors about an attempt on Fish's life and sent you to protect him." Not wanting to be asked any more questions, the Gambler hung up abruptly.

The Gambler's next call was to the Egg.

"I don't trust Scruggs. He is a snake. Send someone to kill him right after this is over."

Egg just smiled, his round face lit up with excitement. He never did like the guy anyway. Agent Scruggs was as good as gone! One less thorn in my side, he thought. Brooder reviewed the president's agenda as he talked with the Gambler. After hanging up the phone, he pushed aside a memo from the White House chief of staff and picked up the phone again to order Scruggs killed.

From the moment Jim Scruggs entered the highly structured parochial school system, he dedicated himself to hard work. He attended Catholic school through high school, always played by the rules, and willingly paid his dues. As the result of twelve years of constant study and determination, he finished in the top 5 percent of a high school class where 90 percent went on to college. After graduating cum laude from college, Scruggs proudly finished at the top of his law school class. Shortly after graduation, he entered the air force, survived brutal fighter jet training, and flew missions in Iraq. He finished his military career by serving in the JAG Corps for four years.

Working for America's oldest government law firm was a great honor, and Agent Jim Scruggs did not take any of his responsibilities lightly. He remembered learning in grade school about the founding of the U.S. Army JAG Corps by General George Washington in July 1775. The story was one that he would never forget, and Jim constantly sought out additional information about the military and law. Even at a young age, when asked what he was going to be when he grew up, he would stand tall and answer—the JAG Corps. Over the years, he discovered the JAG Corps played a key role in the events that shaped our nation and our world while becoming one of our country's largest law firms.

What made this an attractive opportunity for Scruggs was both the responsibility and variety of legal work, and the opportunity to serve not just in the United States but also overseas. Many stories of those he defended touched him profoundly. He sometimes defended men and women who were compromised by orders to behave in a way that would seem unnatural to most of the civilian population. In one of his first cases, he defended a group of Marines accused of murdering civilians. They were acquitted when he proved al Qaeda terrorists who actually committed the murders had set them up.

One of his last cases was arguably one of his most difficult. He was charged to defend a man who was being discharged from the military for being gay. One of the reasons that Jim hated Howard Barker's predecessor, President Bob Clark, was his policy to allow openly gay people to serve in the military—that and the unbearable image in his head of the giggling intern unzipping the president's fly under the desk of the Oval Office. Scruggs admittedly felt uncomfortable around gays, and his first reaction was to ask his supervisor to be removed from the case due to his prejudices. His supervisor's response: "The faggot is lucky he's even getting a trial; so just do the best you can." However, when Jim met with the soldier, he was surprised on several fronts. The defendant was every bit as patriotic as Jim and was highly decorated for valor in two different deployments. He did not flaunt his sexuality; as a matter of fact, his homosexuality only became an issue when his sergeant felt threatened by him and brought up the issue. The defendant didn't lie about his sexuality, and the sergeant broke the "don't ask, don't tell" policy first.

After he vigorously defended that case, his reputation in JAG began to wane. Jim spent less time in court and more time working in the humanitarian side of JAG, but he found he liked that too. Jim experienced a world he could not have even imagined. Not only does the JAG Corps uphold the basic rules of conduct for our soldiers but also the rule of the law in the most important international cases. Military operations large and small have driven the JAG Corps' growth while continually presenting new challenges, roles, and responsibilities. He loved the idea of being involved in and actually making a significant difference in the world. It was known the military could be a cold hard life, and many did not survive in the military world. Jim learned and lived a simple truth: Sometimes the enemy isn't an armed opponent. It can be a force of nature or the face of chaos. The JAG Corps has been actively involved in humanitarian aid, disaster relief, nation building, and peace operations. Jim Scruggs enthusiastically thrived in this high-pressure, high profile environment.

After leaving the military, he immediately applied to work for the FBI. He was offered a lucrative position and decided the challenge would be an upward move. Jim believed he could have even a bigger impact working for the FBI. It was a hard decision, and he regretted it immediately. After reporting to his new job, Agent Scruggs was sent directly to the North Woods. His assignment surprised and disappointed him deeply. He believed with his extensive background that he would never have to spend years in northern Wisconsin tramping around some godforsaken Indian reservation. With his experience and superior references, Agent Scruggs expected a more high-profile assignment and not a tour in the North Woods with a Native people who did not trust or even like most White Men. But if that was what the FBI wanted, he decided to do his duty and perform to the best of his ability. But to his great surprise it turned out to be good for Agent Scruggs.

Having been born and raised on the tough streets of Chicago, he learned of a different kind of guerrilla warfare at an early age—the war of the streets. The reservation had a slower pace, and many of the priorities were different than any he had ever known. He began to learn about the natural world and actually developed an appreciation for it. The idea of slowing down, observing, and developing an admiration for all living things surprisingly appealed to him. He observed the numerous Native spiritual practices and found many parallels between these two different cultures. The culture from which he came and the one to which he was sent slowly merged the intently and upwardly focused White Man with the balanced Native American Red Road.

Even the way people communicated reminded him of the two different worlds. He experienced these people enough to care deeply for the future and that of their children and the world. They felt the same pain and joy in raising kids. Their tears and blood were the same color as his.

As an FBI agent investigating crime, Scruggs quickly learned the underbelly of the Rez. Unfortunately, alcohol, drugs, poverty, unemployment, and crime, as well as distrust of anyone White, colored his early experiences. Much more difficult was understanding a culture that challenged the intellectual and logical mind he had spent so many years developing. The first time he met Lucy Teller of the Menominee Tribal Police, he was amused when she told him she was about to go chasing a witch through the woods to find a kidnapper. He on the other hand followed the evidence, but Lucy ended up being right. Scruggs realized that one of his character defects was to make snap judgments about people, and he tried to counteract that by keeping an open mind and admitting his mistakes.

But Agent Scruggs was not one to give up easily, whereas a lesser man might have quickly requested a transfer. He kept his eyes and ears open while absorbing the culture. He believed we are exactly where we are for a reason. He asked himself many times: why the hell am I here? What in the world could these simple people teach me about life? He did not know it then, but he knew he would stick around long enough for the lessons he was fated to learn.

Scruggs began his cultural education by reading books and observing his surroundings. Then as he grew more comfortable, he took a risk and stepped out of his comfort zone. Slowly, he developed some strong and respectful relationships with tribal members like Lucy Teller. Once he proved himself to be trustworthy, he was invited to participate in the revered spiritual practice of sweat lodges.

Being in the lodge was an extremely cathartic experience. It was hotter than anything he had ever experienced. The prayers and songs touched his heart and soul. He cried, laughed, and sat in awe of the privilege he was given with the invitation to this powerful and ancient spiritual ritual. He was hungry for the teachings that occurred before the sweat lodge. Jim Scruggs hung on every word of the stories told by the respected elder. He was frightened and nervous that he would shame himself and his new friends by failing to remain in the lodge for all of the required four rounds. Each time more hot rocks, called grandfathers, were brought in, making each round of prayers and petitions hotter than the last round. Still, even after all the reading and teachings, he believed sheer willpower would keep him in for the whole sweat lodge.

The respected and wise elder spoke of how one had to give in and surrender to the Great Spirit. When you asked for help to get through the lodge, it was a sign of strength, not weakness, and most would believe in your sincerity. This went against everything he had assumed in his life. He was complimented highly by being asked to represent the east door of the sweat lodge, which is an absolute responsibility and high honor. It appeared to Jim that he felt all the emotions he had ever experienced in life, but all in a period of hours, and strangely felt them almost all at the same time. Some were fleeting, while others seemed to last. But profound fear was the strongest and longest-lasting emotion throughout the teachings and the actual lodge.

He learned that many of the elders believed that this was the time to teach all people, regardless of color, age or gender, of the true Indian way. They spoke often of the Red Road. This was the road of spiritual practices, of making the right choices, doing the right thing. Wishing to help, Jim attended and willingly helped locals set up for powwows. He listened and watched these gentle people live a life he never even imagined. He met many Indians who were trying to rediscover and return to the traditional ways. There were those who shunned alcohol and drugs and tried to follow the Red Road. Jim found himself keenly attracted to them. Of course there was still plenty of crime and domestic abuse. Teenage pregnancies and alcoholism and addictions were burdens on the small population of the reservation. But he was surprisingly drawn only to the healing practices of the spiritual Indians.

Agent Jim Scruggs grew to respect the Red Road, and this helped him to develop his intuitive side as well as a still deeper spirituality to go along with his Catholic faith. He left the Rez feeling centered and stronger in his beliefs and spiritual practices than he could ever remember. Could he hold on to these truths once he returned to the White Man's world?

Scruggs smiled as he snapped his cell phone closed. For the first time since all this started, some things might be going his way. He knew the package would be a tape of Fiddler's son. This was very good news. And it meant two things: first, they might score a lead on the kidnappers, and second—the boy was still alive. Though there were ways of doctoring a tape, he doubted that they would have the time or the expertise to do that.

Scruggs needed some help, and Ray's name popped up first.

"Do you know what Ray has been up to since you spoke to him last night? I could really use his help now."

"No," Lucy replied, "but I'm sure he's been working on this because he doesn't sleep much since he's returned from Africa. And he sounded more engaged in this than anything else in a while."

Confused, Scruggs looked at her and considered inquiring about Ray but decided the current task was too important. He made a mental note to ask her later. He had grown to like and respect Ray during his time on the reservation. Scruggs wondered what might have happened in Africa. But as far as he knew, Ray was a good cop in every sense of the word.

"After we separate, I will call him myself. We need to have people keeping an eye out for strangers who may be buying local papers, or maybe even video equipment."

Lucy suggested a plan.

"The papers will be easy if they buy them in Keshena. There are only two places that sell newspapers. They would have to go to Shawano to get the video stuff, but there are at least five places in Shawano where they could buy equipment. It will be tougher if that's where they go. I know the cashiers in both the BP and the River Mart. I'm sure I could tell them to keep an eye out without making someone suspicious. Most people like to help the police department out here."

"That would be great," Scruggs agreed. "Maybe if we can identify when they buy papers, we could tail them into Shawano to see if they buy camera equipment. Or even those new cell phones that make movies."

Scruggs made a mental note.

"If I survive this, I've got to catch up with technology,"
he told Lucy. But he was really talking to himself.

When Lucy arrived at the point where she usually turned off for her morning smudging ceremony, she and Scruggs split and headed off in different directions.

Scruggs turned around and headed back to where they met. Lucy thought of skipping her morning prayer, but if there was one day she needed the Eagle to bring a message to the Great Spirit, it was today.

Lucy had become even more spiritual in her recovery. She believed deeply in the story about Sunrise Ceremony. The Eagle has been considered a spiritual messenger of the Great Spirit and a symbol of great strength and courage. It was said that if you saw an Eagle while you were praying or participating in ceremony, your prayers would be answered. Lucy remembered being told the story by the elders, one of whom was her mother.

It is said that since the beginning of time, Great Spirit would let the world go on another day if just one person gave an offering with a prayer that morning. The Eagle would be ordered to fly over the world. If he spotted a person or group of people gathered to offer *sama*, or tobacco, the Eagle would then fly and inform the Creator that the ceremony was indeed happening. Greatly pleased, the Great Spirit would grant the world yet another day to exist. Some believed the Eagle carried prayers directly to the Great Spirit, and the day the Eagle could not find anyone offering a prayer—that is the day the world would cease to exist.

Breathing heavily from the run, Scruggs calmly slipped into the woods about a quarter of a mile after leaving Lucy. Concerned someone might be watching, he made it appear as if he was relieving himself. Actually he was calling Ray.

R AY PICKED UP HIS CELL phone on the first ring and was surprised to hear Scruggs. Scruggs quickly filled him in on the Gambler's phone call and the need to stake out stores selling newspapers and video equipment. He shared Lucy's plan for surveillance and the video.

Ray had been on his own stakeout and narrowed down the suspicious cabins on Legend Lake to only two. Three of the other cabins had too many cars parked in front to be a hide-out. So he waited at the first cabin and spotted a young woman with a baby in her arms too young to be Tyler. He moved on to the second property. After hiding at an empty cabin down the street for a few minutes, Ray observed a man climbing into his car. He was in his early thirties and had a heavy build and short hair. If this guy ends up with a newspaper under his arm, Ray thought, maybe he could begin to wake from the nightmare he was living since Africa. He needed to find this kid alive and bring him home safely. Somehow Ray thought a rescue could help him partially heal the deep wounds he still suffered from not protecting his adopted family in Africa.

The suspect parked in front of the River Mart as Ray pulled next to the gas pumps and walked inside to buy more smokes. He saw the man pick up a *Green Bay Gazette* and pay the woman behind the counter. Then he hurried to his car and drove off toward Shawano. Ray impatiently stood at the pump and waited for the attendant even though there was no self- serve at the River Mart. He felt a rush of adrenaline and really wanted to chase this guy, pull him out of the car, and beat him to a bloody pulp. Lighting another cigarette, Ray knew he had to restrain his emotions. After all, it could be an innocent civilian going out for a newspaper.

When the man was out of sight, Ray followed in the same direction, making sure to leave enough distance between them to not arouse suspicion. The man pulled up to a Radio Shack in town, but Ray didn't bother to follow him. He thought, damn, I do need to listen to my gut instincts.

Casually, he called Scruggs and announced, "I think we have our guy!"

Ray quickly returned to the lake and took off in the tribal police boat. He had no trouble finding the cabin by water, but unfortunately the shades were pulled, and he saw no signs of the boy's presence. But at least now he had a visual picture of the cabin from both sides, and maybe the videotape would further confirm that this was the place the boy was being held. Since he also had the fire number and address, Ray decided to check at the lodge for the owner. Immediately, he had all the proof he needed. The cabin was owned by none other than the Gambler!

Relaxed, Alex fish happily arrived in Keshena without fanfare. And he gladly traveled without his capable bodyguards. He wanted an opportunity to see his friends and relatives without the crush of the press. He rarely had the chance to visit without adoring fans eager to shake his hand or pose for pictures with him. The thought of a private conversation with someone other than his political handlers and his campaign manager appealed to the private side of his nature. Even though it ran through his veins, he longed to talk about something other than politics.

For his part, Paul Brandt was a member of the small local group that traveled with Fish. He too had only a small number of people he was actually interested in seeing in town. Besides his family, he wanted to touch base with Lucy Teller. She was his family's heroine who had investigated the death of his brother Scott just outside Keshena. Scott was in a car accident and was fatally injured, not only by the wreck but also by a suspicious car fire, and she solved the terrible crime.

Lucy was the first one on the scene, and the last person to see his brother alive. Paul admired her very much but also felt a pang of envy when he saw her. He wished he could have shared the last few minutes of Scott's life with him. Paul would have told him how much he looked up to him and loved his big brother. At a young age, he learned a very important lesson in life. We never know when or if we will have time with those we love. Any day could be the last.

Paul could remember vividly the last time he touched his brother. Growing up, Scott would wrap him up in an affectionate bear hug, but that was before he left for college, and the family had done the intervention on their dad. When they were younger, he would punch, push or bump Paul gleefully anytime they were in the same room. In his childhood, Paul was irritated that his brother, always bigger than him, could easily send him airborne across the room any time he wanted. Back then, he would dream of the day he would be big and strong enough to return the favor.

Paul remembered the four short words of their last conversation. Scott simply said, "See you later, bro." Paul only answered with a smile and nod of his head. How he wished he could go back and say all the things that he thought and felt. This became a heavy burden that Paul carried every day since he received that tragic phone call. He remembered exactly where he was standing, what he was doing, and even wearing when he heard the dreadful words.

"Paul, there has been an a terrible accident. It's Scott. You've got to come. You need to hurry," his mother told him.

Paul fell to his knees as he stared at the phone for what seemed an eternity. It was a prophetic call, and Paul knew his brother was leaving this world. An immediate hole or emptiness created a void in his body. It was replaced by a longing and heaviness he had never experienced. This pain, a physical and emotional deep scar that never left him, had now become too familiar. It was as if the razor sharp hole took the place of his brother Scott. How he longed to have one more day with him. There were so many things that he wanted and needed to express to his older brother. When Scott left home, Paul always believed there would be other days—other days to harass and joke and wrestle around as grown men who still wanted to act like kids.

Of course, Paul could not realize that was the only day he had left with him. It would be the last time he touched his big brother. Because of that important lesson, he would not let a day go past without expressing his feelings for the people he loved. He constantly made it a point to say, "I love you," when he ended a phone conversation with family. It was a tragic lesson on loss that Paul learned much too young.

Lucy helped his whole family find answers about Scott's untimely death and explain why there were drugs in his system when he should have been clean and sober in recovery. Lucy also reached out to help the Brandt family heal and move on after their unimaginable loss. They buried their child, their eldest son, their brother, their friend.

Strangely, some of the most important facts about the case came to her in dreams. She believed the family needed to know and embrace the whole truth about Scott's tragic young death, and Lucy did what she could to provide them honesty.

Paul also looked forward to touching base with Kathy and Brad. Kathy had been Scott's girlfriend and Brad his best friend since childhood. They were now living together in Shawano and planning their wedding. Kathy and Brad organized an early intervention to get Scott to stop using cocaine. Unfortunately, this early effort failed and Scott continued to use. After Kathy was nearly raped by Scott's dealer and Scott was murdered, Kathy began to rely on Brad more and more for protection and comfort. The dear friendship turned to a tender love. That love only deepened when Kathy was abducted by that same drug dealer and nearly killed. Now Kathy loved this gentle giant even more.

For his part, Brad always felt guilty about loving his best friend's girlfriend even when Scott was alive, but Kathy would always reassure him that cocaine had altered her relationship with Scott. She wasn't sure she could ever love Scott again even if he had lived and continued to recover. Though Scott would always have a special place in her heart, she believed that by starting a relationship with a great friendship and without the baggage of drugs, Brad would make the better lifelong partner. Kathy continued to teach at the school where Scott taught before he died. Though she didn't have the instant rapport with the students that Scott did, with time the students grew to love her.

Returning to Keshena, Paul was reminded of the dangers his family faced while protecting Doc Wolf while Doc trained for and ran a race. It was high risk to keep him safe from people the Gambler hired to kill him. Gambler was in love with Doc's wife Gayle; he saw her as a prize and wanted her all for himself. At first Paul didn't like her, but now also enjoyed seeing Gayle. He recognized that her addiction dominated her thoughts, dreams, and basically her life. She was a beautiful woman struggling to become healthy and save her marriage. Paul respected Gayle's gallant effort to make things right again.

Paul started late with experiencing his own sexuality, and now he found it kicking into overdrive. Through high school, girls had been his buddies, and he enjoyed hanging out with them. He took a date to prom junior and senior year, but they were just friends. Even his first year in college when he began dating, it was more to be part of the fraternity crowd he had joined.

Paul was just not really romantically interested in anyone most of his adolescence. When the majority of his friends wanted to count how many girls they could score with, Paul did not have the drive to participate in the same conquests. He had very different goals and pushed himself hard to reach them. When he started working on Fish's campaign, however, things began to change. He learned that women are attracted to power, and even though he was just on the fringes of that power, they seemed to be attracted to him as well. He began to understand how simple it was for politicians to get caught up in sex scandals. All of a sudden women were looking at Paul differently, and he enjoyed the attention.

Inside, Paul was still a quiet and shy kid, but working on a presidential campaign required him to overcome his introverted nature. His faith in Alex Fish and his stance on the environment was stronger than his anxiety about approaching others. His improved skills in public speaking and engaging others paid off in his personal life as well.

It also helped to have Alex Fish as a role model. He was a man of true honesty and integrity. All campaigns say that about their candidates, of course, but Paul truly believed it of Alex Fish. For Paul, an honest politician seemed unusual—almost an oxymoron. But that was before he encountered Fish.

One ritual that Fish observed during the campaign was his love of running—a throwback to his days as a competitive runner and Olympian. Paul was the only member of his staff who could keep pace with Alex, and it gave Paul an opportunity to speak one on one with the one man whom—perhaps, besides his father—he admired most in the world.

He began to observe that Alex too was really quiet and shy like so many of the Menominee people, but when he spoke of what was important to him, his eyes would light up and his legs would move faster. One day on a run, Alex, looking straight ahead, commented rather casually, "I notice the women giving you the eye."

Paul stammered for a moment, his mind and heart racing, and then he decided to be honest.

"It took me a while to even notice the flirting because I'm not used to that kind of attention. I don't know what to do about it. We're never in one place long enough for me to develop a relationship—not a good one anyway."

"I admire that," Fish said. "There are a lot of young men your age who wouldn't worry about developing even a short term relationship. They would simply exploit the situation and take advantage of the opportunity. Carpe diem and all that."

"A lot of men your age would do the same thing," Paul shot back.

Fish smiled. "You got me there. How about if both of us make a pact to keep our eye on the real prize here and avoid any and all situations that could bring this campaign down."

After that, Paul watched Alex Fish even more closely. He applauded his speeches and showed the same enthusiasm when he spoke on Fish's behalf. He also took hints on how Fish related to women. Although his response was friendly and warm, he was careful not to be alone with them. Alex respected women and made great eye contact. Deferentially, he never let his eyes roam. Often he would ask Paul and a female staff member to attend private conversations with the opposite sex.

Paul, for his part, kept his urges in check and simply developed a rich fantasy life—that is, until he met Judy, a young woman who recently had joined Fish's campaign.

While they were the same age at least chronologically, Judy was more outgoing, experienced, and passionate about politics. She was also tall, blond, beautiful, and full of energy and life. Paul suddenly discovered he really liked tall, blond, beautiful women full of energy and life. She and Paul started off as friends. They engaged in heated political discussions along with the other staff members in their hotel at night that would last for hours. One night everyone gathered in Paul's room, and after a lively debate, one by one the other members returned to their rooms. Suddenly, Judy and Paul were the only two remaining.

Judy's looks had not been lost on Paul, but he had never approached her. He really did admire her from afar. Judy stood up from the chair she'd been sitting on, stretched slowly, and said she was turning in. Tomorrow would be another full day. Paul stood and silently walked her to his door. As he reached to open it, Judy grabbed his right hand and put it on her hip. He felt sparks at the touch of her hand. They stood gazing into each other's eyes, speechless. Just having his hand touching hers made his pulse race. His breathing increased rapidly. She gently put her two hands on either side of his face. They barely touched his warm skin, but he could feel the energy between them.

"When I first met you, I thought of you as a brother. I envied your sister Sally because you are always talking about her. But, as I've watched and come to know you, I realize I'm glad I'm not your sister. You are the kindest, gentlest, dearest man I've met, and I don't want to be like a sister anymore."

Then she closed her eyes and boldly kissed him. Softly her lips brushed across his. He wanted to say something profound but was at a loss for words. It seemed to last a long time, but not long enough for Paul. As she lingered for a moment, which would allow her to turn away if she wanted to, he leaned over and kissed her again. Her mouth was open; she made a small sound in the back of her throat. His heart was racing, his body awake and aroused. As she turned to leave, he wrapped his hands around the small of her back and pulled her gently into him. He had wanted to touch her for a long time. It seemed they were made for each other that they fit so well. Paul was thinking: wow, how corny is that?

She's beautiful inside and out and I am a dork, he thought. Not able to stop himself, Paul kissed her again, softly at first, but the passion and intensity increased, and their hands began to move over their backs and shoulders. Paul was kissing the curve between her neck and shoulders and loved how neatly his face fit there.

Breathing hard, the intensity quickly rose for both of them. She smiled. "I guess you don't want to be my brother either." Their faces hovered inches from each other, and Paul could feel her breath. Softly Judy murmured, "Don't worry. We will continue this at another time."

With a wink, she disappeared. Paul tossed and turned all that night. He ran the scene over and over in his mind and was almost convinced that he must have said or done something wrong that would screw things up. Paul did not want to ruin this one. Judy made him feel and think things he never would have dreamed possible. What a rush of emotions this woman created in him. Could he possibly be falling in love? What really was going on here? He promised Alex this would not happen, but he could not and would not let it stop. Paul knew that he would never again want anyone or anything as much as he wanted this woman.

After that, Paul and Judy were rarely apart, and their sexual intimacy increased in tune with their emotional intimacy. At first Paul was nervous, but his inexperience seemed only to add to his attractiveness in Judy's eyes. Besides, he more than made up for it with his attentiveness to her wants and needs. His slow hand only wanted to please this woman he now knew he loved. They were comfortable exploring each other. For the first time, she shyly but openly talked about what she liked and disliked sexually. They could lie for hours touching, kissing, and bringing each other pleasure and ecstasy even before having intercourse. Paul could not believe the incredible sensations Judy created with seemingly little effort. Their intimacy was natural and without any apprehension. It all just felt so right.

One day on a run, Alex, in his most presidential voice, reminded Paul of a promise he had made.

"Brandt, what the heck happened to our pact? As I remember, we had one."

Paul's stomach flipped, and he began to stutter while he desperately struggled to answer. Suddenly, Alex laughed out loud.

"Don't worry," he said. "You have my blessing, but I don't know who deserves it. Should I give it to you because I think of her as a daughter or to her because I think of you as a son?"

Paul thought back many years ago to the day his sister punched him on the arm and thanked him for saving her life. Just after that, they saw two young loons take their first flight—a metaphor for their new life. He felt that day as if he was flying, and he felt that way again now. He was so proud of his sister and proud to be her big brother. In addition, he was most proud to be with Judy and have Alex's blessing.

"Thank you, sir," was all he could choke out of his dry mouth and throat.

Ironically, that very day Alex was asked by a Christian newspaper reporter if he knew that two of his young staff members were acting as if they were having a secret rendezvous. Maybe they were even sleeping together. Certainly, the exciting energy between Paul and Judy was obvious. Being in the room with Paul and Judy caused one to notice something was going on between the two. When they gazed into each other's eyes, fireworks seemed to be going off for all to see. But they innocently believed the relationship could be kept under wraps.

They did not openly talk about it. They did not touch or flirt in public. But in spite of their conscious efforts, neither one of them was very good at hiding the passion. When apart, Paul easily could remember the ecstasy of their first kiss. He reviewed the events of that late night again and again. The way her skin felt under his hand. The passionate kisses. Were there two or three? The sound she made in the back of her throat.

"I know a whole lot of people who are in relationships that are not marriage," Alex Fish responded to the accusation. "Many are even sleeping together outside of a legal union, but thank you for bringing this up, because I want to speak to your readers. Before I do, I need to ask you some relevant questions.

"I'm not sure to whom you are referring to here, but are the two people you speak of over eighteen? Do either of them have a communicable disease? Is either person being exploited or lied to or forced to be in this relationship? Is one or both being unfaithful to someone else? Those would be the important things I care about. Those would be the answers I would be looking for.

"Also notice what I didn't ask. I didn't ask whether they are the same or opposite sex, because I don't care about that either. I do not believe it is my business to judge others. I may not believe it is all right for me to behave in certain ways. But I am not in charge of others' adult choices or practices. I'm running for president, not preacher. I agree with Jesus when he said, "Give to Caesar the things that are Caesar's, and to God the things that are God's.

"God calls us to be stewards of the earth. Right now I think if we don't begin heeding that as a nation, a lot of people and animals are going to die. Even more than you can imagine have already tragically and senselessly lost their lives. I am concerned about that. I also believe that the rich of this nation are getting richer, while the middle class and poor are getting poorer. This trend has been going on much too long already. Couples cannot afford to have one primary caregiver stay home. Raising good moral children is the most important job I can think of. There is not much above that. Parents need to have two working incomes just to make ends meet. Who are the people raising the children in this country? Is it the child's own loving parents?

"Should they at least be given a choice in the matter? Most would say they have no choice if they want to just survive. I also believe the rich of this country are using their wealth to control our government. I care about that. I also believe that when government spends its time arguing about who should be married, what language should be official, or whether or not people have a right to burn our flag, they are closing their eyes to the real needs of this nation.

"There is so much anger and violence in our streets because we live our lives as a contradiction. We say we are all equal, and we all deserve equal opportunity. That is what we say. How do we live? Racism is real and something we need to change. What religion, what organization, practices equal treatment of all? Not many that I can name. Let's chose our battles. Let's win the war. I don't know if God's on my side or I'm on his, but that's what I'm running on and if you think that's important, please vote for me. And I hope your readers will too. If you are looking for someone to make laws about what consenting adults do in the privacy of their own bedrooms—then I'm not your man."

Alex was angry and on a roll and finally he added, "Let me also say that the two people that you say are in question here, if they are on my staff, they spend long hours all summer to promote the causes they believe in. If I were to evaluate them on my morality scale, I'd give them nine out of ten. I know a lot of married Christians that I wouldn't give nearly as high a grade. Any more questions?"

The reporter left without much to say in defense.

That night at the Wolf's home, Judy and Paul approached Alex, not knowing whether or not to apologize. Since he had given them his blessing, the only thing they weren't discreet about was their feelings toward one another.

"Are we getting in the way?" Paul decided to ask.

"As I told you before, Paul," Fish answered, "you two are like my children, and I'm proud to have you as part of my campaign. You gave me the opportunity to talk about what I believe in and what can be better than that. But speaking about family, I just met your parents, Paul. I don't believe they've had the opportunity to meet Judy yet, and I know they are anxious."

Paul was surprised and elated. He thought that most of the people he was hoping to see were already in the room. Excitedly, Paul took Judy to meet his family and the friends he had come to cherish through Scott's death and the summer's drama with Doc Wolf and his wife Gayle. It was important to Paul for family and friends to meet the woman whom they all soon noticed was the love of his life.

After some socializing, Agent Scruggs asked for their attention. Paul was even more surprised by what he had to say and how he again found himself involved in another summer's drama on the Rez.

CHAPTER **18**

THE NEXT DAY ON THE reservation turned out to be an exceptional hot summer day. The clear sky embraced a few soft white fluffy clouds, but already the heat was building, driven by a hot breeze blowing from the south. What a good day to sit by a lake, Scruggs thought. He wished he could be anywhere but where he was. So instead, he sat on the temporary speaker's platform in the hot August sun, listening to Alex Fish speak words that Scruggs was only now beginning to believe in.

"It's good to be home," Fish began, and already the crowd erupted in cheers. "I promise that no matter where I am and what office I might hold, I will not forget my roots and my mother earth." Again they cheered loudly. Agent Scruggs wished he could concentrate more on what Fish was saying, but his mind was racing ahead. Scruggs was sweating heavily, searching the crowd for faces. Could Egg have sent others to make sure the job was done right? Fiddler was a loose cannon. He knew the Gambler didn't trust him, but then Scruggs didn't trust Fiddler either. At that exact moment, he saw Fiddler slowly and stiffly approach the speaker's platform. He was a familiar sight to most and did not cause a distraction. With people intent on the powerful words being spoken, most did not even notice Fiddler pull out a .357 Magnum. Suddenly, he shot Fish in the shoulder just above his heart and drove him backwards! Most people still did not even know what had happened.

There was a stunned silence. It felt like hours to Scruggs. Alex Fish looked stunned and confused also, as he spun around to face his attacker. In one motion, Scruggs pulled out his own gun and jumped in front of Fish. He got off a round that caught Fiddler in the chest, and he immediately staggered backwards. Scruggs watched him fall almost in slow motion and dark red blood spurted from his chest. At the same time, sparks and smoke seemed to fly from Fiddler's gun. Scruggs took a savage blow, and also staggered backward, and saw his own blood pulsating from his chest as well. He felt no pain as he fell on his back. The warm liquid blood oozed over his shoulder and stained the wood on the platform where he too collapsed.

By this time, the majority of people knew what was happening. At least they knew there were bullets flying around and people were shot. Chaos broke out. Frightened people of all ages screamed and ran in all different directions. Some shouted and others broke into tears.

Scruggs never saw the shot coming. It all happened so quickly. As he lay bleeding on the stage and just before he closed his eyes and drifted off, Scruggs gratefully spotted Lucy Teller, Ray Waupuse, and the other Menominee Tribal Police who had rushed in to keep the crowd away. They pushed and shoved and screamed at the top of their lungs to clear the crowd. The officers desperately made way for the ambulances already on the scene that were staged previously in anticipation of potential accidents or heat stroke in the hot sun.

After some futile attempts to stop the bleeding and administer IV fluids, the three men were swiftly placed in separate ambulances and rushed to Shawano Hospital. Alex Fish was hurried away first. His eyes were closed, and it appeared to all present he might not make it. Crimson bloodstained sheets covered the injured man. People stared in shock; this man they loved was probably mortally wounded. Many cried openly.

It reminded numerous older people in attendance of the tragedies of John and Bobby Kennedy and Martin Luther King. Adding to the tragedies was the fact that the shooter was also shot just as Lee Harvey Oswald was gunned down before the authorities could find answers to that assassination. The people wanted answers.

Not that Scruggs had much choice in the matter. Could he let a man with a loaded gun run loose in a crowd of innocent people and just shoot someone? He could not let that happen. Scruggs believed any choice he may have had was taken away from him. He did not like the feeling of being forced to do anything, let alone resort to violence to solve any problems. He had seen too much suffering to cause anyone physical pain without regret. Scruggs's mind was racing with thoughts and feelings of hope, regret, and fear for the near future.

He longed to take back the day and find another solution to the dilemma. Many thoughts disturbed him. He could not even get the words out of his mouth. He felt trapped in his own head. Maybe it was the fight or flight mode that he had become too familiar with in his combat training. Something had taken over his ability to speak.

Lucy went in the ambulance with Fiddler and her paramedic friend named Ernest. He was a fellow Indian Lucy had known for many years.

ics he did not know. The ride was silent and he watched them closely as they searched for another vein to start an IV for pain management. Paul did not know what he should do with all the emotions that were quickly building up inside of him. He found himself nauseated by all the blood splattered onto the crowd. The antiseptic smell of the ambulance did not help settle his stomach.

In the third ambulance, Doc Wolf went with his friend Scruggs. Within moments of the horrific event, it was all over the news. The media always thrived for more and more shocking things to cover. Doc thought the general public has always needed more bells and whistles. The media needed more and more gore and conflict to get and keep their attention. On the way to the hospital, Scruggs cell phone rang. Dr. Wolf answered it.

"This is Agents Scruggs phone. How can I help you?" There was a pause at the other end. "Whom am I speaking to?"

"I am a doctor attending to him. He's been shot and is unconscious at the moment. Who is this?"

"How serious is he?"

"Very serious. To whom am I speaking?" Wolf asked. The Gambler quickly hung up.

He then called Fiddler, and Lily answered. Again there was a pause.

"Who is this?" "This is Lily."

"Why do you have his phone?"

"He gave it to me in case something like this happened and it has! I don't want to lose him. And I want my baby back! Did something happen to my son? Fiddler did what he was told. Now where can I get my son? He also gave me names to contact in case my son was not returned. I want my son!"

The Gambler swallowed hard.

"I will get back to you with details." Again he hung up. "I want my son, damn it!" she screamed into the dead phone. Trying to breathe and find her voice, Lily roughly wiped away her tears and called Ray Waupuse.

"The Gambler tried to contact Fiddler. I asked about my son and he said he'd get back to me. He said he would get back to me! This is bad Ray, really bad," Lily sobbed.

"I don't think we can wait then," Ray answered.

"Ray, I cannot lose another man that I love. I will die without my son. Tell me this is not happening. Please help me, Ray. Please, Ray."

RAY WAUPUSE QUICKLY CHANGED FROM his uniform into jeans, a flannel shirt, and cowboy boots. Because he worked out intensely to keep himself in shape, his rock-hard body could be used as a very effective lethal weapon. He usually found emotional relief in his strenuous workouts. But after Africa, it did not matter how hard or how long he worked out. The cathartic magic of exercise had evaporated. His physical strength aside, he arranged his firearms for the conflict he knew was coming. He slipped his revolver with a silencer into a holster and tucked it into his pants near his backbone. Another fully loaded Glock went into a shoulder holster. He threw a chainsaw in the back of his truck and drove to the cabin where the men held the boy. He felt in his gut that the little boy was definitely captive in that house. Surprisingly, Ray felt totally calm as he drove into the driveway and blocked any cars from leaving. He walked up the steps and boldly knocked on the door. One of the men, who looked to be the same one he followed into Keshena and Shawano, came to the door.

"I was driving by, and I noticed you have a number of dead trees that are leaning toward your cabin. They really need to be cut down. I will take them all down and haul the brush away, plus cut up the rest for firewood for you for only five hundred dollars."

"Get lost," the man answered. The man was about six feet one and weighed about two hundred and fifty pounds. Ray stood about five feet ten and weighed about 185, but that might have been to Ray's advantage.

Ray smiled easily. "You really should come out here and take a look at these trees. If there is a strong windstorm, you and your family could run into some serious problems. Come on out here and see for yourself."

With that, the man opened the door and stepped out to shove Ray off the porch. With perfect timing, Ray stepped to the side, grabbed the man, twisted his head and deftly broke his neck. Not smiling anymore, he silently dropped him to the ground.

Ray now entered the house and a second man about the same height and weight approached him. Without hesitation, Ray pulled his gun with the silencer from behind him and shot him directly between the eyes. His vacant eyes stayed open as he slowly slid down the wall until his lifeless body stopped into a sitting position against the bloodstained wall. A third man sat on a recliner, watching the news that was carrying the events of the day. Ray menacingly held the gun to his head.

"Where is the boy?"

"What the—! There is no boy! I don't know what the hell you are talking about!" the man shouted.

Ray swiftly smashed the man's nose with the pistol in one fluid movement. There was a loud, sickening thud. Blood quickly filled his hands.

"I said, 'Where is the boy?'"

"Upstairs!" the man answered between moans.

"Get up now!" Ray walked behind the bleeding man up the stairs. He was not moving quickly enough for Ray. So at the top of the stairs he pushed the wounded man forward, using him as a human shield as he slowly opened the door. Opening the door, he was crushed with emotion upon seeing Tyler. Ray roughly shoved the bleeding kidnapper, and he fell face first on the foot of the bed, smearing blood from his face as it skidded across the bedspread.

Ray was relieved to see the child but sickened by the state he was in. The little boy was lying on a bed in the loft with his tiny hands and feet tied spread eagle to the bedposts. He had obviously relieved himself many times right there in his bed. His mouth covered with duct tape, it was clear the frightened child had cried many tears. He looked so small on the stained double bed. Tyler was trembling so hard that he seemed to be having an epileptic seizure. His skinny wrists were rubbed raw by the rope that held him prisoner.

At the sight, in his mind, Ray was back in Africa staring at the naked bloodstained bodies of a loving, gentle mother and her daughter. Without another thought, Ray shot the third kidnapper directly in the crown of his head. Blood spattered across the bed and onto Tyler. He now looked like he had been wounded too. Ray immediately took out a knife, cut the ropes, and as gently as he could, pulled the duct tape from Tyler's mouth. He was scared but didn't fight. Ray picked up the boy and hugged him.

"I'm taking you to your mommy," Ray promised.

Once he had the boy outside and in his truck, he called Lily.

"I got him and I'm bringing him to you. Where are you?"

"How is he? Is he hurt? Where are you? When can I see him? I just want to hold my baby!" Lily was almost hysterical.

"I have him. He is not hurt physically, but he will need a lot of healing. I am bringing him to you and will meet you at Lucy's right away. I'm going to put the phone by Tyler's ear; I don't think he will say anything, but I think he'd like to hear his mother's voice. Right now, I think he is more afraid of me than he was of his kidnappers. Tell you the truth, right now I'm scared of me."

Ray started to cry and put the phone by Tyler's ear. When Tyler heard his mother's voice, tears rolled down his tiny cheeks. It looked and sounded like he was hyperventilating. The boy's chest was moving fast and deep and the first sound he uttered spoke to the terror and relief that seemed too big for such a tiny body. Within minutes, they were at Lucy's, and Lily was waiting for them outside by the drive. She was holding her breath. When she saw her baby's blood-spattered face, she winced and thought she would pass out. Lily put her arm out to regain her balance.

"Is he hurt? Is he all right? Look at all the blood! Where is he bleeding from?" she asked in panic.

"All that blood on him—it's not his blood, Lily," Ray assured her. "Tyler has minor superficial wounds. He is not bleeding, I promise. And he is not hurt physically either, but we need to get him to a doctor for a checkup right now. It's what is in his tiny little mind that I'm worried, like mine, will never heal."

CHAPTER **20**

OUTSIDE THE HOSPITAL IN SHAWANO, a huge crowd of reporters gathered. Curious local citizens also milled around hoping to learn more about the day's events. Shootings and kidnappings and reporters crawling around were hardly everyday events. They had all been waiting nearly an hour when a helicopter suddenly took off from the roof. Shortly after that, Dr. Wolf came to the microphone that had been erected hastily in front of the reporters for an impromptu news conference.

"This will be brief, and at this time I will not answer any questions. Alex Fish is alive but in serious condition. He has been moved to a secure location because we don't know whether there will be other attempts on his life. The two other men involved in the shooting were pronounced dead on arrival. Both of their names are being withheld until relatives can be notified. Thank you for coming. That is all I have to share. Please, no questions." Dr. Wolf was tired and looked drained as he left the podium, facing a barrage of questions, which he refused to answer.

A few days later, the names of the deceased were plastered all over the news. Fiddler was identified and his background as a troubled youth, a Navy Seal, and even a suspected hit man for the mob was described in vivid detail. The picture painted by the media led to much speculation about the attempt on Alex Fish's life. Fiddler's casket was buried privately at a cemetery off Highway VV in Keshena. Since Scruggs's parents were deceased and he had no next of kin, he was buried there also.

Ray and Lucy and her children attended the funerals, as did Lily and her children. Hank and Molly were also in attendance, as were Doc and Gayle. Few others attended, yet many tears were shed. Some curious strangers in suits just watched from a distance. Maybe they're looking for something, Ray thought. The armed personnel that kept them at a distance were obvious and disturbing. Each of the deceased had a closed casket with his picture on top of a simple coffin. A few reporters covered both funerals.

A day after the funeral, Hank, his brother Ken, his son Ryan, and Ryan's friend Zack all started off for the Boundary Waters Canoe Area in Northern Minnesota. The BWCA is a gorgeous area of lakes and woods that features the best in rugged outdoor activity: canoeing, fishing, camping, and the dreaded portaging of canoes and gear.

The trip would be a challenging one, but all involved felt the need to get away, and each of the men certainly had his own reasons for the need for solitude and renewal. Two other friends who were scheduled to join the adventure dropped out at the last minute. Since they had already bought food and paid for six to enter Canada, the group was fortunate to locate two other guys to replace them. It's not easy finding people who want to go to the wilds of Boundary Waters.

Equally challenging would be the second part of the journey into the Quetico region, which is the Canadian wilderness counterpart just across the border from the BWCA. It is also a vast area of lakes and trees that has been returned to its natural state since the heyday of logging in the early 1900s: no cabins, no running water, no electricity, no cell phone towers, not even toilets. Lakes can only be traversed by canoe, and portaging gear the way the French voyageurs did it centuries before is the only mode of transportation between lakes. The designated campsites on the American side consist of a fire grate and a pit toilet dug back in the woods. The campsites on the Canadian side are not designated, and are recognized only by worn spots on the lakeshore where canoes were repeatedly pulled up. And these sites are primitive and certainly not glamorous!

Luckily, Hank found two guys extremely familiar with the outdoors, canoeing, and wilderness survival. They didn't express much interest in fishing, but then they seemed to have a different agenda anyway. The six men drove in one car and pulled a trailer with three lightweight canoes and all the gear and food needed for seven days' survival. They packed fishing gear, freeze-dried meals, cook pots as well as stoves—in case there was a fire ban—and tents. They also packed survival clothes, including rain gear and polypro underwear, in case the nights were cold. They arrived on a Sunday night in Ely, Minnesota—one of the most popular starting points for the hundreds of square miles of wilderness—and slept in a bunk-house that featured two tiny four-person rooms with two bunk beds in each room.

In the morning, they started their day with a huge breakfast and then stopped at the outfitter to pick up last-minute supplies and maps of the areas they would be visiting. They also arranged for a motorboat shuttle across Moose Lake, which would save them several hours of paddling. Finally, the last stop was at the ranger station to pick up the necessary permits to enter the wilderness areas. They watched a film about proper gear, backcountry etiquette, the ban on bottles and cans, and advice on the disposal of fish guts. In the past, it was recommended to leave them on a rock and allow the seagulls to eat them. But then the rangers learned that the gulls were eating loon eggs and disrupting their populations. So the new recommendations involved burying remains in the woods.

Then they told the rangers two lies. First, they provided the rangers with the original six names on their permits even though two of them had been replaced. Then they affirmed that they were not carrying firearms . . . but they were! The rangers didn't check their IDs or bags, so neither lies turned out to be much of a risk.

AFTER DROPPING TYLER OFF WITH his frantic and very grateful mother at Lucy's house, Ray went straight to Lieutenant Moon's office. He admitted immediately what he had done. Lieutenant Moon not only asked him for his badge, but he also placed him in jail and then called Lucy. He then dispatched a squad car to investigate the horrific scene that Ray described. Already suspicious about what she had heard from Lily, Lucy was all too ready to believe the report from Lieutenant Moon. She summoned her mother and children around her. She would need their cooperation and support for what was to come next. She briefly described what she had learned from the Brandts about intervention and asked each of them to write a letter to Ray. Each letter would contain 'I' statements, and though they did not include them in the letter, each would include their bottom lines if Ray was not willing to get help.

She then called Dr. Wolf and described to him what she had observed about Ray since he had returned from Africa.

Dr. Wolf had suspected that Ray was suffering from post-traumatic stress disorder, or PTSD, and he shared with Lucy that Native Americans had the highest incidence of this disorder of any cultural group that was entering combat in large numbers. In fact, nearly 30 percent of them were returning from recent conflicts suffering from the problem. PTSD is an unfortunate mental state but also very treatable.

Lucy immediately suspected alcoholism from his behavior and questioned Dr. Wolf about that. He replied that many of the soldiers used alcohol and drugs to mask their symptoms, so that wasn't necessarily their primary problem. Doc would have to meet with him before he knew for sure, and Ray was the only one who could say he was alcoholic or not. If someone does not believe he has a drinking problem, all the labels in the worlds will not make a difference. But like any alcoholic or anyone self-medicating, he'd certainly be better off not drinking.

Lucy realized that was particularly true if their relationship was going to continue, because she was better off not being exposed to alcoholic behavior or regularly exposed to alcohol. Being in recovery, she was at high risk staying in a relationship with another person who was abusing any substances.

Never having done an intervention, Lucy called Molly to find out how it all worked. Molly in turn referred her to Jack Peterson who had done Hank's intervention. Graciously, Jack offered to meet her at Maehnowesekiyah and volunteered to take her through the whole process of an intervention. Jack understood the urgency of these situations. Meeting at Maehnowesekiyah, he coached her about writing effective intervention letters. He advised her to start out with "I" while de- scribing specific data, and telling Ray about her feelings, and he broke it down into observation, interpretation, and feeling phases. "I observe, I interpret, and I feel." Each letter would start with "Dear Ray, I'm here because I love or care about you and I'm concerned about your recent behavior." All of the data and feelings should be concerned about behavior related to Ray's PTSD and/or possible alcoholism but not referenced by name. It was up to the treatment center to identify the specific problem.

The most important thing was to convince Ray that a problem existed, and he needed help. And first and foremost, they must communicate clearly that they all loved him and wanted only what was the best for him.

Lucy went home and described the process to her children and her mother. Already at work on their letters, they were more than willing to participate. They really missed the old Ray and wanted him back desperately. Since none of this was any secret to Lieutenant Moon, Lucy asked him to participate as well.

"I'd be glad to, Lucy," he answered, "but I'm afraid we have another complication."

Lucy looked at him strangely.

"I can't keep Ray in jail. When I sent a squad car to investigate these supposed shootings, they found nothing!"

"Nothing?" "Nothing, nada."

"But little Tyler was splattered with blood! How could that be? You must have been in the wrong place." Lucy's head began to spin. What was going on here anyway?

"Either Ray made this up or hallucinated this terrible encounter, or some people with a lot of power were able to cover their tracks very quickly," Moon speculated.

"This is all very confusing, and I'm not sure we will ever have all of the facts. When I dispatched a squad to clean up the mess that Ray described at the cabin where Tyler had been held—they found nothing. There was absolutely nothing, not even one piece of evidence. There were no bodies of the three men, no confirmation of blood, or even any sign of a struggle."

Lucy knew the kidnapping was not fiction. She was the one who told Ray about it. She also knew that Tyler was held by a group of men because she talked to the cashier at River Mart who sold one of the kidnappers a *Green Bay Gazette*. Ray had rescued Tyler somehow, and she was positive that he didn't just go up to the door, knock, and ask for his safe return. So what could have happened?

"Lucy, are you there?" Lieutenant Moon asked.

"Yes, I am. I just need to think. Can we talk later? I just need to think." Breathe, Lucy, breathe, she reminded herself.

Then she remembered Scruggs telling her that the men who wanted Fish assassinated were very powerful. She also knew that the Gambler had ties both to the mob and to the federal government. Either one could probably dispatch groups of people there in a hurry. They could have cleaned it all up. But who would have wanted to keep this so hidden? Who in the world would go to this much trouble cleaning up a horrific bloody mess? How could they get it done so quickly? It makes no sense to me at all. Lucy continued her old mantra: breathe, Lucy, breathe. Then she began to worry more and more about Ray. This certainly wouldn't do his fragile mental state much good.

"Lieutenant Moon, does Ray know about this yet?" Lucy asked.

"No, I haven't told him yet."

"Would you mind keeping it from him for a while? Maybe we can do this intervention thing right away. Give us a couple of hours to work on these letters. Then bring him in a squad directly to the Maehnowesekiyah treatment facility."

With pen and paper in hand, Lucy sat down and bared her soul.

Dear Ray,

Next to my children and my sobriety, you are the best thing to happen to me in my adult life. I love you with all my heart, but lately I've become concerned about your behavior. Since you've returned from Africa, I've noticed you don't sleep well. I used to love to spend the night snuggled in your arms. I felt so safe and warm. Now you are restless, and when I reach for you in the middle of the night, you are gone. I feel very lonely.

You are often crabby and irritable, and you started smoking again. I have noticed alcohol on your breath often. Before you left, you didn't drink. When you are unsteady on your feet or slur your words, I feel scared. This frightens me because of my own problems with alcohol and drugs. It is not good for either one of us to be around alcohol.

You've stopped going to church, and prior to Africa, that was very important to you. I'm also concerned about your violence. I know at one time in your life that was a part of you, but you were moving away from it. You told me once that such behavior was not who you are anymore. But it seems to have come back with a vengeance. I am scared.

Most importantly, I'm afraid I'm losing you. Everyone around me thinks I'm crazy, but I even imagine that you fell in love with someone else over in Africa and that you haven't gotten the nerve to tell me yet.

Ray, I love you; and more than anything else, I want you back. I haven't been this lonely since I lost my children.

Please Ray, let the people here help you like they helped me. I want back the man I fell in love with. Please, Ray. Get help. Please!

Jack Peterson was on his way back home when his cell phone rang. He agreed to come back and provide an emergency intervention. It certainly wasn't his preference. Often there was only one chance at these things, and he didn't like feeling unprepared. But given the circumstances, this might be the best opportunity, and at least he could hope for the best.

He met with Lucy, her mother, and the children as well as Lieutenant Moon. Thoughtfully, he decided on the seating arrangement, the order of reading of the letters, and where to seat Ray when he walked in. He confirmed their bottom lines and felt confident that Ray would get help. It was clear to Jack that Ray had quite a lot to lose here.

Some pretty stiff consequences faced Ray if he did not get help. Lieutenant Moon assured him that he'd be kicked off the force and brought up on criminal charges. Lucy would stop seeing him, and that meant he wouldn't see her children either. Luckily, they never needed to follow through on their bottom lines. As soon as Lieutenant Moon finished reading his letter, which mentioned nothing about a bottom line but pleaded with Ray to get help, Ray suddenly asked what they wanted him to do. They asked him to enter Maehnowesekiyah and get treatment to get well.

Ray began to cry quietly.

"This was so kind and gentle after what I've done and after the way I've treated you. Even if I didn't have you guys in my life and even if I wasn't scared to death of losing that, I'd go for help because I just can't go on with this pain any longer. It is killing me. It is eating me up inside. I really need some help. I really need all of you. Thank you."

After a long silent pause, he asked," Now what do I do?"

RAY ENTERED TREATMENT THAT SAME day. Lucy and her family and friends almost collapsed from exhaustion. Their emotions ran at a fever pitch: fear, confusion, anger, love, and compassion. The counselor, Jack, was ecstatic. He wished all the interventions he managed could have this positive an outcome. But he also was very aware that Ray was in deep pain and that the hard part was just beginning for him. But the strong support system of loving people was clear, as he looked the group members in the eye that day. "Ray will need all the help he can get," Jack said.

Staying at the treatment center was difficult for Ray because he watched others go through withdrawal symptoms and change from denial to acceptance. He saw them go through remarkable physical changes as they rid their bodies of toxins and began to eat healthy and work out, but his change was much more gradual. He didn't have to detox from alcohol because he wasn't physically dependent on it, but he did miss the anesthetizing effect it had on his anxiety. He also found himself feeling worse at first because in both individual and group counseling, Dr. Wolf made him relate the painful African story again and again. Rather than attend AA meetings, he attended Al-Anon meetings. He attended them religiously, but most of the time he felt worse rather than better afterward. Sitting in the meetings, he would analyze what was said or judge the messenger rather than absorb the content or meaning. He struggled to get out of his head and into his heart. Emotional thawing was needed in order for that huge wall to break down.

The majority of Ray's life taught him to stay focused and assess a situation rationally. In his military training, he was always prepared and ready at any moment to face a crisis. Emotions were not valuable—in fact, a liability—in his past world. This was such a struggle. It was turning out to be a lot tougher than he imagined, even for a tough guy like him.

Traditional twelve-step work was not enough for Ray. He and Doc knew he needed something more, and that is when he was introduced to the "talking circle." Ray had a vague memory of prior experience with the talking circles. He found them to be powerful and healing. But he worried that the lessons of the circle were lost when he began keeping emotions and people out, and the tall, thick wall was erected. He had taken a huge risk by letting Lucy in and loving her and her family, especially loving her children. But he did let his wall down and kept it down long enough to fall in love. If he did it once, he could do it again!

Ray was reluctant the first time he entered the talking circle or healing circle. He gathered with other people from treatment in a circular formation. A counselor from the treatment center acted as the circle leader who held in his hand an eagle feather, which served as their sacred symbol of his leadership and provided structure and order to the group. The feather, also called the talking stick, ensures a democratic process where all members are expected to contribute and all are equals. Whoever holds the feather is in charge, and the stick is passed from person to person. All deserve equal time to share.

After attending the talking circle several times, Ray called Father Dan and asked if he would hear his confession. In many ways, confession with Father Dan was a continuation of the talking circle because Father Dan listened without judgment. As Father Dan offered Ray grace and absolution with his healing hands upon his head, Ray sobbed openly and another barrier was broken.

When Native Americans engage in conversation, they listen intently. It is common practice to usually look down and not establish eye contact until the person speaking is completely finished talking. Then the next person to talk fully expects to completely finish his thoughts without interruption. For a man who was trained to think on his feet while talking about or facing dangerous situations, it was quite a challenge for Ray.

Opposite of his brainstorming sessions in the military and on the police force, the only one to speak in a circle is the person holding the talking stick. Even if it takes several minutes to think about what they want to say or if there is a pause in the conversation, no one interrupts. Whoever holds the talking stick holds the floor. The talking stick gives each speaker the courage to speak the truth and the power to speak from the heart. Eagle feathers, a rock, sweet grass, or a pipe can be used as a talking stick.

The "talking feather" was Ray's favorite Native object used in the talking circle. Ray somehow found both peace and power in the eagle's feathers. They were not only beautiful, but the eagle is a powerful animal in Native American tradition. The eagle held significant meaning for Ray. Eagles symbolized nature's power, mystery, and majesty. He liked to slowly stroke the feathers solemnly, sometimes holding them in his hand. They were so light yet so powerful.

Some Native American cultures practice a ritual called "what is left unsaid," and it is performed in various ways. The treatment center practiced their own version of talking circle. The group gathered in a circle, going around clockwise, and each patient took turns speaking. Whoever had the talking feather was the one who stated what had been on his mind but had not been said. When he was finished talking, the feather was passed to the next person. Many of the staff desired to extract more delicate information from the patients and would explain the ritual "what is left unsaid" and pass on the feather.

Any negative comments while someone was speaking were absolutely forbidden. Each person would wait his or her turn to speak. Ray struggled with this rule. He felt different from the other residents and challenged what they said. He was accustomed to being in charge and fixing any and all problems he encountered. Ray even suggested that a timer be used to make sure each person had enough time to speak, and he volunteered his watch with a stopwatch setting. Consequently, he was asked to leave the group on more than one occasion. Ray was very angry when asked to leave and loudly protested his expulsions. To other patients or a bystander, he could look very scary, but the staff was encouraged that Ray was actually expressing himself and that the poison of PTSD was slowly leaving his body.

In individual counseling, he was asked to tell his story again and again, and to identify the events in his daily life that made him most anxious. He was sent out in the community and told to stay in those uncomfortable situations for at least a half hour at a time. One of those was playing board games with Lucy and her family. The anxiety was probably caused by his memory of playing games with his African family, but finding out why was not an important part of his treatment. The first time he played, he had to white knuckle his way through the half-hour game. But a week later, he became so engrossed in the game, he didn't want to leave until it was finished. He would also get very anxious putting on his policeman's uniform and strapping on his gun; but he was required to do that every morning. Even though the gun was not loaded, Ray still felt anxiety for the first few mornings.

With the help of staff members, he learned quickly that he had much more in common with the staff and other patients than he imagined. Many of the staff had gone through treatment themselves. Ray also came to understand that using an alarm or timer was inappropriate for the talking circle, because it would disrupt the flow of communication and energy. Ray could smile and joke at his past indiscretions. He decided to try the circle again and this time enjoyed great success. Before long, Ray was helping facilitate the talking circle, and in the fourth week of treatment, he actually called a circle himself.

He explained to some newcomers.

"When the talking feather comes to you, you may talk about anything. You may talk about anything that is in your heart or on your mind. There may be an overall topic that the talking circle is discussing, but patients are not limited to commenting only on something someone had said. You are free to say whatever you desire, without limitation or fear. Talking circles are safe environments, and we should feel comfortable knowing that no one will interrupt or criticize you."

Ray smiled and laughed under his breath when staff talked about interrupting other members. If someone talked longer than what seemed customary, then those in the circle might quietly signal with a cough. Time limits were based on the size of the group and how long the group planned on being in the circle. This was discussed at the beginning of every circle. If you had the feather and noticed that others were coughing, it was time to pass the feather. When Ray finally started self-disclosing in the group, it was common to hear others quietly coughing. It seemed that when he opened the floodgates, there was so much that was never spoken and certainly not healed.

The circle could go around several times or until everyone had at least one chance to speak. Then the talking feather could be passed around once more to assure there was nothing left unsaid. Ray learned he was in charge of putting his wall up and down effectively. He really could let others in and know him. This was a huge release of the burden he carried silently before coming to treatment. He also came to believe there was no urgency to let everything out at once.

People all have a certain limit as to how much they can absorb at one sitting. Ray practiced sharing a limited amount and saved some words for the next talking circle. He made a commitment to the talking circle, remembered its rules, and felt the healing begin. He gratefully found the circle to be both purgative and cleansing. On his third visit to Lucy's, they were able to spend some time alone. Lucy found herself embracing the feelings she experienced in the beginning of their relationship.

"I'm sorry for all you've been through, Ray, but I still feel relieved you didn't find someone else," Lucy said, smiling as she rubbed her hand through his short hair.

"Well, now that you bring it up—there was this tall blond." A look of horror spread across Lucy's face remembering her dream, but then Ray started to laugh, and she punched him in the arm. Ray then put his hands on her arms and looked her right in the eyes.

"I waited way too long to get the courage to invite you into my life. I never want to come even close to losing you again." And they kissed with a passion that had been missing for both of them for too long.

The effect of sharpening his empathetic listening skills helped Ray to learn from others, and he found it to be a blessing. Even he knew that Lucy would benefit from his new skills. Consequently, Ray found the talking circle to be an effective new tool in his sobriety. Because the circle is a form of spiritual healing and also reorganizing the social system, the participant is able to speak honestly about subjects that he or she would normally keep private.

It could be said that the circle is an ancient form of traditional therapy or a community healing process. Ray believed in this ritual so much that he promised to introduce it into his everyday life. He wanted to have talking circle on a regular basis with Lucy and her children. He believed everyone should practice this activity. Its power could heal the world.

AFTER VISITING THE RANGER STATION, the six men drove the remaining twenty miles to the outfitter's lodge on Moose Lake. They jammed their gear into two flat- bottom boats and securely strapped their three canoes onto the racks above their seats. A pair of 25 horsepower outboard motors, the largest allowed on any lake in the Boundary Waters, powered the boats, and even these motors were only allowed on relatively few of the more than a thousand lakes in the region. The first time Hank heard that the boats had only 25 horsepower motors, he was tempted to pocket the fifty-dollar fee and just start out immediately by canoe. But the boats quickly saved at least a half day of paddling and transported him away from the drone of fisherman's motors and into the quiet wilderness he loved. After motoring for a half hour, the guide dropped them off along with canoes and gear at a ten- rod portage into Birch Lake.

For the rest of the day, they canoed and portaged through Birch and Carp Lake and up the Knife River to Knife Lake.

They paddled about ten miles and humped hundreds of rods of portages. Despite a sunny and pleasant day, they were challenged by a strong wind from the east that blew directly into their faces and even created a few whitecaps. The cold wind actually hurt the sensitive areas of their faces and necks and created the potential to blur their vision. Because of the bitter wind, they had to lash down all their gear with ropes and car-abiners—the clips that rock climbers use—to make sure they didn't lose their gear should they happen to capsize. A less experienced man might easily be flipped over. They also put all of their gear in dry sacks—thick plastic bags that closed tight at the top to keep all water out. These sturdy bags also helped to protect their food at night since the tight seal also made it more difficult for chipmunks or even the bears to smell the contents. As an added precaution, they also stored the food in smaller plastic containers.

Weary from paddling and portaging, the men were very grateful to find a nice secluded camp site on Knife Lake protected from the brutal wind. It took another couple of hours to set up their tents, secure gear, and find the right food containers for dinner and breakfast. The first night out they always grilled the steaks that thawed during the day and baked potatoes in the hot coals of the fire and steamed frozen vegetables. They also set aside fresh eggs and bacon for the first morning. The rest of the week would feature a variety of freeze-dried meals. They finished dinner just as the last rays of the sun disappeared over the pine trees. The glowing campfire heated water for the dishes and cleanup and offered an opportunity to meditate about their day and watch the stars at night.

They were lucky that evening to be entertained by a brilliant display from the northern lights. The six men sat around the campfire on their thermal-rest pads, which were used for sleeping but could also be folded into comfortable camp chairs. Each also wore a headlamp on his forehead so he had light to brush his teeth and use the pit toilet before turning in. But now each of the men quietly switched off the lamps, and their faces were lit only by the fire, the full moon, and the dancing stars, which sparked like silver sparks on the lake. With faces dancing with the golden light from the fire, previous experiences in the wilderness caused each of the men to realize such nights should be cherished. Rain or cold or mosquitoes could have just as easily chased them to their tents. The bugs could be relentless when looking for a man to bite. Each one of them had encountered unpleasant camping experiences and was grateful for this more than pleasant night. After a hard day of canoeing and portaging, setting up camp, cooking dinner, cleaning up the food, and packing it away so their sleep would not be interrupted by a black bear visiting their camp and running away with the pack containing next week's food, they were exhausted. But despite their drowsiness, they wanted to enjoy this rare moment.

They all liked fish but didn't want to eat it for breakfast, lunch, and dinner for the next six days—and that's only if they caught fish. The conversation around the campfire was about fishing and all the years spent with those food packs hoping to outsmart the bears. They shared tales of the times they didn't outsmart the bears and the scary visits woodsmen experienced from these crafty scavengers. Conventional wisdom suggests the camper find a tree with a branch at least ten feet from the ground and at least four feet out from the trunk. After tossing a rope over the branch, the heavy food pack is hoisted up above the ground.

Hanging a pack sounds wonderful in theory since the Boundary Waters holds plenty of trees; but the trees grow straight up in a race with the other trees for sun. Most don't grow out, so campers can search for hours just to find a branch long enough and strong enough to hold the food pack. Then there is the matter of finding a rock the right size to tie to the rope to throw over the branch and hope the rock doesn't get wedged in a tree branch. And what about that very smart black bear who now knows exactly which pack is the prize and has long since figured out how to destroy several hours work in seconds and rip open the pack anyway?

Hank developed a simple strategy after struggling with black bears for years. Place the pack into the nearest canoe and drop it off on a nearby island—and then hope and pray the island is free of hungry bears. A hungry human being looks for snacks in the kitchen in the middle of the night and not in the living room. Likewise, bears methodically search the same campsites looking for food. If the bear doesn't find food in his first search, he will simply move on to a new kitchen until he is successful.

As the conversation wore down and the men were all nearly hypnotized from staring at the fire, Hank turned to the two newest additions to their group.

"Are you guys all set to take off right after breakfast in the morning? I enjoy your company, but the time is right for you to get on with your business." The two men smiled and nodded.

"So what's it like to read your own obituary in the paper?" Ken asked.

Scruggs and Fiddler smiled and looked at each other. "It's strange. I never realized I was such a noble, honorable, lovable person," Scruggs answered.

"I, on the other hand, knew I was a screwed-up evil person," Fiddler answered. The close-knit group of friends laughed loudly.

"I must say watching it on TV, I was totally convinced what I was watching was real," Ken said still shaking and scratching his head. "Let's sure as hell hope everyone else did also."

Chapter 24

THE EGG DID NOT BELIEVE anything he saw on TV. Inherently pessimistic and untrusting, he had spent his life in politics distorting reality and manipulating the news media, and so he never believed what he heard or saw.

Within minutes after watching the news, he called the FBI and demanded that they begin to analyze the tape. Egg's gut feelings knew something was up, but he could not really put his finger on it. He even sent his own team of investigators to begin interrogating the police, the witnesses, the ambulance drivers, the hospital staff, and the coroners—anyone who had been involved in the events at the powwow, the assassination, and the aftermath. In spite of his power, the Egg was always frustrated at how slowly things moved in government. Since the incidents happened on a Sunday, it took even longer for his people to respond to his liking, and he became even more livid. The experts at the FBI were in disagreement as to the reality of the events on the ground. He was now officially pissed at everyone. Couldn't anyone just do his job? Why was everyone a screw-up? Besides the people who were in the area as backup, he needed the right people for followup. He had to dump some losers and replace them with someone—anyone—who could get the job done.

Luckily, as soon as he found out from the Gambler that he couldn't contact the kidnappers, he dispatched trusted people to move in and clean up the awful mess that Ray Waupuse had made. The place was a bloodbath, but at least he would not have to take those thugs out. Egg was relieved that they would never be able to talk about the job they were hired to do and failed. At least that is a positive, he thought happily.

He had no authority to exhume the bodies of Fiddler and Scruggs until he had proof and justifiable cause, and the people involved in the incident seemed unwilling to give him the information he needed. Even the whereabouts of Alex Fish were a mystery. This was absurd; he should be able to get any information he wanted. How could he find any competent help with this mess? Even more frustrating was the reality that he didn't have a clue where to find Fiddler and Scruggs if they were alive! Unknown to him, the cell phones he had given Scruggs and Fiddler went unanswered on the bottom of the Wolf River.

All the people Egg saw as pawns on a chessboard weren't moving the way his fat little fingers tried to push them. Spinning had always been his forte, and now he was just spinning out of control, yelling profanities into the phone, and then hanging up.

Slowly, however, answers began to fall into place. A janitor at Shawano Hospital who didn't care much for Lucy Teller ever since she locked up a friend of his, swore he saw Fiddler and Scruggs leave in an ambulance after sneaking out from the back of the hospital. They both were very much alive and well.

Then Egg learned that Lucy Teller often used the Brandts for tasks she couldn't use police to perform, and that Hank Brandt was currently in the Boundary Waters, a perfect place to escape into Canada. This was becoming even messier by the minute. A Forest Service check confirmed the campers, and sure enough, they only found four of the men.

He didn't bother to have the remaining men arrested since in reality no assassination had actually taken place. In fact, Egg didn't want too many people interviewed by the media who didn't agree with his side of the story. Now that he had enough information, he could begin to spread the rumor that Fish had arranged all this to get sympathy and create more media attention for his campaign. Hot damn! He would black-ball this guy if it were the last thing he ever did.

In truth, no outlet could generate media attention like the White House, and the disinformation juggernaut was about to go into high gear.

CHAPTER 25

LUCY AND HER SMALL BAND were also very busy. Gail called the man named Spade in Vegas shortly after the assassination attempt, and he provided the Gambler's cell phone number. She called the number and handed the phone to Gayle. After the Gambler answered, Gayle relied on all of her old behaviors—lying, deception, and charm—to get what she wanted. But in this case, her dishonesty was targeted for the benefit of others and not just about her self-absorbed addictions.

"I've missed you. How are you?" she asked, her voice dripping with love and longing.

"I'm fine," he answered. "I'm lying on a beach in the Caribbean soaking up some of the sun I missed waiting for you to make up your mind. How are you doing? And why are you calling me now?"

"I'm miserable. I'm back working as a nurse. I just hate the boredom. I miss the action. I miss touching and kissing you. I miss you." Gail responded, wanting to throw up.

They continued to talk. Gail was convinced that most of what he told her was a pack of lies, but the longer she kept him on the phone, the greater the chance she had of picking up something in the background that might offer a clue as to where he was. Digging down deep, she kept the charade going as long as she could.

After she hung up and calmed down, they listened to the recording again and again. He was near water because they could hear surf and boats in the background and for brief moment could hear someone speaking French. They immediately took the tape to a French teacher that Kathy knew in Shawano who had spent a year abroad in college in France. The persons speaking on the tape were describing a restaurant they had visited the night before and the French teacher immediately recognized the café as a well-known bistro on the French Riviera.

Lucy quickly forwarded the new information to Hank to pass on to Scruggs. Luckily, they were able to reach Hank by satellite phone as they sat around the campfire.

CHAPTER 26

A COLD, GUSTY RAIN POUNDED THE Boundary Waters the next morning. Hank decided to wait the weather out in the camp rather than risk capsizing in the big water. While Hank actually preferred the small lakes and the quiet serenity they brought, the fishing was often better in the big lakes for the lake trout and walleye they liked to catch. But the big lakes produced bigger waves in windy weather.

Breakfast sizzled under a tarp lean-to they securely erected. And shortly after their hearty breakfast of whole-wheat pancakes and sausage, Scruggs and Fiddler bid the group fare- well and canoed across the lake to Canada. An inexperienced canoeist, Scruggs took the front and became quite fearful of the waves, which occasionally splashed over the bow. Luckily, Fiddler was skilled in the stern, and they safely navigated the first lake. At the portage, they moved quickly and efficiently with much less gear. They each carried a daypack, and Fiddler easily hoisted the forty-pound Wenonah canoe squarely on his shoulders using the padded yoke in the center of the canoe.

Scruggs moved his daypack to the front of his body and slung the large, dry pack on his back.

This portage was the longest and steepest they had encountered, and the ground and rocks were slippery and wet from the rain. With his daypack in front of him, it was also more difficult for Scruggs to see exactly where to plant his feet. He stumbled and slipped on the rocks. They had not even discussed waiting out the weather, given that they figured there was only a small window of opportunity to catch the Gambler—before their deception came to light. The Fiddler was desperate to lay his hands on him one more time. Just one more time, he thought.

They paddled several miles to a takeout point in Canada where an AA friend of Lucy's named Jon met them and drove them to the airport. They quickly changed clothes in the car and soon looked like two businessmen traveling abroad. On the way to the airport, Fiddler and Jon soon shared the closeness of people in the fellowship of AA.

"You American Indians complain about how tough it was to get around the laws of not selling alcohol to Indians, how you had to meet White Men in the woods and drink all they sold you before you got back to the reservation. Hell, in Canada there were one hundred years of prohibition. It was not illegal to sell alcohol to Indians. It was illegal for Indians to drink—period," Jon said with a smile. "Now that was a better idea."

"What difference does that make to you now? You're on self-imposed prohibition. It's funny with all the things White people have done to Indians. It takes two alcoholics to complain about the one thing they may have gotten right. Indians shouldn't drink." Scruggs laughed along with Fiddler and Jon.

The conversation made the ride to the airport go quickly, and soon they were on a flight to Paris. They had fake passports and permits as gun distributors to pack unloaded guns in their stowed luggage. Both Scruggs and Fiddler had a friend in the CIA who they trusted to help them locate the Gambler. He was a person of interest to them anyway, since they knew he was involved in the lobbyist dealing with the Native American casinos.

The Gambler had a busy day lying on the beach, gambling until early morning, and finally bringing a woman to his room. After rough sex, he fell asleep more soundly than usual, still believing Fiddler was dead. Not content to gamble with his own life, however, he still posted a bodyguard to stand guard outside his room for his safety. The bodyguard was diligent for an hour or so until he heard muffled snoring coming from inside the room. Then he pulled up a chair, leaned his head back, and fell asleep.

Fiddler approached the nodding man without a sound. The next thing the hapless guard knew, he had a gun to his temple and a hand over his mouth. Soon Scruggs replaced the hand with duct tape and fished the room key out of his pocket. His huge hands and feet bound securely, the guard was unceremoniously and roughly shoved into a broom closet. Fiddler then entered the hotel room without a sound. The girl was in the bathroom dressing and didn't notice the two men enter. Scruggs slipped silently into the bathroom, grabbed her, and covered her mouth before she could make a sound. Her eyes grew big as the terror of moment overwhelmed her. She faint- ed and her weight tripled in Scruggs's arms. He winced in pain as his back screamed with the additional weight.

Fiddler went silently to the bed where the Gambler was still peacefully sleeping. "Hey, it's my lying, cheating, murdering, kidnapping, pig friend—so happy to be reunited. I told you I'd find you," Fiddler snarled into the Gambler's ear.

Hearing the all-too-familiar voice of this long-time enemy, the Gambler reached a new level of terror. The Gambler had several nightmares featuring the Fiddler's voice, and when he first heard the sound of it, he hoped he would open his eyes and find it was just another bad dream. The Gambler was sure that the Fiddler was dead, and suddenly he was standing there threatening him at the edge of his bed. Terrified, he wet himself.

Scruggs brought the girl out from the bathroom. She was younger than Gayle with blond hair, and though not in Gayle's league, quite attractive. When she came to, her eyes looked dazed as she tried to focus on what was happening.

"Pay close attention, sweetheart. You are about to find out what sort of life form you just had sex with. You really need to change your lifestyle."

The Fiddler interrupted. "Get dressed, Gambler, alias Dealer. We are taking you back to the U.S. where you are going to confess to kidnapping and attempted murder. You are also going to name your co-conspirators."

"You're wrong. I'm not going back with you," Gambler said, trying his best to sound convincing.

"Do you really want to give me the opportunity to kill you myself, which is what I really want to do anyway? Please, give me a reason right now. Just give me the go-ahead, and we can have your pretty little toy here leave. I am sure she has a short memory and will not remember any of this, right?" Fiddler asked.

The young lady shook her head aggressively. She vainly tried to talk around Scruggs's hand. Choosing to ignore her, he turned his focus back on the Gambler.

"You will never be able to get the charges to stick. Do you know who you are dealing with here?"

"That's not my job. I just know you will confess. If you get out, I can always kill you later. And man, I sure hope you get out. You could really make my day."

"Get out of my way, and I'll get dressed," Gambler said, still trying to act tough.

Turning to the lady, Scruggs said, "Get dressed and get out of here. If I were you, I would not mention anything about this to anybody. Do you hear me? You might think seriously about going back to school. This is a world you do not want to be any part of."

The Gambler begrudgingly did as he was ordered and put his pants on right over his soiled underwear. Embarrassed and scared, he did not say a word to the young woman.

CHAPTER 27

WHEN THEY RE-ENTERED THE UNITED States, Scruggs and Fiddler personally escorted the Gambler into custody. Only then did they turn themselves over to the FBI. But by the time they were back home, however, the Egg had his machine working overtime. He had been hoping and waiting for this day.

The national media had embraced as gospel the unfounded rumors that Fish had staged this whole fiasco to get sympathy. Lucy brought the tape to the FBI, hoping to prove there had been a kidnapping, but it only showed a crying little boy in front of a newspaper. After a short investigation and time in the judge's chamber, Scruggs and Fiddler were gratefully released and no charges were filed against them. But astonishingly, the Gambler was also released for lack of evidence!

When the primaries came, sadly Fish lost to a candidate who accepted large sums of money for TV coverage and sound bites from big oil companies determined to invest heavily to stop the Fish movement. Egg was able to get his spin out first.

Since Fish participated in a lie, even though it was to save a child's life, even people in his own party were more willing to accept Egg's version.

As for the Gambler, police were never sure of the motive for his murder. Did he ask the mob for one too many favors? Was the FBI coming too close to him and perhaps therefore to them? Did Fiddler not want to risk another attempt on his children? Nobody could be certain, but the Gambler was discovered executed in gangland style in the trunk of his rental car.

Howard Barker did restore a small amount of Scruggs's faith in him as an honorable man. He called Scruggs to apologize for the situation in which he had been placed. "Even though Egg would be enormously helpful to me in the upcoming general election," Barker said, "I'm going to ask the Egg for his resignation."

"I feel I must ask him to leave before I have no self-respect left. I know all presidents have handlers these days, but I feel I'm being handled right into hell. And I can't live with that!"

"Is it customary in those situations for him to be escorted out of his office?" Scruggs asked.

"I could arrange that if you would like," the president answered.

"I would like that. I want to be transferred back to Wisconsin, but it would be great if that could be my final assignment in Washington."

The next day Scruggs met the president in Robert Brooder's office.

"You will regret this!" the Egg retorted as Scruggs escorted him out in handcuffs, but the president smiled as he watched him walk away.

Egg's popularity in the White House was exemplified as the staff lined the halls and applauded as he was leaving. "Don't let the door hit you in the ass," a few mumbled.

As soon as they were in the back of an unmarked Secret Service vehicle, Scruggs unlocked the cuffs. "You are not under arrest, but being sportsmen we just thought we would have some fun keeping a vicious predator from law-abiding citizens." The car stopped in front of a large open field outside Washington. A helicopter hovered above the car. "Run as fast as you can and you may want to swerve back and forth so you are not such an easy target. In the interest of sportsmanship, they are going to give you a head start." A look of terror came over Brooder's face as he realized what was happening.

"You can't be serious?" Brooder blurted out. "Do you know the contacts I have?"

"Maybe you can text them as you are running. At any rate, if somehow you survive this, e-mail me and let me know how the wolves feel."

Brooder started running, and Scruggs laughed as he waddled slowly across the field. After about fifty yards, the helicopter started to move, and soon Brooder grabbed his chest and fell. When Brooder didn't get up, Scruggs was surprised because he knew there were no guns in the chopper. Scruggs jogged to Brooder, who was clearly in deep pain, probably from a heart attack. "Help me," he whispered.

"I will call an ambulance," Scruggs said as he walked back to the car. After climbing in the back seat, Scruggs pulled out his phone and called 911, but by the time paramedics arrived Brooder was dead.

"The experience for me was bittersweet," Paul said to Judy in their apartment back in Colorado. "I feel bad that, in my eyes, the best candidate by far did not win. I believed this was a loss for so many—me, the country, you. I'm proud of this country, but I feel like big business, the lobbyist, and the spin doctors are becoming way too powerful and that the average citizen is not working hard enough to stay informed. On the positive side, though, I learned a lot about government and decided that it was better to be a part of it and try to make a difference than to turn it over to people like Egg. I also met you, and you've taught me so much about adult relationships."

"Well, I've learned a lot from you, too," Judy replied. "So much has changed since we first started enjoying each other's company. I decided to transfer to the school you attend here in Colorado, and here we are living in the same apartment. I never thought I could love somebody this much, and I love your family as well. By the way, your mother said if only one of us could afford to fly home for Christmas, I should come and leave you here."

Paul laughed and grabbed her, pinning her to the couch, but their wrestling soon turned to kissing.

"I just can't get over the feeling that so much is left hanging in my life," Ray said to Doc Wolf in one of their regular conversations. "And that so much of what I did was for nothing. I tried to help bring peace to Africa, but that seemed like a bottomless pit. Countries keep pouring resources in, but nothing changes. Alex Fish didn't get elected, and except for the Gambler, no one seemed to get what he deserved, good or bad. And what have all these wars gotten us besides more people who hate us and more people like me feeling their effects."

"Well don't forget about Brooder," Dr. Wolf said, "and most importantly you saved a little boy's life. Indians have been suffering from the effects of war probably since we evolved from that bear. Johnny Cash sang about us in the "Ballad of Ira Hayes." How many people look at those soldiers raising the flag on Iwo Jima and know a Native American was one of the men raising the flag and what it cost him? If you believe the Pentagon, about 40,000 soldiers are returning from the current conflicts with PTSD, but independent sources say it is more like 300,000. The Pentagon says some 105 soldiers committed suicide in the last year, but that only includes those who are on active duty. We have no idea how many veterans commit suicide annually. Though a large number of soldiers come back from any conflict with PTSD, Native Americans suffer the highest rate. Nearly a third of Native American soldiers are coming back from the most recent conflict with the disorder—some after being deployed for the third time in five years.

"From what I have read, no one knows why, but some speculate that Indians tend to identify more with the people being invaded." Doctor Wolf worked hard to find some hope for Ray to embrace. "You saved a boy's life, and you are working to get your own life back, and perhaps it's best if we have a government that we can't rely on, because maybe it's time we take personal responsibility for our lives and our environment. Make your life what you can, Ray. I believe you can help yourself and those you love."

"I think it's time I put my energy toward life rather than death. I am going to give it a try." With both a tear in his eye and a smile on his face, Ray left Doc and headed for his new family.

Ray also was able to drop his guard—his wall—and allow Lucy back in. If he had not found his emotional bottom, Ray was not sure where he would be. Probably end up an an- gry, lonely old man, he thought. He believed he was, for the first time in his life, able to let someone in fully. Lucy, her children, and family, welcomed Ray back with open arms, and he was indebted beyond words. Lucy and Ray talked about the possibility of marriage and even adopting a child from Africa. They believed there were orphans who could benefit from being a part of their family. Lucy knew her children would gain from knowing a child from another part of the world. They could teach each other so much, Ray thought—yeah, even how to always win at all the games!

CHAPTER 28

IT TOOK A FEW MOMENTS for the sleep to seep from Kathy's brain after she opened her eyes in the room where she had slept for most of her young life. Her father had been making subtle noises, hoping to wake her. He didn't have the heart to just go to her room and knock on her door. He sat in the kitchen sipping coffee and cherished the moments of the last night his daughter would spend with him as a single woman. She had been his whole life since his wife had died of cancer when Kathy was only in junior high.

Once the realization popped into her mind that today was her wedding day, Kathy jumped from her bed and parted the blinds to see what kind of day the Lord had made. The sky was dark blue, but the frost still hid behind chimneys and behind the trees blocked from the sun. The weatherman predicted that the temperature could reach the mid-sixties today, but Kathy thought that even with the bright sun, fifties might be somewhat optimistic. Still, she smiled at the blessing she felt she'd been given.

She donned a pair of running shorts, a sports bra, a Wisconsin sweatshirt, and socks and then quietly walked to the kitchen. Her father sat with his back to her as she entered the room, and she sneaked up to him and placed a hand on his shoulder. He responded in kind by putting his hand on top of hers and giving it a squeeze. She then reached over and kissed his cheek and tried not to notice the smile on his face and the tear in his eye. Playfully, she rubbed the top of his head.

"My gosh!" she said, pretending his bald spot was a crystal ball. "I can see my entire future and that of your grandchildren up here."

"You are not too old for me to wash that smart-aleck mouth of yours with soap."

"Dad, you never even did that to me when I was little." "Well, I should have. That could have added to the list of resentments you have for me."

"Dad, maybe you have some regrets, but I don't have any resentments for how you raised me. I think you were the best dad a girl could have."

"Go back to the smart-aleck comments. I will never get through this day if you keep making comments like that," he murmured, with a tear rolling down his face.

Changing the subject, she observed. "I wish I did have a crystal ball so I could know if anything bad was going to happen to the people I love. Maybe like what happened to that little Tyler. I don't know if I could survive that."

"What if I had had a crystal ball to know your mother was going to die when you were still in grade school?"

"Would you still have married her?"

"In a heartbeat, but I don't know I would have been as happy for all those years we were together if I had known I was going to lose her."

"I guess it's better we don't know and just take what we have. Right?"

"You're pretty smart for a bald guy," Kathy continued with a smile. "One more thing. Thanks for all you've done, and I love you."

All he could do in response was to pat the hand that still rested on his shoulder. That was all he needed to do. She never questioned how he felt.

"Wait! I do have resentment! Where did you put my running shoes? You are forever hiding them on me."

"I probably hid them by the back door where you took them off yesterday. If you remember, it was raining and you are never satisfied running on the sidewalks and streets like normal people. No, you always have to head off into the woods and jog on the hiking trails, even when they're muddy."

"Well, OK, but that still doesn't account for that time in junior high when you really did hide them."

"If you remember, you had a hundred and one temperature and still wanted to run in a track meet. And I didn't hide them. I locked them in the trunk of the car because you wouldn't take no for an answer."

"Yes, and it is all your fault we lost the relay race that day."

"Sorry about that deep emotional scar."

"Yeah, well now that I got that off my chest, I'm going running as soon as I scrape the mud off my shoes. You wouldn't still have an extra pair in your trunk would you?"

"Not since your fever went away."

She kissed him again and this time on top of his head. "You are the best dad and the second-best mom ever."

"Have a good run, honey" was all he could choke out. Kathy knew just where to run to find her friend. And sure enough, just as she reached one of the larger trees in the woods, Kathy spotted her with her back against the tree, drawing the smoke of tobacco and sweet grass toward her with her outstretched hands. Kathy waited patiently as Lucy put the contents she didn't burn back into her personal bundle.

"I still prefer my brand of perfume."

Startled, Lucy turned and smiled at her friend.

"I believe the Great Spirit prefers mine, but since it is your wedding day, you are allowed to wear any fragrance you like," Lucy advised as she joined Kathy running down the path. The two ran together for about five miles before returning to the front of Kathy's house, where Lucy left her to return to the hotel where she, Ray, and the kids were staying.

At the wedding, Lucy sat with the community of people who had developed a close bond with one another through a number of trials. Gratefully, most of their combined efforts continued to bear fruit.

Fiddler, Lily, Kaitlyn, and Tyler were all together, and Tyler clung even closer to Fiddler. Joining them were Doc Wolf and Gayle, who sat together and held hands. The Brandts sat together except for Molly, who would be playing the organ for the ceremony, and Bobbi and Ryan, who were in the wedding party. Kathy's class made a lasting impression at Scott Brandt's funeral, and they were all abuzz since they were now part of Kathy and Brad's wedding as well. This whole group took up about a quarter of the church on the bride's side, beginning a few rows from the front and ending several rows from the back. By the time the ceremony began, almost the entire sanctuary was filled.

When the limo pulled up in front of Kathy's house, her father said, "I wonder if the back end has left Minnesota yet."

As they sat in the back on the short ride over to the church, her father started to say "I wish" several times. The rest seemed caught in his throat.

"I know, Dad. I wish Mom could have seen this day too, but I think she is here in spirit."

Everyone stood and watched as Kathy and her father walked down the aisle. Brad looked lovingly as Kathy approached him.

"Who gives this woman to this man?" Pastor Brooks asked.

"Her mother and I do," Kathy's father answered in a strong voice.

After the vows, Pastor Brooks went to the pulpit. "We have a special treat today. Ray Waupuse has been asked by the bride and groom to say a few words."

Ray walked to the podium. Though he was used to standing in front of the church at St. Michael's, he only passed out communion wafers and didn't have to speak. He was happy to be back doing wafers again, but this speech was another matter. His hands shook noticeably as he clutched the sides of the podium.

"It's really not true that Brad and Kathy asked me to talk. It's more like I asked them, and since I saved Kathy's life once, she really couldn't refuse me." A chuckle spread throughout the guests.

"Besides, I'm not doing this so much for them as I am for myself and many of the people I have known over the years who not only can't be here today but also can't be anywhere on this earth because they've died in war. You might be thinking to yourself what a terrible thing to bring up on this happy occasion of marriage, but that is exactly why I do bring it up. To me, nothing should be more opposite of war than love and marriage. Yet, too often what starts as love and marriage soon becomes hate and war, separation and divorce."

"Kathy and Brad, whatever you do, don't let that happen to you. We must promote peace, because I'm here to say I don't think war works as a way of making peace. I would never say that I think my comrades died in vain, because they may have protected our freedom or in some cases even our shores. They have eliminated evil dictators and governments that exploited people. They have killed terrorists who spread nothing but hate and fear and destruction, or maybe they did what they had to until we can find a better way, but for me I agree with Chief Joseph: I will fight no more forever. Let's start here today to make peace in our own lives. Let us use the strategies and skills of love and peace in our lives rather than the weapons and destruction of war. And let me tell you that words can be either. I've seen men killed by the weapons of war, but I've also felt the devastation of words. Both are destructive. I don't want to be part of destruction anymore. I want to be part of creation. Join me in being part of creation and love, and all of you out there join me in love.

"Brad and Kathy, make your lives full of richness and joy. Do it for yourselves because it feels good, but on the days that you want to lash out at each other— and there will be those days— do it for all the people who war has prevented from having the chance you have. I'm not just talking about the soldiers who died. I'm talking about the beautiful African family that I knew who were all killed because they were on the wrong side of war. Do it for them and for so many other victims like them. Do it for the walking wounded, like the ones I came very close to becoming. Do it for those who are so mentally and spiritually damaged by the atrocities of war that they are incapable of being in a relationship. Do it for the children who grew up without parents because of war, the parents who were called to duty, the parents who never came home, and the parents who came home in body but not in soul and spirit. Let's make their lives matter by making our lives better. I wish you love and peace."

With that Ray left the podium . . . but the silence, which was present from the time he started, remained.

Kathy and Brad, Ray and Lucy, the Brandts, and Fiddler and Lily did not live happily ever after. No person does. But Ray's words echoed inside of them, and they did their best to live in peace.

THE END

Other Books By Robert Bollendorf

Sober Spring

Sober Spring tells the compelling story of the Brandt family's struggle with the tragic uncertainties of alcoholism. The book brings to life the torment of a father's addiction, the pain of a family's recovery, and the healing of a community's deep inner trauma.

Flight of the Loon

This sequel to Robert Bollendorf's *Sober Spring* chronicles the rebuilding of the wounded Brandt family, and shows how events, even tragic ones, can hasten the family's healing.

Autumn Snow

Autumn Snow, written with Donna Gluck, is the third novel in Robert Bollendorf's addiction and recovery series. The Brandt family faces its greatest crisis when Scott, their eldest son, is involved in a terrible car accident and drug use is suspected. Officer Lucy Teller feels there is more to the story and sets out on an investigation that uncovers disquieting facts about the accident and truths about herself.

Witch of Winter

Witch of Winter, written with Donna Gluck, is the fourth novel in Robert Bollendorf's addiction and recovery series. It continues the story of the Brandt family and Officer Lucy Teller. Involved in a harrowing investigation set in deep Wisconsin winter, Lucy learns a great deal about relationships, recovery, and the true meaning of love.

POST-TRAUMATIC STRESS DISORDER

IN THE BOOK *THE CHALLENGER*, one of the major themes is that of post-traumatic stress. One of the book's characters, Ray Waupoose, who had shown many signs of personal strength, integrity, and balance in previous books, began showing signs of aggression, anxiety, and violence. This happened to Ray after he returned home from a military peacekeeping mission to Africa, where he was subjected to scenes of great brutality and inhumanity. This was particularly painful because the people brutalized were not soldiers, but women and children who were simply trying to survive.

When Ray returned to the reservation, he was a different person and showed many of the signs of post-traumatic stress disorder (commonly known as PTSD). In *The Challenger*, Ray was returning from a military conflict. We wanted to focus on this because PTSD has become a growing problem among military personnel, given the recent U.S. involvement in two simultaneous wars, and because Afghanistan is the longest war in which we have fought. In 2012, the Department of Veterans affairs reported 22 veterans a day were committing suicide.

It is important to point out early that PTSD can be a result of anyone, of any age, who experiences a traumatic event. It does not have to be a military engagement. People also experience PTSD as a result of sexual, physical or psychological abuse. It is much more likely to occur in situations where there is no easy way to escape, where someone perceives their life or someone they care about as being in danger. It is also true that PTSD can show up either shortly after the event, or many years later. It is interesting that many Vietnam vets have recently begun reporting PTSD symptoms now, even though the war ended some 40 years ago.

Recovery from the event is much more difficult if the person is unable or unwilling to talk about it. For anyone who has experienced an accident or been a crime victim, one of the things they may notice is the desire to tell other people what happened. The person may find themselves describing the incident to almost anyone willing to listen. Afterward, they may ask themselves why they did that, or worse, rebuke themselves and feel guilty for wasting someone's time.

The truth of the matter, though, is what they are doing is good and an important step toward emotional healing. It is the person who does not do this who is much more likely to experience PTSD, which is one of the reasons that it occurs so frequently in the military. Sometimes, the person who does this is perceived as weak. Oftentimes, the soldier is afraid to talk about what they might be experiencing because he might be afraid of being kept from battle, which may result in a feeling of guilt for abandoning one's platoon brothers or sisters. In some cases, the person who hopes to make a career of the military may be afraid to talk, worried about leaving a black mark on their record and keeping them from advancing.

In Ray's case what he did was a violation of his orders, and could have led to criminal charges. In Ray, we see the result of the trauma and his silence leading to a number of problems when he returned. The reader should have noticed a number of symptoms, including sleep disturbances, which are often the result of waking from bad dreams in which the person relives some part of the traumatic event.

The person may experience tremendous anxiety. This is particularly true when subjected to a situation which has any similarity to the trauma. For instance, if someone was injured in a roadside bomb in Afghanistan, he may have difficulty driving or riding in a car back home.

But other things even less related may also cause problems. Ray had trouble putting on his police uniform, or even allowing Lucy's children to leave the house. This is usually referred to as generalization. In one famous example, a subject named Albert became afraid of his pet rabbit after hearing a loud noise behind him. He soon generalized that fear from the fur of his rabbit to the fur of his mother's fur coat and became afraid of her when she was wearing it (Rayner & Watson, 1920). This generalization can even reach the point of being anywhere but home, and even there being depressed, anxious, and even suicidal because there seems like no way out of the endless pain that visits, even in sleep.

One of the common responses to these feelings besides suicide, which is a threat that the counselor working with PTSD patients must always keep in mind, is self-medicating. In Ray's case, he turned to alcohol, but any central nervous system depressant may be used, which can have both a short-term effect on the anxiety and also increase the depression related to PTSD. Any drug going in also tends to have the opposite effect going out, therefore once the anti-anxiety agent begins to wear off, the anxiety may become worse.

There are a number of treatments that have been found to be beneficial for PTSD. Cognitive and Mindfulness, to be covered in a later article, or telling the story over and over again in both individual and group therapy, is one part of treatment that helps, and in Ray's case, fit very well with the talking circle, which seems to be an effective treatment, especially for Native Americans.

Bibliography

Green, J.W. *Cultural Awareness in the Human Services: A Multi-Ethnic Approach.* (1995) Needham Heights, MA: Allyn and Bacon

Hammerschlag, C.A. *Healing Ceremonies: Creating Personal Rituals for Spiritual, Emotional, Physical, and Mental Health* (1997) New York, NY: Perigee Book

Harper K.V. and Lantz J. *Cross-Cultural Practice: Social Work with Diverse Populations* (1996) Chicago, IL: Lyceum Books

Robinson, R. and Rutledge D. *Center of the World: Native American Spirituality* (1992) North Hollywood, CA: Newcastle Publishing

Zoladz, Phillip. "Current status on behavioral and biological markers of PTSD: A search for clarity in a conflicting literature." (June 2013) Neuroscience and Biobehavioral Reviews 37 (5): 860-895. PMID 23567521 (https://www.ncbi.nim.nih.gov/pubmed/23567521. Doi:10.1016/j.neubiorev.2013.03.024 (https://doi.org/10.1016%2Fj.neubiorev.2013.03.024

Friedman, M.J. "Finalizing PTSD in DSM-5: getting here from there and where to go next." (October 2013) Journal of Traumatic Stress. 26 (5): 548-56 PMID 24151001 (https://www.ncbi.nlm.nih.gov/pubmed/24151001)

Rayner, Rosalie and Watson, John B. "Little Albert Experiment" Journal of Experimental Psychology (1920)

Rothschild, Babette. *The Body Remembers: The Psychophysiology of Trauma and Trauma treatment. New York* (2000) W.W. Norton & Company

Fullerton, C.S., Ursano, R.J., Wang, L. "Acute Stress Disorder, Posttraumatic Stress Disorder, And Depression Disaster or Rescue Workers" (2004) Am. J. Psychiat. 161 (8): 1370-1376

Olde, E, van derHart, O, Kleber R., van Son M. "Post-traumatic stress following childbirth: a review" (2006) Clin. Psychol Rev. 26(1): 1-16

Shalev, A; Liberzon, I; Marmar, C. "Post-Traumatic Stress Disorder." The New England Journal of Medicine. (22 June 2017) 376 (25): 2459-269

Hollifield, Michael; Warner, Teddy D.; Lian, Nityamo; Krakow, Barry; Jenkins, Janis; Kesler, James; Stevenson, Jayne; Westermeyer, Joseph. "Measuring trauma and health status in refugees: a critical review" (2002-08-07). JAMA. 288 (5) 611-621

Mason, Fiona; Lodrick, Zoe. "Psychological consequences of sexual assault." (February 2013) Best Practice & Research, Clinical Obstetrics & Gynecology. 27 (1): 27-37

Pitman, R.K. "Post-traumatic stress disorder, hormones, and memory." (1989) Biological Psychiatry. 26 (3): 221-223

Yehyda, R. "Biology of posttraumatic stress disorder." (2001) J Clin Psychiatry. 62 Suppl 17: 41-6

Zohar, J.; Juven-Wetzler, A; Myers V.; Fostick, L. "Post- traumatic stress disorder: facts and fiction." (January 2008) Current Opinion in Psychiatry. 21 (1): 74-7

Heim, C.; Ehlert, U.; Hellhammer, D.H. "The potential role of hypocorticolism in the pathophysiology of stress-related bodily disorders." (2000) Psychoneuroendocrinology. 25 (1): 1-35

Beard, C. "Beyond generalized anxiety disorder: psychometric properties of the GAD-7 in a heterogeneous psychiatric sample." (Aug 2014)

Dixon, Laura. "Lance Corporal Johnson Beharry accuses Government of neglecting soldiers." (February 28, 2009) The Times. London. Retrieved 2009-08-29

Andreasen, Nancy C. "Brave New Brain: Conquering Mental Illness in the Era of the Genome." (Feb. 19, 2004). New York: Oxford University Press. P. 303. ISBN 978-0-19-516728-3

Shay, Jonathan. "Achilles in Vietnam: Combat Trauma and the undoing of Character." (1994) Scribner. pp. 165-66

Holmstrom, Lynda; Lyttle; Burgess; Wolbert, Ann. "The Victim of Rape: Institutional Reactions." Wiley-Interscience. ISBN 0471407852

Printed in the United States
By Bookmasters